After the Smoke Cleared

JACK KUPER

First published in 1994 by
Stoddart Publishing Co. Limited
34 Lesmill Road
Toronto, Canada
M3B 2T6
(416) 445-3333

Canadian Cataloguing in Publication Data

Kuper, Jack
After the smoke cleared

ISBN 0-7737-2832-5

1. Kuper, Jack.   2. Kuperblum, Zelik.
3. Holocaust, Jewish (1939–1945) — Poland —
Personal narratives.   4. Jews — Poland —
Biography.   5. Holocaust survivors — Canada —
Biography.   6. Holocaust survivors — Soviet
Union — Biography.   I. Title.

DS135.P6K8 1994   940.53′18′092   C94-931324-6

Jacket Design copyright © 1994 Jack Kuper
Typesetting: Tony Gordon Ltd.
Printed and bound in the United States of America.

The names of some of the people in this book have
been changed, as well as some of the details of their
lives, for their protection.

Stoddart Publishing gratefully acknowledges the
support of the Canada Council, the Ontario Ministry
of Culture, Tourism and Recreation, Ontario Arts
Council, and Ontario Publishing Centre in the
development of writing and publishing in Canada.

In memory of my mother,
whose voice was stifled in mid-song.

And for my father,
who sang no matter what.

Long after the war, men will not be
able to look each other in the eye
without reading the question:
How is it you happened to survive?
How did you do it?

Janusz Korczak

1

IN LUBLIN, POLAND, 1945, a small crowd gathers at an intersection to listen to a boy singing in Russian. He is accompanied by a blind accordionist. The old man's calloused fingers dance across the black and white keys, his body bending to the rhythm. Where there should be eyes there are only eyelids, and a mouthful of rotting teeth protrudes when he parts his lips.

In a torn cotton shirt and patched trousers, the barefoot lad croons sorrowfully:

> The night is dark
> Only the bullets are wailing in the Steppe,
> Only the wind is droning through the wires,
> Dimly, stars are winking.
>
> On this dark night
> I know, my beloved, that you are awake,
> And sitting by the crib,
> You are wiping away your tears.

Revealing a mop of tangled hair, the singer works the assembled crowd. "Thank you and God bless you," he intones to those who toss coins into his oily cap.

If I had an accordion, I muse, I'd never go back to the orphanage.

An imposing portrait of Stalin on the side of a building dominates a square. I'll write him. He'll send me an accordion. I break into a gallop. I am flying, the instrument strapped to my body, the strains reaching heaven and God's ears. Below, their necks straining, the inhabitants of Lublin applaud.

As I near the orphanage, screaming voices draw me to the back of the building. I am just in time for soccer.

"I'll take him," says Motel, the partisan, pointing to Sampson.

The other captain indicates Horse.

"The Professor."

"Rabbit."

Motel screws up his face. "Cat."

One by one, they fall out of line. There are three left. Motel parades before us.

"Let's move it," prods his counterpart.

Motel pauses in front of me. I flex my meager muscles. "I'll take a chance on him." I step forward. "Not you, Jesus." His hand shoves me back. "That one." He beckons to a boy with missing fingers.

The other captain slaps Bones on the back. "You, come with me." Motel kicks the ball into the air and the players disperse across the soccer field.

"What about me?" I say, choking. "It's not fair." I run after them.

"Get lost." A finger pokes my nose.

I stand my ground.

"Go play with your cross."

"He can take my place," says Rabbit, the lanky boy with almond-shaped eyes, and he stomps off the field.

The ball is in the air. It bounces off someone's forehead, then suddenly Motel has it, playing with it like a cat with a ball of wool. Our defense rushes to block him, but he leaves them behind.

"Check him, Jesus," scream my teammates.

"Try and stop me, Jesus," taunts Motel, charging like a bull. Suddenly everything turns upside down. I am led off the field, clutching my genitals and cringing in pain.

"Jesus! Jesus!" A little girl runs towards me, her long, reddish hair reflecting the afternoon sun. She tugs at my sleeve and studies my wet eyes. "You're wanted in the office."

Looking disapprovingly at my demeanor, the house-mother points to a man in a chair puffing nervously on the butt of a cigarette. "He doesn't speak a word of Yiddish," she informs him and leaves.

"You're from Pulawy?" asks the visitor in accented Polish. He studies me with weary eyes, inhaling and swallowing the smoke. "Do you remember your father?"

A shiver storms through my body. Could this be Papa?

"What's your name, child?"

"My real name?"

He looks puzzled.

"Jankel Kuperblum. At home they called me Jankele."

"And your father's?"

"Zelik."

He gasps, "You're Aaron Zelik's son?" and butts the stub with his thumb.

"You know him?" A shard of hope flashes across my eyes.

"Your mother, too. She had a voice like a canary . . . a beautiful woman. I can picture them wheeling you in a carriage through the park." A sad smile spreads across his face. "What happened to . . ."

"Papa escaped to Russia," I volunteer. "Mama and my little brother Josele were deported to Sobibor."

He blows his nose. "And you? How did you survive?"

"Among peasants."

"They weren't afraid to keep you?"

"They didn't know." I smile impishly. "I tricked them. I went to church and prayed to their Jesus."

"How old are you, Jankele?" He touches my cheek.

"Thirteen."

"Thirteen." He extracts a faded photograph from his inside breast pocket. "He'd be about your age now." Tears descend his cheeks. I glance at the image of a child with a teddy bear. "I'm like a ghost . . . a shadow, propelled by bitter memories. Searching, knowing I won't find." He speaks as if to himself. "I went back to Pulawy. Not a Jewish face. The synagogue in ruin. And the peddler who used to sell sour apples, you probably don't even remember him, well, ah . . . it doesn't matter." He wipes his eyes and rolls a fresh cigarette. Polish Jews are returning from Russia, and it is only a matter of days before Papa will come to claim me, he says.

THE DAYS DRIFT into weeks, then months, until one morning we are escorted to the train station. By evening the city of Lublin is far behind us.

I lie on a bed of straw, sharing a blanket with someone whose face I can't see. Sleep will not come. Names of towns, villages, cities float past in my mind. Is it possible I've just been away on a summer vacation and am returning home? Will my family recognize me? These past years have been nothing but a nightmare. Maybe it's still 1939 and I am seven years old.

The train chugs, exhausted, into a damaged station. Why isn't my family here to greet me? In place of Pulawy, an obscure name is lettered above the entrance. Russian soldiers, some on crutches, others with bandaged heads or arms, scrutinize us.

"This way, children. This way." A chaperon guides us to an army truck. My eyes glued to the flaking sign, I follow the others and stumble.

Tall birch trees shade the highway, and in the distance beyond barren fields, mountain peaks loom. We motor into a small town, its cobbled roads lined with elegant two- and three-story mansions. All the signs are in German. Shutters are closed and doors bolted.

We pass a small, desolate park dominated by flocks of pigeons. A church comes into view. The fragrance of flowers drifts into our nostrils. The truck races along and comes to a halt in front of a white stucco building, a welcome banner strung across its front.

A small woman in a Polish army uniform, bedecked with medals, epaulettes, and a pistol, materializes. She surveys us like a general inspecting the troops.

I am indeed back home in Pulawy, and she's the midget with the painted face and baggy pants, luring us to the wonders to be found inside the Korona Circus.

She positions herself on a wooden crate, under a flag that is snapping in the breeze. Placing one hand on her hip, leaving the other free to gesticulate, she orates: "Until recently, this town was known as Peterswald, but thanks to the glorious Red Army and our illustrious leader, Comrade Stalin, it is now Pietrolesie, part of Polish soil." We cheer wildly.

"You are the hope of tomorrow!" Her words are amplified through a megaphone. "You, the remnants, the young, the orphaned, the scarred, will prove once and for all that in a socialist state, everyone can live in peace and harmony, as equals, as brothers. All working hand in hand to rebuild our beloved homeland."

I see myself atop a high structure, hammer in hand, nailing shingles, while all around, red flags ripple in the wind and thousands of white doves take to the sky. Accordion airs echo throughout the land, and workers embrace, dance, and throw bouquets of flowers at a passing parade.

The little general extends a clenched fist. "Never again will anti-Semitism raise its ugly head in our midst! Never!"

She stamps her foot, and the wooden box gives way, sending her plummeting to the ground.

Two Polish soldiers, stopping to gape, break into derisive laughter.

"Our national anthem, children," the little one thunders. We snap to attention, our eyes affixed to the shimmering red and white flag, and with raised voices sing:

Poland is not yet lost
as long as we're alive.

"Jews!" one soldier spits out.

"I thought Hitler had killed them all," his companion says. "And here they are, crawling out like bedbugs from inside a mattress."

MOST OF THE TOWN'S stores are padlocked. The occasional one that still carries on business has hardly a customer and not much of anything to sell. Two stale loaves of bread keep each other company on a bakery shelf. A husky butcher is alarmed when he catches sight of us peeking in his window. We stop to look at a photographer's display of smiling babies and happy couples in wedding attire. The German citizens of Pietrolesie stare at us in stony silence.

A boy in short leather pants, riding a bicycle with one hand, gripping a bottle of milk with the other, is almost upon us when Motel the partisan thrusts a stick between the spokes of the front wheel. The rider topples over, the bicycle on top of him. The bottle flies through the air and falls in fragments on the road.

"Watch where you're going," Motel hisses. The boy lies twisted on the sidewalk, milk running down his ruddy cheeks. "You'd better apologize," growls Motel. The victim's eyes fill with terror. "Apologize, you bloody fascist!" Motel screams.

A refined gentleman, walking a dog on a leash, observes

from across the street. Apprehensive faces peer from behind lace curtains. Eyes strain in our direction, but no one comes to the boy's aid. Where are all the fearless Germans? Are they afraid of Motel, of the others, of me? Me?

The boy scrambles to his feet, wipes his bleeding knee, and apologizes. Gripping the handlebars, he tries to pass, but Motel blocks him.

"Let's see your permit." We laugh. "Oh, so you don't have a license for your bicycle?" The bully takes hold of the bike, but the boy won't submit.

"My mother's sick. She's waiting for me," he pleads.

Motel sticks his right hand in his jacket pocket, creating a bulge. "I'll count to three, and if you're still here, little Hitler, I'll put a bullet through your fascist head." Terror rises in the boy's eyes. "One." The boy releases the handlebars. "Two." The vehicle falls to the ground. "Three." He is running around the corner.

NEXT A TRUCKLOAD of Russian soldiers pulls up across from our building, and with rifle butts, they smash the doors and break the windows, leaving twisted hinges and shattered glass in their path.

"The Hitlerites didn't leave their keys," complains one, machine gunning a lock to one of the abandoned residences.

We join the pillage. The furnishings inside are covered with white sheets, and portraits in gilded frames gawk from high walls.

"Take. Grab what you can," urges Horse, laden with stamp albums.

"Look what I found." One exhibits a typewriter above his head.

"I saw it first. It's mine." A quarrel develops into a scuffle.

I pull out drawers and scavenge through cupboards. Gowns, suits, fur coats, compete with necklaces, broaches, gold earrings, and pocket watches on long chains. I slither down a set of stairs and fly out one door and through another. Roaming, sweating, panting, I snoop under beds and tap walls for secret passages.

A complete orchestra of instruments stares at me in an attic. Violins, tubas, trumpets, horns of every description, even a harp. Pick me, they beg. But no accordion. A Russian soldier, guzzling vodka from a bottle, is perched on the piano, pummeling the keys with his boots. He jumps down, then smashes the instrument with a sledge hammer. One leg of the piano caves in, and it tilts. Another blow, another leg, and it lies on the ground like a wounded beast. The drunk man tears out the strings with his bare hands. The cords, looking like animal innards, are coiled around his feet. The keys are scattered across the room. Exhausted, he falls to the floor, moaning.

My heart skips a beat when I spy an ornate accordion atop a baby carriage laden with goods, wheeled by a grand-mother. I raise my arm, but instead of stopping her, I wave. I take a giant step and mumble, "Do you have a license for the accordion?" A small package falls from the carriage. I grab it and run.

Our dormitory becomes a bazaar. Two boys are playing marbles with gems, while Motel struts around in a fur coat, hat, and high-heeled shoes.

"I'll swap candlesticks for a harmonica," a voice sings.

"Leather boots."

"Umbrella."

Professor is deeply engrossed in a photo album of Hitler. Rabbit displays a gold watch for all to admire, while Bones jingles a pocketful of rare coins. I climb up on my bunk and unmindfully open the package in my hand. A collection of embroidered ladies' hankies tumble out. I blow my nose in one, discard it, and shred the others, one by one.

STRANGERS SHOW UP at the orphanage in search of a lost child. "What's your name? Where do you come from?" Eyes peer through me, and hopes fade when I don't produce the answers they long to hear. Tomorrow will be my lucky day, I keep telling myself, and in the dark of the night I imagine the encounter:

A platoon of Russian soldiers comes into view. They march in step, their voices resounding in song. "Jankele!" I hear my name and pivot. One falls out of line, gripping a mandolin. "Jankele, my child!" He bounds towards me. "I knew I'd find you!" I am enveloped with kisses.

"Papa!" A myriad of polished medals dangle from his uniformed chest.

"My dearest Jankele!" He tunes the mandolin.

"Papa, everyone's dead!"

"I fought in Stalingrad. I was the first one into Warsaw. And who do you think leveled Berlin?"

"Oh, Papa!" I hug him. "I knew you'd find me!"

Every man in the distance looks like him. I follow strangers. His face is everywhere. When I spot it on a poster in front of a movie theater, I enter and occupy a seat, front row center. The theater fills, but no one sits beside me. How considerate of them to leave the best seats for latecomers. Germans are indeed polite, well-mannered people. I don't dare glance back at their scornful faces saying, Look at that ill-mannered Jew grabbing the best seat for himself!

The theater darkens, the red velvet curtains part. People larger than life magically appear. Everything looks lop-sided, about to collapse into my lap. My eyes strain, my neck is stiff; I look back. The rows behind are all occupied.

I am mesmerized by *Two Soldiers,* the story of two comrades defending the homeland against the fascist invaders. During a lull in the fighting, they find shelter in a dimly lit bunker. The one who looks like Papa reaches for his guitar and begins to strum. The smoke from the cigarette dangling from his lips glosses his eyes. He stares into space and sings "Dark Night," the song that's been haunting me since I first heard it on the streets of Lublin. It is Papa, all right!

It's only a film, you fool, and the man is only an actor.

Papa could have become one. Everything is possible in Russia.

Since when does your Papa play guitar?

It's not all that different from mandolin.

Suddenly a shell lands on the bunker. My heart jumps. Explosions tear the earth apart. Dust and smoke blanket the giant screen. Miraculously, the comrades rise from the debris, their guns at the ready, the guitar intact. Relieved, I cheer them on.

They throw themselves into battle and fight gallantly. When it's over, the fields are strewn with demolished tanks and thousands of enemy soldiers with frozen noses are being led by a handful of Red Army infantrymen. But there's no sign of Papa.

A figure appears, frantically running across the scorched landscape. "Arkady!" he hollers. It's Papa's buddy. He scans the devastation. "Arkady!"

Suddenly he comes upon a curled figure, blood trickling from the mouth, the guitar fused to a clenched fist. Tears appear in the soldier's eyes. I wipe mine. He slings the body over his shoulder and reaches for the guitar.

"The battle is won, but you're dead," he moans, approaching the crest of a hill.

"Who's dead?" Papa's voice interrupts. "How can I be dead when there are more battles to be won? Let me down, you fool, Stalin is counting on me."

The friends embrace and the music rises in a crescendo. I leave the theater in a blizzard of hope.

THE STREETS OF Pietrolesie are covered in snow, icicles hanging from rooftops. Inside, the orphanage is warm, the food plentiful, and the little soldier, a familiar figure, is speaking.

"My dear children," she begins, and then waits until the din of voices and rattling of dishes subsides. She reminds us of the debt we owe the Polish government, the Red Army, and especially Comrade Stalin.

I have visions of her sipping tea with the benevolent leader, reporting how we are faring; how each of us is progressing in school; whether we are in need of anything and how we are responding to our fresh surroundings. "How is Jankele Kuperblum?" I can hear his voice: "His request is on my desk, but as you know, the accordion factories are still in ruin."

Bundled in winter attire, charity from America, we trudge to school. Screaming, yelling, and hurling snowballs, we attract disapproving glances.

A sour teacher, ruler firmly planted in hand, walks between rows of desks, lecturing under the watchful eyes of framed photographs of Stalin, Lenin, and Marx. Names of kings and heroes who have sacrificed their lives for Poland, echo through the room. I wait for the name of my ancestors to appear on the blackboard. "Kuperblum" is never even whispered.

I long to be back in the small, gloomy *cheder** where the elderly rabbi with a long beard and black caftan sits behind a desk on a platform. The pungent odor of onions frying in chicken fat drifts down from upstairs. From dawn to dusk, the rabbi directs the frightened collection of scholars. When his head is buried in a book, someone sticks out a tongue, makes a face, or plays a practical joke. If caught, the unfortunate prankster is called to the front to receive a flogging with a cat-of-nine-tails.

I am feeling neglected and wonder if the rabbi even knows my name. Just then he thunders "Jankele!" and

*   religious school

beckons me with his middle finger. "Come here!" he commands. I approach cautiously, restraining onrushing tears. "Closer!" He motions with his head. "Up here!" He points to the chair beside him. Eyes downcast, I sit down. "Read!" He shoves a dog-eared prayer book into my hands. The Hebrew letters dance before me.

Twirling his earlocks, he recites, his voice slowly fading as mine takes over.

"I can read!" I cheer.

"Why not?" He pats my head.

Pulawy, the unventilated *cheder* with its rabbi, and even the nauseating body odors are so endearing. I can read, and someday I'll understand the mysterious words. When I get older, I'll take my place in the synagogue and sway my body in prayer and God will listen.

Mama beams, but Papa continues pressing his foot on the treadle. Later, an eerie silence takes its place.

"What's he going to grow up to be? A man with a beard and a skullcap?" His salvos reach my ears after I am tucked into bed.

"A Jew has to learn *Torah*,"* Mama argues.

"Much good that will do him! Public school will broaden his horizons."

"At least let him attend Hebrew school."

"A Zionist?"

AS IF PARACHUTED from the sky, shadowy figures appear in our midst. I hear whispers, but when I stretch my neck, conversations quickly change to Yiddish. I awake to urinate and find my roommates dressed and packing. Glances are exchanged all around me as I dress and gather my belongings.

Like commandos we slip out of the darkened corridor to

* Bible

a waiting truck. Our view is obstructed by drifting snow. The wind whistles a symphony. The wheels turn, telephone poles speed by. Dawn is just breaking.

We board a train. Passengers layered in heavy apparel traipse back and forth, rubbing their hands and stamping their feet. Our noses are numb, our hands frozen. The train pulls out of the depot and speeds across the frosted landscape. We hardly speak.

The endless journey is interrupted by delays, stopovers, and the changing of engines, but eventually the rhythmic clanging ends and a conductor's voice hollers, "Lodz!"

Dazed, we ramble through a train station, get onto a crowded streetcar, transfer to another, and after several stops, continue by foot. Our footsteps produce jarring sounds in the crisp snow. Swearing and cussing, a drunk urinates at the side of a building.

"Where are we going?" I ask the one leading, as we pass tall chimneys protruding from industrial buildings.

"Jews built these factories and made Lodz world famous for linen," he tells the group. Shortly after, he knocks gently on a heavily hinged door in the entrance of a darkened courtyard.

"Password," demands a voice from inside.

"*Amcho!*"*

With the crank of a key, a wooden door creaks open, revealing a boy with large, sad eyes. In one hand he holds a book, and in the other, a Luger. I think of running, but the door is already fastened behind me.

In the morning a radio is reporting the news. I vault from the bunk and jump into my trousers. Through a clearing in a frosted window, I peek at children going to school.

"Heads up high! Stomachs in!" a husky voice commands. "Right turn! Left turn! Forward march!"

I open a door and at the end of a narrow hallway I come

* your people

upon an assembly of boys and girls in gray shirts and blue neckerchiefs, stepping in pairs, the floor creaking under their determined gait.

"One, two, three! One, two, three," a young woman instructs. Portraits of unfamiliar faces adorn one wall; a blue and white flag with a star stretches across another.

I am in the Warsaw Ghetto. Mama carefully pins the white armband with the six-pointed star onto the sleeve of her threadbare coat.

"Your name?" A husky voice brings me back to the present.

"Jankel."

"From now on your name will be Jaakov. We'll not only change your name, but your life as well. And when we're finished, you'll stand tall for your people and *Eretz*[*] Israel." My blank expression prompts her to add, "Palestine."

"Who wants a tree in Palestine?" asks the pretty young woman in a colorful dress, her hair swept back into a bun. She mesmerizes us with tales of a distant land where Jews till the soil, pick oranges, and drain swamps. The *Tarbut*[**] Hebrew School is clean, spacious, and filled with natural light. Counting the raised arms, she distributes booklets. "Each space is reserved for a stamp that costs only five *groszy*. Once your book is filled, it will be sent to Palestine, and a tree will be planted in your name."

It holds little interest for me until a schoolmate boasts he is already on the second page.

"Drink your milk, Jankele!" Papa pleads. I clench my teeth. "How do you expect to grow up healthy and strong?" He holds the glass out to me.

"Papa, I need five groszy."

"Sweets will ruin your teeth." Seeing the tears collecting in my eyes, he fishes out a coin and holds it between his

---

[*]   land
[**]   culture

thumb and forefinger. "Drink your milk and it's yours." My eyes fixed on the shiny coin, I reach for the glass, but the mere thought makes me want to gag.

"You must try!"

I close my eyes, allowing the dreaded liquid to trickle down my throat.

The teacher separates a colorful stamp from the perforated sheet. Licking it, I affix it ever so carefully to the first square. For each bitter infusion of milk, another fascinating stamp occupies a space, until the book is almost filled with animals, birds, trees, unfamiliar fruit, and heroic pioneers. I wander far away to a beautiful sunny land where my tree, with *Jankele Kuperblum* engraved into its trunk, is growing taller and taller, until it reaches the heavens, disappearing beyond the clouds.

"Drink your milk, Jankele!" Another coin. Another stamp.

I sleep under my tree. Its branches protect me from freezing snow, drenching rain, and sweltering sun. One more space to fill.

I wait for night to pass. Finally, a ray of sunshine peeks through our tiny bedroom window. Before Papa finishes saying, "Drink your milk, Jankele," it has evaporated from the glass. But his hand does not dip into his pocket. I wait, hedging around.

"Tomorrow will be a brighter day, you'll see, Jankele. The factory will pay what they owe me and my pockets will jingle again."

"Then I drank it for nothing! I only need one more stamp." I snatch the album from my schoolbag.

He leafs through the pages, his eyes burning. "This is what you did with your money?"

Suddenly Mama is at my side, pressing the precious coin into my hand. I wipe the tears and my nose on my sleeve and run out.

A shrill siren sounds, followed by bombs plummeting

from diving planes, shattering my illusions into smithereens. People run, the earth shakes, and after the smoke clears, the *Tarbut* Hebrew School lies in ruin, the pretty teacher dead, my beautiful stamps turned to ashes along with everything else in our flat.

UNLIKE THE ORPHANAGE, the preparatory kibbutz at 49 Kielinskiego in Lodz is impoverished. Powdered milk and eggs, marmalade, and wilted potatoes are the standard fare. We cook, wash dishes, launder, scrub the cold floors, and rotate guarding the premises against attacks by anti-Semites. Before our arrival, a grenade, delivered through a window, killed several members.

One of our leaders, a deserter from the Red Army, pens Russian letters on my behalf, to the Red Cross, the Polish Embassy, and a missing persons bureau, all in Moscow.

With hope, I join the eager hands reaching for the daily mail, only to walk away disappointed. Perhaps tomorrow will be my lucky day! Tomorrow becomes the day after, and then the day after that. How envious I am of the lucky ones! Oh, to see my name on an envelope!

"Could I read one of yours?" I beg the comrade in the upper bunk. His expression implants itself in my memory. A letter taken from under his mattress attaches itself to my hand. Behind the toilet door I pore over the words of endearment, imagining that they are from Papa.

In a makeshift school we study Hebrew. Slowly, I find my Yiddish tongue.

Teachers speak to us of Herzl, Trumpeldor, the Macabees, and twenty-one-year-old Mordecai Anilewicz, who led the uprising in the Warsaw Ghetto. We listen to the poems of Chaim Nachman Bialik and tales of prophets who once roamed our Holy Land. We drink and devour whatever is placed before us, then hunger for more.

Emboldened, we take part in a parade. The streets of Lodz are lined with curious onlookers; children wave flags, streamers on balconies shimmer in the breeze. A Polish Army band leads the procession, followed by contingents of tanks, cavalry, infantry, nurses, firefighters, scouts, and factory workers. Somewhere at the end of the snaking line is our motley group, in gray blouses, short pants, and blue neckerchiefs, stepping along the cobbled road. I am in the lead, carrying the blue and white flag with the six-pointed star.

Deafening applause precedes us, but as we come into view, we are met with silence. Though we tremble inside, we hold our heads up high. At the turn of a bend, a man in a wheelchair applauds.

Centuries earlier, the Jews arrived in Lodz at the invitation of a kindly king with a vision. They built factories and introduced trade and commerce, and a village mushroomed into a city. The newcomers married, had children, circumcised their sons, and sent them to study *Torah*. Slaughters and infernos followed, turning everything to ashes. The offspring buried the dead, rebuilt the factories, created more lavish synagogues, and offered even larger sums to the new ruler. Just when the second Garden of Eden towered on the horizon, new pogroms spread. The Jews were blamed for plagues, personal misfortunes, poor crops, droughts, floods, and the murder of God's only son.

Our home is across the sea, waiting for us to return. Come, Jaakov, I hear it call. If my forefathers were tillers of soil, there is no reason for me to be a herring merchant. If Jewish kings ruled and made wise judgments, why should I not aspire to noble deeds? Why have we waited so long, repeating the same mistakes, obliging one persecutor after another, providing them with an endless parade of sacrifices? I long to be comfortable in my own skin.

"Jews, *Eretz* Israel is your homeland!" we holler at the Lodz railway depot, greeting Jews returning from Russia.

"Join *Hashomer Hatzair!*"* I trumpet.

"Don't listen to Zionists! Don't swallow their propaganda. Poland is your country!" a fashionably dressed little man shouts. "You can't trust communists!"

"Jews, it's hot in Palestine!"

"Jabotinski is a fascist! Join us, not *Betar!*"** shouts a man with a speech impediment.

"The *Bund*† is the answer!"

The platform gyrates. I jump from one coach to another, stepping over sleeping bodies, and mothers with exposed breasts feeding their young.

"Zelik Kuperblum . . . anyone here know or heard of a Zelik Kuperblum?"

They shrug, shake their heads, and raise their eyebrows. "Zelik who?"

*   the young guard
** youth organization of the Zionist Revisionist Party
†   Jewish Socialist Party

2

ON THE SECOND DAY of Passover, the melting snow turned the streets of Lodz into rivers of slush. Birds chirped, plants sprouted on windowsills, and lines of wash were strung across balconies. Curious faces peered out and snotty-nosed children stood idly by, watching us lugging our belongings.

The train jerked and began to move. The outskirts of the city came into view and just as quickly vanished, to be replaced by wet fields. Passengers sat on wooden benches and suitcases. Others stood. By midafternoon, the crammed coach was polluted with human stench and cigarette smoke.

A bulbous-nosed farmer with a bushy moustache conversed with a younger one beside him. "Who do you think is running our country? The Yids."

I thought of the Jews arriving in Lodz centuries earlier, dragging their feet along the flooded fields, pulling carts loaded with meager possessions. And of baffled Slavs scrutinizing the strangers with long beards, phylacteries binding their arms and foreheads, their shoulders draped in prayer shawls.

We conversed in whispers and munched quietly on *matzah*,* but the passengers eyed us suspiciously. They reminded

---

* unleavened bread

me of the friend with whom I had tended cows in the village of Kulik during the war. He believed that Jews killed Christian children and used their blood to bake *matzah*.

"Jews to Palestine!" Distant voices rung in my ears. I ran, fearing to look back. "Jews to Palestine," the voices pursued, and a stone whistled by.

Mobs had run through the streets of Pulawy in 1938, smashing windows and clubbing Jews to celebrate the Polish Army's entry into disputed territory in Czechoslovakian-held Silesia.

The butcher's daughter had her skull split in half and the entire *shtetl** attended her funeral.

How incongruous! Now that we wanted to leave for Palestine, they stood in our way.

The train chugged along, puffing and coughing, and on a dark night pulled into the Szeczecin station. It was humming with activity and buzzing with sailors. However, the streets were deserted, save for the military patrolling the port. A courier in a shabby raincoat met us, and without ceremony, signaled us to follow. He led us through unlit streets and up a set of creaky stairs into a dark room. When someone struck a match, he erupted in fury. Our exhausted bodies collapsed on the bare floor.

Daylight filtered through the shattered windows. Chunks of plaster hung suspended from the ceiling, and the damaged walls exposed a jungle of pipes and wires. Outside, a once beautiful city lay in ruin, the scars of battle everywhere. Polish soldiers guarding a spared structure across the street traded stories and reeled with laughter, their merry voices echoing, stabbing our hearts with fear. Like mice in an attic, we envied the pigeons fluttering about on the outside.

Hungry, our nerves strained, weeks later we were still waiting for Moses to part the sea, when a powerful fist rapped at our door and a voice shouted, "Open up." Our faces lost

* town

their pallor. Thunderous army boots rushed up the stairs and a Russian soldier burst in, accompanied by a civilian.

"Destroy all documents, photographs, anything that can identify you," he ordered, crisscrossing the room, tearing precious possessions from our hands, ripping them to shreds. "You're not to speak Polish, Russian, or Yiddish, only Hebrew. They'll think it's Greek. In case you're caught, you're orphans, returning home from Auschwitz."

We were packed into a truck like sardines. A tarpaulin enveloped us in darkness, the fumes nauseating us. The motor drowned out all grievances, and except for the drone, a nervous silence prevailed.

"Papers!" A border guard's gravelly voice made us flinch. The canvas shot up and a blinding flashlight slashed across our faces.

A prison cell flashed before me. "You Jankele?" a tender voice questioned. "When I saw your name on the list, I could hardly believe my eyes." I glanced through the steel bars at the laughing eyes, the familiar moustache, the benevolent face, so unmistakably Stalin. "Your father will be terribly disappointed when he learns of this."

"Potatoes it is!" boomed the voice, and the tarpaulin fell.

Gears grated and the vehicle took off, shaking, jolting, and swaying our frail bodies. When we stopped at a railway line, the Russian dumped us, as if we were indeed potatoes.

A yellow sun rose, devouring the morning dew. Laborers carrying lunch pails and picks waited on the platform jabbering in German. When an assembly of flatbeds inched into the station, the workers jumped on. We dispersed among them.

"Nice morning," said one beside me.

"Greco," I said, avoiding his eyes.

Several stops later, we arrived at a chaotic terminal with rails crossing and twisting in every direction.

Famished, weakened, supporting one another, we emerged days later from Berlin's underground. Street after street lay in ruin. Block after block of desolation and death. Hitler's capital flattened. The few structures that had miraculously withstood the assault were boarded up. A child's face peered out from a cellar. On the hood of an army jeep, a French flag shimmered in the morning breeze. The soldiers surveyed us with frozen expressions.

A flea market of survivors, babbling in a myriad of tongues, queued up for nourishment, which was dished out from a cauldron by a woman with warts on her nose and a hairy chin. Squatting against the walls, with plates in their hands, they cursed the ones in charge.

"Spinach again!"

"Thieves!"

"Where's the food from America?"

After devouring mine, I fell into line once more, evading detection. The column for food was short compared to the one for the only functioning toilet. Those waiting squirmed, danced, and twisted every which way. A hysterical woman threatened to relieve herself if she wasn't granted entry. Loose excrement oozed down a pair of skinny white legs.

In desperation I ran to the dormitory, spread a newspaper, and splattered the day's events. Strolling along with the neatly wrapped package under my arm, I encountered suspicious looks from gendarmes.

Placing the package at my feet, I sat down on a park bench. Minutes later I strolled off, whistling nonchalantly, but a man sharing his bread with starving pigeons pursued me. "Hey! You forgot your lunch. Here."

Stepping gingerly over the charred debris in the remains of an ancient church, I saw my opportunity to dispose of my package. An upside-down Christ dangling from a rafter brought me to a stop and something brushed against me. Startled, I turned to catch sight of a ragged urchin taking off with my treasure.

Black giants with glistening white teeth and friendly

expressions came for us in American army trucks. Listening to their clipped speech, I wondered how they could possibly understand each other.

My friend Itzchak, who had lived in our courtyard in the Warsaw Ghetto, knew everything. One day he told me that Hitler had choked on a chicken bone and the doctors couldn't save him. According to him, America had a secret weapon: black warriors who could tear Germans apart with their bare hands.

"Gum?" said the driver of the vehicle I was in. He laughed as he watched us swallow the mint-flavored sticks. We tried to bite into the chocolate bars he distributed, but they were as hard as wood. One sip on the bottled drinks and we spat out the medicine-flavored liquid.

"*Broit! Chleb!*"* we cried at a stopover.

Instead, an elegant lady in a UNRRA** uniform distributed cans labeled "Peanut Butter." We dug into the gooey substance with our fingers, turning our intestines to concrete.

In the streets of Munich, uniformed GI's promenaded arm in arm with short-skirted *frauleins*. Thick-necked, bald-headed men sat in beer gardens guzzling and singing. Lines formed outside movie houses and radios blared renditions by Harry James. The dance halls were full, and the sun shone on, unaware of what had taken place.

Not so at the railway station. German POW's returning from Russia were disembarking from an incoming train. Some on crutches, some blind, others sheathed in bandages. Wading through the throngs, a woman held up a photograph. "Does anyone know my Gert?"

"My God!" cried another, hugging a veteran without a nose. "What have they done to you?"

"This is your Papa," a mother told her little boy. The father squatted to kiss the child, but the toddler retreated.

---

*   bread
** United Nations Relief and Rehabilitation Agency

One man on crutches rolled a cigarette, scanning the platform. Hours later, as our train pulled out, he was still there.

JORDENBAD, A RUSTIC hamlet of gingerbread structures in the French zone, was a fairyland isolated from the world. A gentle stream flowed through a valley permeated with scented flowers in a rainbow of colors. It was surrounded by high mountains of pine forests. Cloaked in habits, nuns floated about weeding the vegetable gardens, tending the orchard, and pruning shrubs. They cooked, baked, and served hardy meals on cloth-covered tables laden with crystal and sterling in a serene dining hall. Supposedly, Hitler had once vacationed at this famous spa. No doubt he would have had apoplexy seeing the present guests stamping their feet to the *hora.* *

We splashed in the river, camped in the nearby woods, kicked a soccer ball, and at the slightest excuse, broke into song. Often a visiting dignitary from America or an UNRRA official would become infected with our spirit.

In my head, my nimble fingers flitted across the black and white accordion keys accompanying the circle of dancers. But as time went on and my prospects dimmed, I shared my dream with those in charge. They listened, but their minds were on more pressing matters.

Skipping class, I crossed the bridge, passed the goats grazing in the lush pasture, and before noon entered a village boasting a church with a high steeple, a bell, and a fountain cascading water from a mermaid's mouth. Pedestrians exchanged pleasantries before immaculate gardens with storybook homes. I headed up a hilly street dotted with shops. As I pressed my nose against the glass of a barber shop, I spotted an accordion.

* a communal dance

"For sale?" I asked in my best German.

The barber sized me up in the mirror. "For trade. Men's shoes." Rummaging through a drawer, he handed me a length of string. "This size."

For a short eternity I walked about swinging the piece of string like a pendulum, eyeing everyone's feet. UNRRA trucks arrived regularly bringing supplies of food, clothing, games, and reading material. In time, a cargo of shoes screeched to a halt.

"I'm next! I'm next!" Arms reached for the footwear from America. A lifetime later, my name was being checked off the list.

"Try these."

"They're too small."

The American slipped a shoe onto my foot. "Next!" he called, handing me the mate.

"My feet swell up in hot weather." I begged, "A larger size, please." Rejecting the second pair as well, I presented him with the strand. A thin smile crossed his face.

I was convinced if I closed my eyes and let my fingers loose on the keyboard, the rest would take care of itself. It worked for the blind man. Why not for me?

My friends plugged their ears, stuck out their tongues, and snickered.

"Give me a try." Hands pulled the shoulder straps.

"I'm first!"

"And me."

"Don't even touch," I shrieked.

"What's yours is ours." Motel the partisan's nose rubbed mine. "This is a kibbutz. Remember?"

"All for one and one for all!" they all sang.

I stood firm, guarding my prized possession. In the dining hall, when I asked for food to be passed, they pretended not to hear. By the time it reached me, the dish was empty. Not a soul spoke to me, and humiliating messages appeared on the bulletin board deriding my selfish behavior. Exiled, I caved in, and like a good comrade smiled at the line of would-be accordionists pounding the keys and violently pulling at my treasure.

A GIRL RETURNING from the Poking DP Camp in the American zone reported coming across "Kuperblum" on a list. The words had barely left her mouth when I ran to the office begging for bus fare.

The very next day I left for Poking. Looking out the bus window, I saw an endless procession of Kuperblums parade before me. Some, I remembered from a wedding, a sickbed, or a Sabbath dinner. The face was always Papa's.

Shutting my weary eyes, I tried to sleep, but my mind refused to relax and I fidgeted nervously, chewing on the end of my coat sleeve. As fast as the bus raced, it appeared to be standing still and even regressing.

It was well past midnight when I was let off. I asked the frazzled driver the way to the DP camp. Following his directions, my path illuminated by a crescent moon, I groped my way and knocked on a door. A man in longjohns cradling a crying baby stood before me.

"Are you Kuperblum?" I asked foolishly, immediately recognizing my Uncle Shmil-Leib.

I saw him running in a field of clover, laughingly pursuing a girl in a multicolored frock, her long black tresses tied back with a red velvet ribbon. The two floated above the ground as if carried by the wind.

"Yes," he replied, shoving a pacifier into the screaming baby's mouth.

"Do you know who I am?"

"I can't even see you!" he said, beckoning me to enter. Hoisting a naphtha lamp, he squinted his eyes. "For God's sake, boy, who are you?"

It moved me to tears, and I saw him lifting me above his head, asking what I was going to be when I grew up.

"I'm your nephew." The words clung to my throat.

"Favel's son David?"

I ached. "No. I'm Jankele."

"Jankele?" He was lost.

"Once when I had a fever, you brought me an orange from Warsaw."

He had trouble articulating. "Sonia, my brother Zelik's son!" he called out to the reclining figure at the end of the dimly lit room. "Are you hungry? Let me scramble a couple of eggs for you. You must be tired! How long can you stay? I'm so mixed up, so confused, I don't know what I'm saying!" Placing the baby in the crib, he pulled me towards him and choked on his own tears. Odors of unwashed feet, smelly socks, and rotting teeth assaulted my senses. But I put my arms around him and squeezed.

"How did you survive?" I asked after the baby had fallen asleep.

"In Russia."

"With Papa?"

"We wrote to each other." He yawned. "Then we lost contact. If he's alive, for sure he'll make his way to Belgium."

"Where?"

"Our eldest brother left for Brussels before you were born."

Over breakfast I shared my hopes and dreams. His mind was in a million places. "Very nice! Why not? Your father played mandolin. How he played! The girls were just crazy about him." He tousled my hair. "I'll buy you the biggest accordion, Jankele."

His wife erupted in laughter. "An accordion yet? He'll only break your young heart, Jankele. Look at my shoes." She reached under the bed. "The heel is broken on one and the strap is torn on the other. Would you like to guess how many times your millionaire uncle promised to buy me new ones?" She threw them at him.

"Sonia, this . . . "

But Aunt Sonia wasn't about to be stopped. She catalogued

everything he had vowed and not delivered. "The baby needs diapers, shirts . . . and look at me. I can't even get dressed because I have nothing to wear." She pounded him with her fists.

"She doesn't mean any of it," said Uncle when we were alone. "She misses her family in Russia, and she almost died giving birth."

On the subject of *Eretz* Israel, he raged, "What have they put into your head? Your father would die if he knew his son had become a Zionist. I won't allow it! There's going to be a blood bath in Palestine, Jankele, and I don't think our family can afford to spare another Kuperblum. You're coming with us to Belgium!"

THE ROOFTOPS OF Jordenbad were covered in snow. Intricate frost patterns attached themselves to windowpanes. In a matter of weeks we were to board a clandestine ship for the Promised Land. I imagined the nuns setting the tables for breakfast and discovering we were gone. Jews! Didn't say goodbye.

Forms had to be completed, stamped, and dated. A doctor and nurse arrived. I stood in line, squirming every time a needle jabbed an arm and blood filled the vial.

"Next!" Feet shuffled forward.

"Next!" Antiseptic odors reached my nose.

"Next!" I spun around and ran to the back.

"Next!" Horror! I was three heads away.

"Next!" a hand gripped my arm. With baggy eyes surrounded by liver spots, the physician raised the hypodermic. The needle vibrated in his quivering hand. A bullet pierced and I fell, splattering the Negev Desert. I jerked free and fled.

Storming into the dorm, I began to pack. My comrades looked askance when I announced I was leaving. But when I reached for the accordion, I was surrounded.

"It belongs to the kibbutz," said one, and I was freed of it.

A train whistle blew in the distance, and from the forest the disturbing caw of a crow was heard. I boarded a coach and stared at my reflection in the window fusing with the naked forest, snow-covered fields, and farm houses nestling in the valley. I intended to disembark at Ulm and take a bus to Poking, but when I awoke, I found myself in Munich. Like a zombie, I boarded a streetcar. In the blur of shuffling pedestrians and moving traffic, I recognized a face. Squeezing through the wall of bodies, I vaulted and fell into Uncle Shmil-Leib's arms.

"Uncle! Uncle!" I yelled, trying to catch my breath.

"Jankele, what are you doing here?" His raincoat barely protected him from the severe cold.

I stared at my feet. "Aren't you happy to see me?"

"Jankele . . . " He blew into his cupped hands. "In a couple of hours I'm leaving for Belgium."

I began to sniffle.

"Damn you!" he cussed. "Why do you jump to conclusions? Don't I have enough troubles with that Bessarabian bitch? Just in case, fate sent you along. Between the two of you, for sure you'll destroy my nerves." He closed his eyes. "Jankele, forgive me." He didn't know how to leave. "Go to Shmulik Zaifman in Neufroiman. I'll be in touch." And he was gone.

A streetcar took me to the Neufroiman DP Camp on the outskirts of Munich. When I asked for Zaifman, the guard at the gate studied me with his small eyes and pointed to a cluster of cottages.

"Look for a house with shutters. Upstairs you'll find Shmulik. Upstairs, not downstairs . . . got that?"

An open door exposed a bed and a table, and by the cracked window sat a shoemaker with a shock of red hair, spewing nails into a sole. Patterns, tools, and pelts hung on the walls.

"You must be Shmulik, the shoemaker?"

"Do I look like a tailor?" He continued to hammer.

"I'm Jaakov Kuperblum."

The implement dropped from his hand and before I knew it, he was rubbing his stubbled chin against my face. "Sarah, come quick," he shouted.

I heard the sound of feet charging up the stairs and a pretty woman entered. She pinched my cheeks. "A beauty! A picture to behold! But skinny like a scarecrow."

Food appeared. Neighbors and friends were summoned. In the hubbub of voices, I heard the name of Gershon, a Warsaw butcher who was raking it in on the black market.

"Why is this night different from all others?" I asked at the Passover Seder in 1940. Papa had already left for Russia, and we were living in Warsaw with Mama's family on Pawia Street. The two-room basement had been scrubbed. Everything sparkled and smelled fresh. Near the *matzah* was a plate of hard-boiled eggs in their shells. Uncle Moishe, only three years older than I, made faces causing Josele to laugh. For the hundredth time, I reached under the table to finger the leather boots *Zaidy*,* mother's father, had handcrafted for me.

"And the Lord took us out of Egypt with a strong hand, and with an outstretched arm, and with great terror, and with signs and with wonders." Moses was parting the sea as sounds of marching Germans and strains of *Deutschland Uber Alles* reached our ears.

Aunt Fela's fiancé, Gershon the butcher, sat beside her. Strong as a bull, he lifted me high up to the ceiling. I shrieked, begging for more, but Fela pulled him away to take her for a walk. As soon as they left, her brother Moishe signaled me. We followed, taunting them and refusing to leave until Gershon flipped us a shiny coin.

I remembered Gershon, all right. The next day, when I rapped on his door, a young woman in a short-sleeved

* grandfather

30

sweater and tight slacks answered. Toying with her long black hair, she ran her tongue along freshly painted lips. Beside a number branded into her flesh, a gold watch sparkled with diamonds.

"I'm looking for Gershon," I announced.

"It's for you, darling." She stood aside, revealing two men in blood-soaked aprons dismembering a cow. Its intestines protruded all over the floor.

"Yes? Dear God!" The color, save for a few spattered droplets of blood, left his face. "Jankele!" He ushered me out the door. "I'm in such a terrible predicament. My wife knows nothing. I'm building a new life for myself and want to forget that I was ever married to your Aunt Fela or that we had a baby." He pulled out a roll of money. "How much do you need?" I felt faint and walked away. "I'm still your uncle," he begged, running after me.

A POT-BELLIED English Jew in a long coat showed up at the Zaifmans, introducing himself as the *macher*.* Uncle Shmil-Leib had sent him. While I was packing, he sat himself down and with his index finger, purged the wax from his ears. In discreet tones he talked of a mistress, a blonde, blue-eyed German bombshell. As if the photograph he displayed was not enough, he produced several strands of pubic hair. Sarah looked the other way. Shmulik almost swallowed the tacks clenched between his lips.

"I don't know why you're leaving," Sarah lamented. "We may not have much, but we love you. You are our Jankele!" She pulled a sweater over my head and pressed a bag of food into my hand. She hugged, then kissed me, then hugged and kissed me again.

* fixer

3

BY THE TIME THE TRAIN pulled out of Munich, night had replaced day. Stuffing his mouth with bonbons, the *macher* handed me a passport. "Your name is Marcel Halpern, born in Brussels in 1932 and lived there until the Germans deported you to Dachau." He pointed to a middle-aged couple facing us. "These are your parents."

The man had a bulldog face with dots for eyes. His partner, wrapped in a moth-eaten fur coat, looked me over.

"You've got to look happier than this," the *macher* directed them. The woman adjusted her outlandish hat and both squeezed out a grin.

At the crossing into France, the *macher* was hauled off by the gendarmes. I expected them to return for us at any moment, but surprisingly the *macher* reappeared. "Whores!" he swore under his breath. "No matter how much you smear, it's never enough!"

Night had descended when the train reached Brussels. I saw Uncle Shmil-Leib running towards me. "Jankele!" He planted kisses on one cheek, then the other. He had so much to tell, but I was in a daze, and tuned out.

We boarded a streetcar. A city with pedestrians arrayed in their finery, crowding the wide avenues. The brightly lit stores were filled with merchandise, and the cafés and restaurants swarmed with patrons. Voices laughed, music blared, neon lights danced in the sky. A world I could never have imagined.

"We'll have to be quiet," whispered uncle, when we neared our destination. "There's a vicious dog on the main floor." We tiptoed up a flight of stairs. He flicked on a light. "This is your Uncle Jankel's apartment. He now calls himself Jacques."

Curtains adorned windows, carpets covered floors, photographs and mementos crowded the tops of dressers. A collection of ties was draped over a chair. Dishes and utensils were stacked on a kitchen counter and a bouquet of red flowers graced a large table.

"In case you wonder why my brother wasn't at the station, let me tell you right now. It's not his fault. He would have foregone all the festivities, I'm sure, but celebrating the New Year means more to his wife than greeting an only surviving nephew. Why am I telling you all this? It's best you shouldn't know."

He signaled me to follow him to the floor above. "This is where we live. I promised Sonia I'd wake her when you arrived, but I don't think I should. You'll sleep over there, Jankele." He pointed to a folding bed. I undressed and slid under the covers. Suddenly the baby started to cry. Outside, voices ushered in 1947.

When I awakened, smiling eyes were staring at me from behind thick lenses. "I'm your Uncle Jacques," a man said, and his lips descended on my cheeks. "Come," he beckoned. I slipped into my clothes.

"Our child!" Auntie Chela shrieked as I entered the room and bombarded me with kisses. As if her short stature weren't enough, nature had blessed her with bowlegs and a head of barbed wire. "Look at him! So gorgeous! So handsome!" She held me at arms' length. "How we worried about you! We couldn't sleep . . . we didn't eat. Thank God you're finally with us." She pushed me into a chair.

"François! Jacquy!" she screamed, dishing out scrambled eggs. "You must be starved, child. Eat as much as your heart desires. Don't be shy."

I was about to butter a chunk of bread when she leaned over, breathing on me. "What do you make of that bargain your Uncle Shmil-Leib found in Russia, eh?"

I looked up bewildered.

"Don't worry child, you'll eat with us, and if we had a little more room down here, you think we'd let you sleep with them?"

"Chela, please!" Uncle threw her a stern look.

"Sooner or later he'll find out." She put her hand on mine so I could not lift my fork. "The stories I could tell you, you wouldn't believe. After all we've done for them, and neither one has spoken to me in weeks. Now I ask you, is this the kind of gratitude I deserve?"

"Bonjour!" A boy my age joined us, and after kissing my aunt and uncle, he stood staring at me.

"This is André," said Uncle. "His parents were deported."

"A terrible character," said Auntie with a grimace, quickly adding, "Don't worry, Jankele, he doesn't understand one word of Yiddish."

Uncle closed his eyes. "Chela!"

"A self-centered egomaniac. He stands in front of a mirror like a girl, combing his hair. Believe me, Jankele, we treat him like flesh and blood, but nothing good will come of him. Look at the way he eats. Still has one piece of bread and already reaches for the next. The other day I caught him red-handed, devouring the last apple. Didn't even ask permission. Selfish, I tell you. Sometimes I hate myself for feeling this way, but believe me, Jankele, his own parents didn't care much for him either."

A basketball whizzed by, bounced off a wall, hit Uncle's head, dislodged his glasses, and landed squarely in the frying pan, flecking the wall and Aunt's face with egg. Two pajama-clad boys rushed in and covered her with kisses, coaxing a laugh out of her.

"What do you think of your cousins?" she beamed. They shook my hand, and lifting me above their heads, stomped around the room.

An enraged voice bellowed from the apartment below: "The ceiling is caving in. The entire building will collapse. You're not fooling me, Kuperblum. You're turning this place into a DP camp."

"The dog!" said Uncle. "So many decent people were murdered, yet he managed to survive not one, but three concentration camps."

Uncle told me about the occupation, describing the work he had performed for the underground, and how his sons had survived in the care of a heroic Gentile woman. François was sixteen and his brother, less exuberant and sporting a moustache, was a couple of years older. Their laughter was spontaneous. They were uncomplicated. I couldn't imagine inner voices or nightmares haunting them the way they did me:

Like a stray cat, I roam a large metropolis. Suddenly a figure falls upon me, sending me reeling to the pavement. I look up, and in that split second, I recognize the intruder. It's Papa. He glances at me elusively and crashes his way through the swelling crowd. I pursue and catch sight of him a little later, slipping into a darkened doorway. I cross the slippery street and follow him. My heart is pounding. I ascend the worn stairs as if in slow motion, feeling my way through the blinding darkness. From above I see the glow of a light, and inch towards it. It's a naked bulb suspended from a flaking ceiling. I tiptoe along the corridor and come to a stop at a door. Strange chanting emanates from behind it. I press on the handle and the door creaks open. Facing me is an assembly of bearded faces, one looking like all the others, their heads draped in prayer shawls, holy books glued to the palms of their hands, swaying back and forth in feverish lamentation. Suddenly the chanting comes to a halt and they gape at me. Their eyes are familiar. I know them well. They evoke the happenings the tongue cannot express. They are my Zaidy's, the baker's eyes, Papa's eyes, and the very ones I see every time I look in the mirror.

One takes a step towards me, followed by another, and soon I feel arms locked around my shoulders. I'm being pulled and pushed and made to kick my feet in joyful dance. The door shakes, the walls tremble, the crystal chandelier shows signs of coming away from the ceiling. But the congregants show no concern. With closed eyes and raised arms they pound the floor, chant with ecstasy, and bless the Almighty for having spared me.

"A Jewish child! A diamond!" a voice intones and a kiss descends upon my cheek. My face is irritated by a brittle beard. I look up. Our eyes meet. It's Hitler in the garb of a *Chassid.* *

"What about the future, Jankele? Have you thought what you want to do with your life?" Uncle Jacques asked.

"Play accordion."

"I mean a profession, so you can earn a living."

"I'd like to go to school."

He removed the spectacles. "It's a struggle just to keep alive."

The next day, Uncle Shmil-Leib and I breakfasted on pieces of stale bread topped with marmalade, and like burglars stole our way down and out the door. Day was barely breaking; the streetlights were still on. Half-empty streetcars made their way along the wet tracks. Here and there a figure emerged from a doorway, umbrella in hand.

"*Bonjour,*" greeted a milkman, high atop a horsecart.

"*Bonjour,*" replied a plump woman, who stopped to chat.

I had to run to keep up with Uncle. "I told him you're an obedient boy, Jankele, and that your life's dream is to be a

_____

* a member of the ultra-religious Chassidic sect

tailor. So don't make a liar out of me." He rubbed his chafed hands. "Don't think it was so easy to get him to agree to a weekly salary of fifty francs. This character doesn't part with money. You should be thrilled." We passed a statue of a naked boy urinating. When I stopped to stare at a shop window displaying musical instruments, uncle yanked my arm. We hurried for several more blocks. "To look at you, one would think it's the end of the world."

We entered a tailor's shop. "Good morning, Baruch!" shouted uncle in a booming voice, halfway up the steep stairs. "I forgot to tell you, Jankele, he's hard of hearing."

The man was a bear, with a mop of gray hair, a carrot for a nose, and oversized feet. As befitted a tailor, he wore a pair of worn, baggy pants held up by suspenders over a flannel undershirt. He was bending over, attempting to kindle the stove.

The cold was not the worst thing. A stench of odors, as if uncorked from years of imprisonment, invaded the place. Somewhere a child cried, someone sneezed, and a cat meowed, brushing against my leg.

"So this is the boy," muttered the boss without looking at me.

"Our Jankele."

"What?"

"I said his name is Jankele."

"You said something, Shmil-Leib?"

The cramped room served both as kitchen and workroom. Miraculously, it accommodated Uncle, Baruch, his wife, myself, a cat, the stove, utensils, bolts of cloth, several tailor's dummies, two sewing machines, and three other tailors who arrived shortly afterwards. Later we were joined by the two children, who spread out on the floor. Their father threatened them, ordering them out, but they ignored him.

Uncle stitched the lapel of a blue-striped jacket and hummed a bouncy tune as the machines whirred and steam rose from the hot iron. No sooner would the *patron* be explaining some tailoring detail than the doorbell would summon him to the shop below. And so it went, all day long.

Uncle tossed a piece of fabric onto my lap, fitted a thimble on my middle finger, and ordered me to practice with an unthreaded needle. In, out, in, out. Watching me from the corner of his eye, he'd lean over to offer a pointer.

"I've mastered it," I announced a short while later.

"You're a genius, Jankele! It took me seven years." The laughter spread like typhus, but Baruch rescued me, sending me out for cigarettes.

"Be so good, Jankele." The wife presented me with a broom. Then she asked me to peel potatoes, dice carrots, and chop onions. Then it was time to diaper the baby again.

"Keep your eyes on the fire, boy, or we'll freeze," hollered Baruch, charging down the stairs.

"You've got talent," shouted Baruch, when we called it a day. "Stick with it, you'll make a fine tailor one day!"

I had most of my meals with Uncle Shmil-Leib and Aunt Sonia. The baby cried endlessly as did Auntie. "In Russia I went dancing, to the opera, to concerts. What have I got now? I sit in this God-forsaken attic washing diapers! No one even to talk to. Why did he drag me here? Back home I had my family, my friends. That son-of-a-bitch uncle of yours, I used to be beautiful." She looked at her image in the mirror, biting her lip, and ran a hand down the side of her curved figure. "Men used to kill themselves for me. I could have had any one of them, but like a fool, I chose a loser. I'm old before my time!" When Uncle finally came home she would pound him with clenched fists.

"I've got to find a Sunday job," he uttered to himself. "I'd rather sweat it out bent over a machine than spend a day with you."

"Take me back home."

"Go! I don't care!"

"Goddamn it, I never see you! You're not a husband!"

"What do you want of me? You think the *macher* smuggled

us for your looks? My brother put up the money, but now haunts me for it. Even for Jankele's share." He held her firmly by the arms. "Look at me, Sonia! I'm sweating day and night. For who? For myself? You think I enjoy going without sleep? Without food? Without you?"

She spat in his face. "Who is she?"

His fist landed at the side of her mouth. She recoiled. He took her in his arms.

They made up, blaming the flat, the dog, and Aunt Chela's poisonous tongue.

That week Uncle Shmil-Leib went out and found a third-floor flat on Rue Blass. He invited me to inspect it. There were two rooms with a common toilet on street level. Worn linoleum covered the floors and the wallpaper peeled from dampness. "Would you like to move in with us?" he asked while I studied an insect scaling a wall.

"She doesn't know how to care for her own child, how will she look after you?" I smelled Aunt Chela's breath. Uncle Jacques advised me to stay put. I remained, and soon afterwards, my cousins joined me in the garret.

"Her parents are away in Paris." Jacquy was whispering, so as not to wake me. "I walk her home, and before I know it, I've got her naked, like the day she was born. Wow!"

"You think that's something?" François said. "Jules and I meet this number at a dance, and less than an hour later, we are giving it to her."

"Ooh!"

They had no time for me, pushing me onto André, who resented it. But after Uncle's nudging, my cousins took me out one evening.

Leaving the brightly lit boulevard, they led me through narrow, winding alleys with faintly lit cafés. An accordionist serenaded patrons in a tavern with "Seul dans la Nuit." Cats scavenged inside garbage cans and the aroma of *frites* drew us to a kiosk. A lover's quarrel was drowned out by the clanging bell of a racing fire engine.

"Take your pick, Jankele." Jacquy pointed to scantily attired women with hard and grotesque powdered faces, reeking of a thousand fragrances. They were everywhere; in windows, in doorways, along the sidewalk, winking, beckoning, puckering lips, and blowing kisses.

"Their husbands send them out to peddle their asses," François informed me. "After liberation there was screwing on the streets."

"Want to get your little thing wet?" Jacquy teased. "Don't worry, they'll show you what to do."

"No one has to show me."

"Oh!" Eyebrows raised.

"I've seen it."

"You've watched?"

"Horses!"

"Horses?" they looked at each other.

"Dogs, too," I added for good measure.

I could have told them, but didn't, about the young woman who lived in our courtyard at 32A Pawia Street in Warsaw who was often visited by a dapper-looking suitor bearing gifts. Once, my friend Itzchak invited me to the third floor to share the visual feast through the keyhole.

Next, my cousins treated me to a film. The action inside the movie theater was infinitely more interesting than the pair of comics on the screen. A boy's tongue was in a girl's mouth, his hand traveling up her skirt.

"How would you like to shove it into this one?" asked Jacquy later, at a night-club entrance, stroking a life-size cut-out of a show girl in high-heeled shoes and ostrich feathers.

I leaped into the air.

"What if I told you she's a he?"

I lay awake troubled. How little I knew about life!

AT THE SOLIDARITET, the club Uncle Jacques belonged to, one could eat a hearty meal in the basement cafeteria for a few francs. Small wonder the place was packed! The library was on the top floor, its walls lined with Yiddish books, miraculously saved from the Storm Troopers. There Uncle spent pleasant hours reading the leftist Yiddish press from Paris, playing chess, and debating politics.

He introduced me, boasting about how I had survived by my wits. I was impressed with the many people he knew and the high regard they had for him.

"Your uncle is a hero. Were it not for him, I would not be alive today," more than one told me, out of Uncle's earshot.

In his youth, he had worn a skullcap and attended synagogue until he discovered Zionism. "By reading Marx and Lenin, it became clear to me that the Zionist vision was too narrow," he related. "What was needed was not just a solution to the Jewish problem, but for all mankind. If the world were run by the proletariat, racism wouldn't exist." He wasn't opposed to a Jewish state, but didn't advocate it. "Instead of creating new borders, we should be tearing down existing ones."

It made sense. Why did we need a country? A flag? An anthem? How easily one could be misled! It felt good to know what was right. Not only for me, but the entire world!

The fifty francs I earned at Baruch's were barely enough for a movie ticket. Even then, there were times he made no move to part with my wages. I lingered, then went home empty-handed. Uncle Shmil-Leib had found a better job, and with Baruch continuing in his amnesia, I summoned the courage to face him.

Screaming, stamping his feet, spewing venom against Uncle for leaving him at the peak of the season, he turned on me. "The *chutzpa!* Your uncle begged me, literally begged me to take you. My parents had to pay when I apprenticed. You hear? Pay! What I give you is charity, out of the goodness of my heart, because I pity you."

"He'll never amount to anything," I heard Aunt Chela say behind closed doors when I quit my job at Baruch's.

By chance, Uncle Jacques ran into a comrade who happened to be looking for an assistant. He lived in an apartment reserved for the well-to-do, but which was now deteriorating. "Your uncle tells me you're a tailor." He spoke softly, warmly.

I nodded and looked about.

The work area, a section of the living room with a southern exposure, provided an abundance of natural light. I sipped on the tea I was offered.

"What did you learn at Baruch's? You stitch?" he asked.

"Naturally!"

"Use the machine?"

I smiled. "Of course, and I sweep floors, peel vegetables and, if you like, can help your wife with the children."

"I'm alone," he said, picking up the tea glasses. Then he hollered from another room. "If I give you three hundred a week, will you be happy?" I didn't reply, fearing the trap I had laid for myself. "Perhaps you were expecting more?" He re-entered. "In a month or two, if you work out, we'll talk about a raise." He shook my trembling hand.

It didn't take long for the truth about my skills to surface, but he threw me a net. "If Baruch doesn't know, how could he have taught you?" Patiently, he showed me how to affix buttons, stitch buttonholes, and operate the machine. He was interested in my story, and in turn, related his own experiences in the Belgian resistance. I could clearly picture the setting, the time of day, the color of his pursuer's eyes, and hear the background music. Not unlike the adventures Alan Ladd portrayed on the screen.

"Now that you're earning a few francs," said Uncle Jacques, "you should give your salary to your aunt." She left me with fifty, for pocket money.

"Shameful! I'm embarrassed for my brother." Uncle Shmil-Leib was livid. "But rest assured, Jankele, it's not his doing. This is not an act our family is capable of. Her entire family was like that. Stingy penny pinchers, but I never thought she would stoop this low. Are you sure you're telling me the truth?" He cupped my chin in his hand. "Come live with us. It's not luxury, but whatever we eat, you'll eat, and we're not starving. Your money will go towards an accordion."

"You didn't arrive at this on your own," said Uncle Jacques when I announced I was moving.

Jacquy and François couldn't have cared less, and Aunt Chela refused to look at me. "I treated him like my own flesh and blood and this is the thanks I get." Only André seemed pleased, watching me carry my belongings down the stairs.

I slept on an army cot in Uncle Shmil-Leib's kitchen. The money in my pocket made up for the discomfort. I treated myself to the cinema two or three times a week, to ice cream, chocolate, *frites,* and Coca-Cola. On other nights I listened to Aunt Sonia cursing her ever-absent husband. I offered to babysit, but she didn't bother even to get dressed.

"Where can a woman go by herself? They'll think I'm a whore."

Late in the night, when Uncle dragged his feet up the stairs, I heard them duel. "I'll leave and you'll never see me or the baby again."

Uncle yawned. "Do what you want."

Eventually there was no dialogue at all. "I doubt if they'll want her back," Uncle said when I told him she had contacted the Russian Embassy. "Let her frighten the bedbugs," he scoffed when I gave him the message that she was leaving.

As I was dressing for work one morning, she said, "I won't be here when you come home." Her voice was bereft of emotion. She kissed me.

That evening, when I found the flat deserted, I pushed the bedroom door open. "Auntie Sonia," I said. In the wardrobe, Uncle's suit and a tie dangled from wooden hangers, but there were gaps where her dresses had once hung.

Night descended on the city, but there was still no trace of her. Stretched out on my cot, I was blinded by the naked bulb. I expected the door handle to jiggle and to see her enter, the baby in her arms. Hours later, a key turning in the lock brought me to my feet.

"She'll be back," Uncle grumbled. But as the night wore on, he bolted the door. "Jankele, how about something to eat?"

I opened a can of sardines, diced an onion, sliced a loaf of bread, and brewed tea. He attacked the food, reminiscing between bites. "At eleven, I left school and went to work. After my bar mitzvah I left for Warsaw. What can I tell you, Jankele? I found employment and a place to sleep. Hmmm, sleep? A blanket on a bare floor. So as not to worry my parents, I wrote them glowing letters. When your *buby*,* may she rest in peace, asked for a winter coat for my father, I thought I'd go out of my mind." He lit a cigarette. "You know something, Jankele? You're a better cook than Sonia." The cigarette fell from his lips. Sinking his teeth into the back of his hand, he tried to stifle the onrush of tears.

BY SPRING OF THAT year my movie attendance had expanded to nightly, twice on Saturdays, and three screenings on Sundays. I breathed the world of cut-throat pirates, captive maidens, stormy seas, and flaming ships sinking with treasures in their holds. Galloping with cowboys along western plains, I shot villains, massacred savages, and rode off into sunsets. Sometimes I gallantly fought the German army, dropped bombs, machine-gunned entire regiments, saved my buddies, and returned home a hero without a scratch and not a hair out of place. To be Frankenstein's creator was infinitely more exciting than my life in the damp flat on Rue Blass.

*　grandmother

Easing into a seat at the movie house, I brushed my knee against the girl next to me, placed an arm around her shoulders, and drew her closer. If it led to our lips meeting, my hand would nervously creep up her skirt. After the movie, she would go her way and I mine, without a word having passed between us.

Uncle relied on me to do the chores. The menu consisted mostly of canned goods. I saw less and less of him, eating alone and leaving his portion on the stove. When I caught up with him, he looked haggard; he would collapse face down on the bed, flinging his arms at his sides.

"You know something, Jankele?" he said one Sunday before leaving for work. "Maybe what I'm about to tell you is none of my business. After all I'm only an uncle. But there isn't a film in the whole of Brussels you haven't seen at least twice." He stopped to collect his thoughts. "I have a proposition: I'll give you spending money out of my own pocket. You give me your salary and I'll save it for your accordion." He pulled open the table drawer. "Right here." Reading the gratitude in my eyes, he tweaked my nose. "That's what uncles are for."

THE DAYS WERE hot and humid and the nights no different. Fans swirled in open windows and doors were left ajar. Men drowned themselves in beer and women cradled their young. Foul odors emanated from plugged toilets. Cats chased one another and stray dogs rummaged through the garbage dumped at the curbs.

The merry-go-round music filtering from the nearby boulevard was hard to resist. A ride in a bumper car was all I could afford, leaving only enough for the week's streetcar fare. I stopped to listen to a barker's voice extolling the wonders on the inside when I sensed someone staring at me. It was a girl with rosy cheeks. She was smiling. Within minutes we were looking down from the top of the Ferris wheel. Her laughter made me want to melt, and when she squeezed my hand, I was as tall as the Ferris wheel. She lived in a village and had come to the fair for the day. After one kiss, I was prepared to give my life for her, so when she asked for another ride, I gladly emptied my pockets, except for my handkerchief and the key to the flat.

"How old are you?" She tickled my nose.

"First you tell," I managed in lame French, suspecting she was older than my fifteen years. She was turning eighteen on her next birthday.

"I'm also eighteen." I swallowed my breath and kissed her again.

"Where you from?" she asked as we wandered through a labyrinth of trailers.

Pressing her against a tiger painted on the side of a van, I slipped my hand inside her white blouse and massaged her nipples. To the beat of the midway dissonance, my hand traveled up her legs, inside her dainty pants. I thought she would claw me to pieces.

"What are you doing?" she writhed, reaching for me.

"Let's find a better place." I quickly buttoned up her blouse.

"Where do you live?"

"Not far."

The midway was boarding up for the night. Save for isolated pedestrians, the streets were bare.

"There," I pointed to a darkened window.

"Good. Let's go."

"My uncle . . ."

"You said he often doesn't come home."

"He might be there. Asleep."

"I'm afraid you're stuck with me, Jacques. I don't have car fare."

"Wait, I'll get some." Like a kitten she followed me up the darkened stairs. I switched on the light and breathed again when I saw Uncle's room in the condition he had left it that morning.

"Fancy," she said, throwing herself onto Uncle's untidy bed, pulling me on top of her.

"Better go before the streetcars stop running."

"You foolish child. The last car left over an hour ago." Again she teased with her tongue. Before I knew it, she had slipped off her underpants and was unbuttoning my fly. I had visions of her parents, armed with pitchforks.

"But your mother . . . ," I could barely utter.

"I'm at my girlfriend's."

"What if my uncle . . . ?"

"What if? I don't care," she breathed heavily. Two writhing dogs, locked in copulation in an isolated Polish village, pursued by stone-throwing children, burst forth in memory. I jumped off the bed. "You're mean!" she purred with injured pride.

"I'll give you money for a taxi."

"It'll cost a fortune."

"I don't care." I ran to the kitchen. The shock on my face brought her to my side. We stared into the empty drawer.

"I guess you're stuck with me, you silly Pollack!" she laughed.

On the verge of tears, I heard approaching footsteps. I jerked her arm, switched off the light, and led her to the landing above. Through the banister dowels I could faintly see Uncle Shmil-Leib shuffling his feet and unlocking the door with his rusty key.

Whatever was left of the night, we spent on a park bench. At dawn, after panhandling the cost of a streetcar fare from a passing night worker, I walked her to the stop. She could hardly keep her eyes open. No words were exchanged between us. I waited for the vehicle to arrive and watched her select a seat in the almost empty car. As it pulled away, she raised her arm, waved, then blew a kiss in my direction.

I was relieved to be rid of her, but by the time the streetcar had turned a bend and vanished from my view, I longed to hold her again, and touch her breasts.

"YOU DON'T THINK I spent your money, Jankele?" Uncle was hurt. "I just thought it would be safer in the bank. Anytime you want it, just ask." I was ashamed for my thoughts. "One thing you should know is that Kuperblums, and I mean all the Kuperblums, the entire family, have always been hard-working, honest people who never deceived anyone. No Kuperblum has ever shamed us. You can be proud of that name. I want you to know that because someday you'll have children and you'll want them to know it too!"

Saturdays the old market spilled over onto Rue Blass where farmers peddled produce from behind makeshift stalls. Large-boned ladies wrapped in shawls sat on stools, surrounded by bundles of flowers. Hucksters attracted crowds with knife-sharpening and cabbage-shredding gadgets.

In the market proper there was more to be had: American army surplus, old stoves, brass beds, tarnished goblets, figurines, damaged portraits, bottles filled with buttons. Next to a corroded bust of Napoleon I spied an accordion in an open case. Sitting on a crate, chewing a clove of garlic, and assessing my interest was the dealer, her hair straw-like, her face pockmarked.

"How much?" I stroked the keyboard.

"Expensive! But if you're really interested, on account it's been damaged, I'll make it affordable." She pointed to a hairline scratch. "It belonged to a beloved café musician who committed suicide over a deceiving woman. For you . . . ," she stared at my eager eyes, "for you . . . if you promise to study hard and take good care of it . . . and if you buy it right now and if . . . nine thousand francs."

"Uncle! Uncle!" Breathless, I fell into the room. His face

lathered, he tested the blade. "I've got to move fast." He scraped the razor along his cheek. "Only nine thousand," I brimmed. He stared at himself in the mirror, wiped his face on a towel, then combed his thinning hair. "Uncle, I need my money!"

"What money?" he dabbed cologne on his face. "This apartment is not a gift from God, and food doesn't come from heaven."

I screamed but nothing came out.

THE FLAT COLLECTED dust, and dirty dishes were piled in the sink. I refused to cook and ate at the Solidaritet. Saturdays I would stroll through the market to visit my instrument until it was no longer there.

Days and sometimes weeks went by without my ever crossing paths with Uncle. But there were signs of his presence: a wedge of lemon and a cigarette butt floating in the remains of a glass of tea, stale smoke, bread crumbs, a half-empty can of sardines for the rats to feast upon. Periodically, I caught glimpses of him endlessly inhaling cigarettes. Not a word was exchanged. Our eyes refused to meet. Each pretended the other did not exist.

In spite of his seeming interest, I had the distinct feeling my employer thought little of my musical ambition. I could almost read his thoughts: He'll grow out of it, he'll grow up and become a tailor like me. But one morning, noticing my bloodshot eyes, he handed me a violin case. Inside was a fiddle, a bow, and a yellowed music book.

"Bravo! Jascha Heifetz!" the tailor cheered when I ran the bow along the strings, making a grating sound. As if something was blocking his windpipe, he said, "I've kept it, hoping against all hope, that one day he will walk through the door. I still have trouble understanding what those beasts had against my eleven-year-old son."

Sheltering the instrument under my raincoat, I ran in a downpour for the streetcar.

The waitress at the Solidaritet, eyeing the case, was impressed and brought me a side order of pickles, saying it was on the house.

"I was hoping I might find you here," said Uncle Jacques, lowering himself into the chair beside me. He watched me eat, telling me about an interesting book he had just read. He then leaned across the table. "There's a woman I know . . . a bright, intelligent, very wealthy lady." He shifted uncomfortably in his chair. I gaped. "She lives alone in a very large house, except for a servant. She has everything — stores, factories, investments, I think even in America. But no family. They all perished. She has seen you here and would like to adopt you. When she dies, you would inherit everything." He removed his glasses, fogging them with his breath. "What do you think, Jankele? You'll get the best education. You won't have one, but ten accordions. If I could bring myself to believe in God, I'd say it's a godsend!" He cast his eyes away. "The only . . . well . . . you would have to change your name."

"What will Papa say?"

"I doubt if he's still alive."

"My name is not for sale, Uncle, and neither am I!"

"Jankele . . ." He reached for my arm as I stood up to leave. I jerked free, grabbed the violin case, and headed for the exit. Something prompted me to look back. A reflection from a light danced on the surface of his polished lenses.

I FELT MYSELF being carried by the late autumn wind like a leaf falling from a tree along the boulevard. The reason for my numbness was that I was dead, I concluded, witnessing my own funeral procession. Among those carrying my casket was the blind accordionist from Lublin.

"You don't remember me, eh?" smiled a young man

standing beside me on the streetcar, holding onto a safety strap. "Jacques Vogler. We met at the Solidaritet." I tried to affix a name to the face. He told me he was emigrating to Canada. "They're allowing in a thousand Jewish orphans."

"Canada? Where's that?"

"In America."

"What's there?"

"Bread, milk, butter . . . lots of it."

"And the girls?"

Grinning, he jumped off the moving vehicle.

"No other tailor in the whole of Brussels could have made this!" My employer stood back admiring the cream-colored suit on the dummy. "Look at it! Fit for a king!" Ordered only days earlier, we had executed it with great speed, both of us working late nights. "Feed the iron. When I get back from the bank, I'll press it." He slipped into his heavy coat.

Through the window, I saw him boarding a streetcar, and my eyes shifted to the suit, imagining his surprise when upon his return, he would find it ready for delivery. "I don't believe it! Congratulations, boy! I'm doubling your salary."

The iron was heavy, and the steam clouded my vision. I smelled smoke and faced a hole the size of a large coin. The overfed city official stood in the doorway. The tailor's face crimsoned, his body trembled. "A thou-ou-ou-sand par-d-dons, *Monsieur,* but the most un-unfortunate acci-dent-ent-t accident occurred, but rest assured that, that, that . . . if monsieur will give me an extra day, I'll have it corrected!"

"My daughter's wedding is tonight, you stupid, stupid, stupid Jew!"

"Monsieur is right. I am stupid for ever having taken pity on this imbecile!"

"You'll pay for this!" the pompous official foamed at the mouth. "Swindler! Conniver! Speculator!"

Perspiration pouring down my brow, I looked up and saw through the window my mentor approaching with bounding steps and swinging arms. I reached for my coat and flew out the back door.

"I must go to Canada," I announced at the Jewish agency.

From behind a desk, a dapper young man hurled questions at me. When he got to "Profession," he said, "I'll put down tailor. We need tailors in Canada."

"But I am a tailor."

"Of course you are," he winked. In answer to another question, I told him I was a communist.

"That's not funny," he said.

UNCLE SHMIL-LEIB ROSE, splashed his face, and warmed his innards by slurping a glass of tea. Disregarding my packed suitcase, he was about to close the door when I called out, "Goodbye, Uncle." Perhaps he didn't hear!

Carrying my fiddle and the gray cardboard valise I had purchased at the old market the day before, I left the flat on Rue Blass for the very last time.

"Good grief! Fifteen and going into the world all on your own," wept the Flemish woman next door.

Uncle Jacques was at the train station. "I read there's a large Jewish community in Canada, and many Poles. You'll feel right at home." After counseling me to associate with decent people, take an interest in books, and improve my chess, he presented me with a brown fountain pen. "Write a few words when you have a moment. Who am I to tell you not to go, Jankele? The decision is yours, and it may prove to be a wise one."

He kissed me on each cheek and left, so as not to be late for work.

4

"NAME?"

"*Ton nom?*" Mademoiselle looked at me.

"Jacques Kuperblum."

"Age?"

"Fifteen."

"Country of birth?" the immigration officer droned on.

"*Pays de naissance?*"

"*Pologne.*"

"You only speak French?"

"Polish, Russian, Yiddish, Hebrew, German, Ukrainian . . ."

He poked the peak of his cap, tilting it to the back of his head. "Any English?"

"English?"

"You do speak English!"

"Little bit."

"Why didn't you say so right away?" He imprinted my passport with an oval-shaped stamp: LANDED IMMIGRANT. CANADIAN IMMIGRATION, DEC. 20/47. HALIFAX, N.S. He extended his hand.

"Little bit." I shook it.

"Next!"

I pushed along with the others, my light coat offering

little protection from the gusts of wind. Seagulls swirled above. Perched on a hill, small dwellings lay buried in snow. The horizon was as distant as ever.

During the war, the *Aquitania* had transported troops to battle zones in Europe. Now she carried the dispossessed to Canadian shores.

After we boarded in Southhampton, the seasoned ship set sail. The first evening at sea when the bell rang, I joined the stampede for the dining room. But just as I was about to sit down at the table set as if for royalty, I looked up at the port-hole and caught a glimpse of the enraged ocean at an askew angle. I ran like a hellcat back to steerage and there remained on my cot for seven days and nights, kept alive by bits of food smuggled in others' pockets.

Now the ship stood anchored at Halifax, the waves beating against her bow, as if bent on her destruction.

Although the age limit for Jewish war orphans entering Canada at the time was eighteen, I suspected that many in our group were older.

"Keep together, children," Mademoiselle's voice reverberated. She could not have been more than twenty herself. We followed in pairs. A native of Montreal, she said, "It's a beautiful city, where many people speak French." On board ship she had offered us a choice: Montreal or Toronto. I saw little sense in starting all over with yet another new language, so I opted for Montreal.

"How will we get there?" asked the Greek girl.

"Train."

"Is it far?"

I butted in. "Will there be seats?"

"Not only seats, but beds as well."

What did she take me for? I knew a thing or two about trains. Passengers with strength to push and elbow landed seating space. Others stood like sour pickles in a jar.

When our train came into view, all hell broke loose. The black porters looked horrified and blocked our path as we stampeded towards them. To my astonishment, I was helped with my luggage, offered a stool to step up on, and assisted into the coach, as if I were a nobleman entering a carriage.

This one had ample leather upholstered seats, a scrubbed floor, and the smell of detergent still lingering in the air. Not even a thumb print on the pristine windows. Levers, handles, chains, and hooks, made of copper and brass.

I claimed a seat with a view. Maurice sat next to me. He had anchored himself to me when we'd boarded the ship in Dover. One year older and at least a head shorter, he spent an inordinate amount of time in front of a mirror, inspecting his receding hairline. On the stopover in London, when he was getting ready for bed, I noticed a number branded just above his wrist.

Passengers bundled in winter apparel were scooting by, lugging their possessions. Some had infants. On board ship, I had studied their faces and listened to their conversations. They avoided my gaze. Collaborators with forged documents.

In the summer of '42, Red Army soldiers who had escaped from the POW camp in Chelm roamed the nearby villages. In exchange for sharing my lunch with them, they taught me songs and offered hope of my seeing Papa again.

One, a happy-go-lucky Ukrainian with an enchanting voice, turned himself in to the Germans. Later, we heard he had become a brutal guard in Sobibor.

I closed my eyes. What are you doing here, Jankele Kuperblum?

I won't stay. I'll just look around.

I imagined the edge of the earth beyond which only an abyss existed. My mind veered: Why does it rain? Snow? Thunder? How do butterflies manage to fly? Why do fish live under water? Where does the sun come from and where does it go?

A manicured and jeweled hand tugged at my sleeve. I

looked up. "Take." A large red apple was under my nose. She was followed by a fur-wrapped, perfumed companion in high heels, distributing magazines. Both were from the Halifax Jewish community, obviously unaware of what had occurred over there.

Maurice immersed himself in a *Captain Marvel* comic book. I sank my teeth into the apple and thumbed through *Life*: pictures of extraordinarily joyous people driving automobiles, smelling coffee, tasting soups, washing dishes, and sipping Coca-Cola. Holding up a tube, a freckle-faced youngster brushed his teeth, grinning from ear to ear. A buffoon of a man hugged his wife as she waxed the floor.

The engine revved, the whistle blew and the doors were bolted. The train started to move. Buildings, forests, houses floated across the winter landscape as if in a dream.

"Look." A hand pointed to children with sticks skating on a frozen pond.

Someone whistled a familiar tune. A girl recited a poem. Closer, a voice recalled the thrill of seeing a dancing bear on a Budapest sidewalk. Conversations bubbled in a stew of languages, switching from one to another, like shifting gears.

"See the one in the rabbit coat?" Maurice gestured to a girl with an oversized bosom. "I spent an entire night with her in Paris," he whispered. "She was completely undressed! Now she pretends not to know me."

My eyes opened wider. "What was it like?"

"She was afraid, so we just held each other." He stared at me. "Ever do anything?"

I thought of those I had kissed and others who didn't object when I touched them in restricted places. Then the out-of-town girl came to mind. I didn't have her address. I didn't even know her name.

"Jacques, come to Toronto," Maurice jabbed me. "With your looks and my irresistible charm, we'll score big."

Telephone poles zipped by. The train sped into the night.

"Dinner is being served in the dining coach." A porter in a white jacket strolled through. Pushing my way along with the others, I expected to face a grisly man ladling out meager portions of watery slop into dented canteens. Instead I found linen-covered tables with cutlery, glassware, plates, and yellow flowers. Waiters pirouetted with silver trays, weighed down by mountains of food, the aromas invading my nostrils, teasing my appetite. Is this a dream? One tap of a wand, and it will all disappear.

I attacked the roasted chicken with bare hands and wolfed down the creamy potatoes, green peas, and cubed carrots. I devoured everything that was placed before me. Tomorrow I may not be so lucky.

Maurice and I had returned to our coach when Zygmunt, who on board ship had shown interest in my violin, stopped by and bombarded me. Who had I studied with? Who was my favorite composer? He reeled off peculiar names.

"What's your favorite piece?"

"Dark Night," I blurted.

"Who wrote that?" He rolled his eyes.

A voice intruded. "Where are the beds you promised, Mademoiselle?"

"On the roof," someone answered.

We were still convulsing when the porter appeared. Pressing a button here, a lever there, he converted the seats into beds.

Maurice dived into the lower berth. I flew to the upper. The linen was freshly pressed, the pillows soft and fluffy. I had forgotten about comfort and warmth. I pulled the covers over my head and cried.

In the morning the beds reverted to seats. Outside, the frozen landscape blasted past. Cities, forests, factories, popped up from nowhere, and in between, billboards with the same forced smiles. In late afternoon the train slowed and inched into a depot.

"Those for Montreal, detrain," Mademoiselle commanded.

"I guess this is it, then." Maurice held out his hand.

I pressed my violin case under one arm and clutched the coarse rope securing my suitcase, which contained a shirt, much too large, a few pairs of socks, and twenty-three Canadian dollars knotted in a handkerchief. As in the past, I now saw myself as a rabbit at a crossroads, sniffing the terrain for what lay ahead. My eyes fell to my feet.

"Jacques!" Mademoiselle yelled, waiting for me to get off. "Hurry!"

"How long is the ride to Toronto?"

"Overnight."

"Beds?"

She lifted my chin and curled her lips into a smile.

5

PEDESTRIANS SCURRIED ABOUT, their arms laden with gift-wrapped packages. Santa Claus rang a bell at one corner and at the next, a uniformed band lured coins into a cauldron. Rows of one-story houses were interrupted by banks, churches, and an array of gas stations. A man sold evergreen trees from the back of a truck parked at an intersection. Store windows glittered with Christmas ornaments. Toronto. A village, I concluded.

In a three-story house on the corner of Markam and Harbord, a motherly type received us with kisses and hugs. The rooms upstairs had bunk beds, and in the kitchen, an assortment of breads, buns, and bagels lay on the counter. The fridge was stacked with milk and butter.

Coiffed women came to chauffeur us around. At a factory on Spadina Avenue, a Yiddish-speaking man outfitted us with shirts, underwear, hankies, socks. A few blocks away, we tried on suits. When I faced the mirror in a pinstripe I had plucked off the rack, the owner asked, "For your father?"

Next were coats, followed by a stop for shoes and one for ties. "You're too young," advised one of the chaperons, watching me admire myself in a fedora at a milliner's.

Sunday, I put on a white shirt with cufflinks, slipped into the suit and gleaming shoes, knotted the wide, colorful tie around my neck, and donning the winter coat, marched out onto the street, fedora in hand. I hardly encountered a soul. When I gazed into a store window, I saw Humphrey Bogart's reflection. At the movie theater, the doors were locked. Everything was locked on Sundays.

Visitors invited us to their homes. And when they all served turkey, we concluded it was the national dish.

"Is it true what happened there?" inquired some.

I welcomed the questions, hoping to unload my emotional burden. But often I sensed my story was not believed, and those who did not question its veracity made me feel I should apologize for having survived. But most simply didn't ask, didn't want to know. They were looking for Hollywood heroes who stood up to the Germans.

Girls in loose-fitting sweaters and ankle-length tight skirts, shuffling about in flat-heeled shoes, also came to take a peek. They played records and taught us to dance. On weekends they held parties. I tagged along in my Humphrey Bogart outfit.

"How old are you?" asked one I had difficulty leading in a foxtrot.

"Twenty-one," I answered, my head resting on her bosom. "And you?"

Organizations and businesses donated tickets to films, concerts, and other events. In a mammoth ice stadium, spectators cheered opposing teams on skates, fighting with sticks over a small black disc. I was baffled by heavy balls being rolled down wooden alleys, dislodging the bottle-shaped objects at the other end. Day after day and week after week, the same song came from the radio: "You can have her, I don't want her, she's too fat for me."

The social worker I had been assigned to, Miss Spivak, petite and bubbly, suggested I call myself Jack. Glancing up from my file, she said, "A family wants to meet you."

She left and soon re-entered, presenting me to three immaculately groomed and dressed people. The man, his bush of frizzy hair combed to the back, wore freshly pressed slacks and a corduroy jacket with leather patches on the elbows. His delicate wife was attired in a gray two-piece suit, a string of pearls around her slim neck. The daughter, in a plaid skirt and white satin blouse, her dark hair falling loosely below her shoulders, studied me.

"I understand you want to be a musician," the man intoned in a nasal voice, more in German than in Yiddish. "I'm with the Toronto Symphony Orchestra, first violin in the second row." When I didn't so much as blink, he came closer. "I'm not just an ordinary fiddler, the kind who play at weddings where you come from. Not a *klezmer*,* you understand? I'm an artist, a classical musician. I play Schubert, Beethoven, Mendelssohn, Bach, B-a-c-h." He breathed on me. "Do you understand?" After adjusting his glasses on the bridge of his pronounced nose, he recalled his days in Berlin, where he had studied with a most renowned professor.

"Enough, Harold!" his wife motioned.

Mr. Sumberg cleared his throat. "Would you . . . I mean . . . we would . . . like . . . ?"

The fiddle on my lap, I sat in the back of the taxi, listening to Miss Spivak's reassuring words. The cab came to a stop and the social worker pointed to a house with a high angled roof burdened by snow. We mounted the steps to the veranda, Miss Spivak lugging my suitcase, and I behind, the violin under my arm. The buzz of a button, followed by a dog's bark, brought a smiling Mrs. Sumberg to the door. Before I found my bearings, the social worker bade me farewell. Mrs. Sumberg pointed to the mat for my galoshes, and to a velour-covered bench for my belongings.

"Quiet, Chester," she addressed the dog enclosed in the kitchen. He leaped at me, but she calmed my fears. He was so unlike the vicious dogs in Polish villages.

* musician

A sandwich and a glass of milk appeared on the chrome table. Sliced diagonally, each half of the sandwich was topped with a peculiar, green, oval-shaped fruit, spiked with a toothpick. I yanked one out, smelled it, then set them both aside. Imprisoned between the bread was a slice of processed cheese and a lonely leaf of lettuce. Through the milk-clouded glass, I caught her look of surprise when she saw the plate was empty.

"I'm full," I replied, when she offered more, hoping she would press further. But she took me at my word.

"No one ever eats them," she complained, catching me eyeing the wooden bowl filled with walnuts. While she recounted her family's history in Russia after the revolution, I reached for the nutcracker buried in the bowl. She lashed out at the Bolsheviks and Stalin, likening him to Hitler. Nor was she enamored of Zionism. Her family were all socialists. She talked and I cracked nuts. At one point I sensed a disapproving glance, but charged ahead. By the time her daughter Cora had returned from school, only shells remained in the bowl.

Later, when Mr. Sumberg came home, he took me on a tour. In the elegant living room with a fireplace and baby grand piano, he pointed to a cabinet with dials. "Radio, r-a-d-i-o. Do you know what this is?" Paintings, drawings, and sculptures vied for attention. The artists, he told me, were their personal friends. Explaining everything in its minutest detail, he made me examine and touch, informing me what was rare, handcrafted, and valuable. Each book in his library had a sticker with his name on it, while in the basement, a rack held corked wine bottles labeled, *Sumberg — 1946*. On the way to the second floor, he pointed out his award-winning photographs, which lined the staircase. A music stand, violins, photographic lights, a case with a camera, and numerous lenses occupied his study.

After parading me through three bedrooms, we entered yet another. "This is where you sleep." In the washroom, he turned on the taps, activated the shower, and demonstrated flushing the toilet. "I hope you know what this is." He tore off a piece of toilet paper.

Bombs were falling and Germans were on the run. Returning from the town with their spoils, the villagers scratched their heads. Adam Kozak, the wise man of the village and my employer, was summoned. He studied the rolls of paper, while the crowd, like a flock of geese with necks outstretched, waited. "Obviously, the Germans ran out of cotton bandages and had to resort to paper." He ripped off a section, filled it with tobacco, sealed it with his tongue and lit it.

Turning to Mr. Sumberg, I answered, "It's for rolling cigarettes."

Mr. Sumberg sat at the head of the table, his wife at the opposite end, and I across from Cora. After sharpening the silver-plated knife, the maestro carved the chicken with much ceremony, skilfully dissecting the bird. Ever so gently, he lifted the slivers of meat with the serving fork, placing them onto plates.

"Oh, Harold, enough!" His wife held up her hand after the second slice.

Luckily, I was allotted three. There was a carrot for each of us. Of the five dwarfed potatoes nestling in a fancy tureen, Mr. Sumberg asked for a half and his wife took one. I was the recipient of two whole ones. I stared at my plate, thinking I could devour the entire bird twice with all the trimmings. The clock chimed, and the conversation was sparse. They cut their meat into morsels, chewing so elegantly, barely moving their lips, pausing only for a word between bites. I intended to emulate them, but once I lifted the fork, I lost control.

"Too much for me," sighed Mrs. Sumberg, pushing away her plate. Cora's carrot was untouched. "A little more?" Mrs. Sumberg asked me.

"I'm full," I said.

After dinner, the doorbell rang, and a teenager, fiddle in hand, was admitted and sent scurrying up the stairs. Jarring strains, interspersed with nasal instructions, drifted to the kitchen where Cora and I were doing dishes. We conversed using a concoction of French, with a sprinkling of Yiddish, but mostly, we used our hands.

Just as we were getting to know each other, her mother summoned Cora to attend to her school assignments.

"We only listen to live music in this house," an alarmed Mrs. Sumberg said when I attempted to turn on the radio in the living room. I took myself to my room until hunger brought me down to the kitchen. "A glass of milk and a cookie," counseled Mrs. Sumberg. "It's unhealthy to eat before bedtime."

Following André's example when saying goodnight, I approached a seated Mrs. Sumberg and leaned over to plant a kiss. She offered me her cheek. Her husband backed up and held up his hand like a traffic cop. "That's not necessary!"

They presented me to their family, friends, and colleagues as "our Jack." Cora referred to me as, "My brother, I guess!" It was up to me, they said, what to call them. I swallowed hard, and called them "Mom" and "Dad."

At a department store, Mr. Sumberg bought me a knickerbocker suit. He said it was more fitting for a fifteen-year-old than my pinstripe. It made me look like a little boy, but I accepted it graciously.

Cora accompanied me on my first day to attend special English class for newcomers. And when she saw me struggle with homework, she came to my aid. In time we exchanged views, laughs, and when her parents were out, we treated ourselves to take-out from the Seven Seas, around the corner. Sitting cross-legged on the staircase landing, we licked our fingers on fish and chips dripping in oil. Although we were careful to dispose of the evidence, her parents were mystified by the odor when they returned.

Unlike most families, the Sumbergs refused compensation for my keep from the Jewish community, and every Friday I would find a five-dollar bill on my dresser. I pocketed the money, picturing Mr. Sumberg talking his heart out for an hour or sweating at a rehearsal. He set aside Sunday mornings to teach me, passionately trying to instill in me a love for the violin. By the sixth week, we both gave up. When I was stuck for a word or bruised a sentence, he took dictionary and encyclopedia in hand and spelled the word, gave me a synonym or antonym, or corrected my pronunciation.

Mrs. Sumberg also tried to elevate me, showing me how to eat with fork and knife and how to chew with my mouth closed. She complained about my smelly socks, begging me to change them daily. Some mornings my socks, underwear, and shirt were missing. "They were so dirty they crawled away on their own," she said, straight-faced.

A gift-wrapped package sat by the side of my dinner plate on April 16th. Over a cake with glowing candles, the three sang "Happy Birthday" to me, and I was told to make a wish. I did, and couldn't hold back the tears as I opened the small box. Nestled inside was a watch.

Relieved of dish duty, I went to see *Monsieur Verdeaux,* a Charlie Chaplin film. Spotting an appealing girl, I sat beside her, and when the theater darkened, I put my arm around her. Then I heard a scream and felt a slap.

For weeks, I feared to so much as glance at a female until one evening, noticing a young woman gazing into a shop window, I summoned new courage. "Can I buy you a Coke?"

She looked me over. "I'd love it, only I'm married."

Those with whom I had crossed the ocean seemed to be luckier than I. One lived with a family whose playroom was equipped with a complete soda fountain. I shared my feelings with Miss Spivak and she offered to arrange a transfer. I considered it for only the briefest moment. How could I hurt them like that?

As the warm weather approached, bicycles appeared on the streets. There was no prospect of one for me, but Cora's was deteriorating in the garage and she offered it to me. With the rust scrubbed off, the chain oiled, and a renewing coat of paint, it looked new and rode like a charm. When I was met with snickers, a length of a broomstick across the frame changed the bike's gender.

With the special English course behind me, I was placed in grade one and promoted a few weeks later. In this manner, I reached eighth grade within months, and left before exam time as Mr. Sumberg had enrolled me in a summer work camp run by the Farm Labour Service Force, an agency created during the war to assist farmers.

"Where you're going, there's an army camp nearby, Camp Borden — B-o-r-d-e-n," Mr. Sumberg informed me on the day of my departure. "During the war, many girls in that vicinity got themselves into trouble." He threw me a covert glance. "Do you know what I'm talking about? Condoms. C-o-n-d-o-m-s!"

Most of the recruits were school dropouts. As I lay in the bunk, watching them get drunk and inhaling cigarette smoke, one asked, "What's your name?"

"Jack Kup," I answered, gripped with anxiety.

"What kind of name is that?"

"Polish," I said.

To make it sound more familiar, a few days later I changed it to Kuper.

The work was taxing and boring, and the pay, fifty cents an hour and all one could eat: juice, hot and cold cereals, bacon and eggs with fried potatoes, mountains of foamy white bread and heaps of fresh butter for breakfast. A copious bagged lunch accompanied us to the fields, where, bent in half, we picked lettuce. Dinners were sumptuous: chicken or beef, overflowing platters of vegetables and potatoes, jugs of fresh milk and home-baked pies.

Like a squirrel, I saved my earnings, only occasionally

treating myself to a chocolate or candy at the tuck shop. One day, three fresh recruits, immigrants themselves, arrived and greeted me in Polish.

"You're a Jew-boy!" one sneered when I answered in their tongue. Word spread, and I feared for my life. Surprisingly, the others couldn't have cared less.

MY BODY TANNED, muscles toned, a few pounds added to my slight frame, I returned to Toronto in time to enrol in the commercial art course at Central Technical School. With no primary school diploma, I was placed in a special class. A ragtag band of rejects, we were treated with disdain by teachers and students alike, and exposed to a smattering of everything, from auto mechanics to home economics — subjects I had no aptitude for or interest in. However, when Miss McCarthy of the art department told me I showed promise, I reached out to her. Thanks to her vigorous lobbying, I was rescued. Riding the streetcar with an art portfolio under my arm, I felt at least a foot taller.

I was irritated by the mechanical spacing, poor color, and lack of design in the signs fronting the stores I passed. The buildings, the street, the streetcar itself — all begged to be redesigned. Everything waited for me to make it right.

A man sitting next to me on a streetcar invited me to his home to meet his beautiful daughter, who had polio. On the same ride, two Italian immigrants, gesturing with their hands and speaking loudly, were confronted by an irate old lady. "Speak English, you bloody foreigners!"

When our English teacher, Miss Prior, assigned us to write a composition on "How I spent my summer vacation"; "My favorite sport"; or "My brother," I chose the last. I recounted how when my brother, Josele, was hungry and crying for bread, I placated him by drawing and telling him stories. Though I received a high mark for my effort, I was not invited to read my story to the class as the others were.

Later that year when I submitted a poem for the school yearbook, *The Vulcan*, about a boy cigarette seller in the Warsaw Ghetto who starves to death for lack of customers, I was thrilled that it was accepted for publication. But when I saw it in print, I could hardly recognize its title or my first name.

THE RAIN

By John Kuperblum

The sun has hidden his face,
Beyond the clouds of the north;
The wind is taking its place:
The rain is coming forth.

Moving across the sky,
Blowing the woods and grains;
People they run; birds they fly:
For it rains, how it rains.

On the corner of the street,
Near the church where people pray,
Stands a girl with bare feet:
"Buy my flowers" I hear her say.

And cruel is the wind that blows,
And cruel the torrential rain,
The girl shivers in her rags,
Again comes that piercing pain.

The girl is no longer there;
Her story you know too well,
A story as old as time,
And only the rain can tell.

Later I wrote a one-act play, *The Number.* Set in the red-light district of Brussels where I had gone with my cousins, François and Jacquy, it dealt with a man who, after agreeing to go to bed with a prostitute, recognizes her as his mother by the concentration camp number tattooed on her arm.

After showing it to a classmate, a line formed to read it. During a life-drawing class, while we were struggling to capture the form of our seminude model, Mr. Ross, our instructor, sat in the corner, his eyes buried in my manuscript. When the bell rang, he asked me to stay behind. Handing me the play, he said, "I suggest you don't expose your writings to these children. They don't understand."

It was a jolting reminder that if I desired acceptance, I had to blend in — a condition I knew something about from my years on the run in the skin of a Catholic orphan. My accent worried me, and I had difficulty with pronunciation. When purchasing art supplies, I'd ask for six shits of paper, or I'd suggest to a friend, "Let's go to the druckstore for a cock." As hard as I tried to shed the past, it intruded.

Besides accommodating my art supplies, the knapsack I carried to school contained my lunch: two sandwiches, an apple, and a couple of cookies. Between scrawny buttered pieces of whole wheat bread was a slice of processed cheese, or chopped egg mashed with mayonnaise.

My mouth watered as I watched others nibble on chicken legs, chomp on bagels with cream cheese topped with lox, and wolf down chunks of salami smothered with mustard pressed between hand-cut slabs of Russian rye. Swapping was common, but when I offered mine, there were no takers. "Yesterday you had egg, so it must be cheese." On occasion, my classmate Manny Silver's mother would take pity on me and throw in an extra bagel, a juicy thick burger or chopped liver on pumpernickel. "For the greenhorn," she said. I chirped, as did the birds pecking on my discards.

To satisfy my curiosity, one day, instead of taking my lunch, I snatched Cora's. It was cheese, as I had been expecting, but instead of two, there was only one sandwich.

To abate the pangs of hunger, daily I treated myself to three-for-a-dime danishes from a shop near the streetcar loop. At the beginning of May, as I emerged from the patisserie, my eyes zoomed in on the headline in the *Toronto Star*: "Newborn State of Israel Attacked by Six Arab Armies." I stopped in mid-bite. Deserter! Coward! distant voices resounded.

A GALAXY OF YOUNG MEN, each with his own scent of aftershave, arrived to date Cora. The Sumbergs scrutinized the suitors, reminding their daughter to be back at a decent hour or find herself locked out. These escorts came and went. Except for Phil. Decked out in navy uniform, shoes smelling of polish, he became a regular. He had lost his mother at a young age, and had later been abandoned by his father. Determined to become a doctor, he had joined the navy, who sponsored his education.

"He's a strange one," the Sumbergs whispered, watching Cora leave arm in arm with him.

I passed my first year and went looking for summer work in a safe environment. Miss Spivak recommended me to a Jewish golf and country club on the city's outskirts. After a wait, the manager appeared in bathrobe and slippers, one eye ringed by a monocle. Eric von Stroheim.

My accent and limited vocabulary were disconcerting to me, until *he* spoke. As he ate his breakfast, he outlined my duties, my pay, and assigned me a bed in a trailer.

Members arrived at dawn to tee off, caddies behind them, lugging heavy bags. At lunchtime the waiters busied themselves serving three-decker sandwiches, salads, soups, and fancy pastries. The dinner crowd was larger and noisier. Guests shouted greetings from afar. I had trouble relating to these Jews. The manager, bathed in nauseating perfume, a cravat tucked into his collar, table-hopped, shaking hands and sprinkling compliments.

To Ezio Pinza's "Some enchanted evening, you will meet

a stranger, across a crowded room," I maneuvered the tray laden with dirty dishes, as if through a minefield.

Compliments were sent to the chef, and diners would summon him to extol him. He knew how to take a bow, look humble, and speak with a Parisian accent. Once he flipped a filet mignon onto the floor. But he scooped it up, garnished it, and sent it out. I felt guilty watching the waiter carrying it to the table and appalled when the customer handed him a five-dollar bill to take to the kitchen.

By week's end all the staff, except for me, had left. I quickly progressed from busboy to waiter to head waiter, to the only waiter. Club members took note of me, giving me pointers. At night, when the place cleared, the kitchen closed, and the manager retired, I was left to look after a group of card-playing ladies who didn't want to go home. They tossed their money freely into my already bulging pockets.

With my elevated status, I was now invited to join the manager and chef for an occasional beer. They talked about this and that, but mostly about the members, with whiffs of disdain.

Truckloads of supplies arrived and an army of waiters was bused in for a Saturday night affair. The dining room was adorned with candles. The taskmaster strutted about like a peacock, inspecting every detail through his monocle. By sundown, the room had filled with elegantly dressed ladies and escorts. The orchestra struck a chord, a singer imitated Ezio Pinza, and the chef, sweat pouring from his body, performed culinary acrobatics over hot coals. The waiters rushed about, while the white-suited manager, a boutonniere growing out of his lapel, greeted arrivals, bowing from his waist and pressing his fleshy lips into unblemished ladies' hands.

"Your favorite table is waiting, Mr. Rosenberg."

"How lovely you look in this exquisite gown, Mrs. Horvath!"

The guests were blind to his smiles. In this bedlam, I searched for the president, a gaunt man with eagle eyes, and found him whispering into the manager's ear.

"Jawohl, Mr. Schwartz." The compliant servant clicked his heels.

As Alan Ladd, I neared the president, and looking askance, said in a conspiratorial tone, "I have something very important to tell you."

"If you have a problem, tell Mr. Glockenspiel."

"He's an anti-Semite," I breathed fire.

"He's the very best manager this club has ever had," he said, and whisked past.

IN THE MORNING, with a worn brush and some black paint I'd found, I smeared the interior of the trailer: "Death to all Nazis!" Then I pulled out my suitcase, which was brimming with crumpled bills, threw in my belongings, and headed for the bus.

When Mrs. Sumberg saw me bouncing up the front stairs, she looked disturbed. Taking the hint, I jumped on a train bound for another Farm Labour Service Force camp — this one at Harrow near Windsor. To buttress myself, I persuaded two classmates to join me: Manny Silver, who without glasses resembled his idol, Danny Kaye, whom he imitated unerringly, and another boy with a classic case of acne. On board, we met another member of the tribe, Sid Furie, brought up in comfort in Toronto's Forest Hill Village. At camp we selected adjoining bunk beds and shared a table in the mess hall. As soon as we hit the fields, my buddies complained, and by day's end they could barely drag their feet. In the morning Sid left without a word. A day later, their backs breaking and scorched by the sun, the other two departed.

I stretched to make friends. One French Canadian could barely wait for Friday night to hit the local scene. "After a few beer I find me a chick, stand her against a tree, and give it to her," he crowed. But when we got to the local bar, with not a conquest in sight, he got so plastered I had to carry him back.

The girls were to be found working in the fields. That's how I met Margaret. I took a shine to her, and when I asked her for a Saturday night date, she told me that was when she worked at a drive-in. I arrived at midnight and anxiously waited outside, watching her on roller skates serving a stream of screeching cars. At two in the morning, when we arrived at her darkened house, instead of stepping into the shower to wash and change so we could go dancing, she fell onto the bed. I felt her naked body against my pounding heart, her lips pressing against mine, and thought I had died and gone to heaven.

After breakfast, I escorted her to church. We sat in the back row of the balcony, and while the priest performed theatrics, I toyed with her hair and whispered sweet endearments. Days later when she confided she had missed her period, I packed my bag.

"You can't stay here all summer," lamented a startled Mrs. Sumberg when I arrived home. "I need a rest."

THIS TIME I HITCHED a ride to a vacation spot one hour's drive from the city, where many of Toronto's Jews owned summer cottages. I walked into a deli and asked for a job.

To support a wife and child, the proprietor, an aspiring cantor, was trying his hand at business. He wanted to hire me but couldn't afford to pay. Nor did he have a place for me to sleep. From scraps and discards, I built a shack for myself behind the store. I washed dishes, cleaned tables, and advanced to short order cook, boiling hot dogs. Soon salads were added to my repertoire; I turned them into dazzling creations.

My days off were spent at the Red Barn Theatre. I felt

honored to sweep the stage, paint scenery, or just hang around the magic. Hearing audiences laugh and applaud, I knew that's where I belonged.

The actors were American, treating the detour into the wilds of Canada as a summer respite. The director's wife, who with layers of make-up portrayed the frightened old lady in *Night Must Fall,* encouraged me, intimating that if I came to New York, they would send me to an acting academy.

Her co-star, Tim, a deli food addict, would often drop by the restaurant and I'd load his plate with extras. I offered to introduce him to a few girls. Smiling politely, he told me he had someone special in New York.

Placing his wife behind the cash register for one day, the cantor kissed his daughter and asked if I needed anything from the city. The glint in Colleen O'Grady's eye and promise of ecstasy in her gait came to mind. Tall, with long auburn hair, she sat beside me in class and thought my accent was sexy.

"Call my girlfriend, Colleen, and say hello for me," I said.

"Consider it done." He turned the key in the ignition. I extracted my little black book and was searching for a pen. "I'll just take this." He yanked the book out of my hands and was gone.

When I returned to school in the fall of 1949, Colleen gave me a chilly reception. "What a creep!" she said. "He wouldn't take no for an answer, and the next thing I knew he was knocking on my door."

Almost every girl in my book told a similar story.

That summer, Cora and Phil had exchanged vows.

"It was just a small family affair," explained Mrs. Sumberg. "We didn't want to drag you back just for that."

The hit parade blaring from Phil's radio made the Sumbergs grit their teeth, but they held their tongues. The table conversation was more lively, with Phil telling jokes and pulling pranks. But there was hardly any extra food for the additional mouth.

In the evenings Phil would occasionally accompany me when I took Chester for a walk. Pungent whiffs from the corner deli pulled us. Staring through the window, we watched the aproned man behind the counter, an Auschwitz survivor, slicing the steaming brisket. We would empty our pockets and share a spicy sandwich, topped with a dill pickle, then wash it down with a Coke. Saturday mornings the two of us would bike down to the Crescent Grill in the *shmata** district at Spadina and College to gorge ourselves on kaiser buns drenched with butter, sausages and eggs, and side orders of fries.

That's where I ran into Mussy, a girl I knew from public school, and her two friends. One's birthday was approaching and they were scouting for a place to celebrate. Without thinking, I offered the Sumbergs' rec room.

The Sumbergs were unbending in their opposition to the idea until Cora intervened.

Chaperoned by Phil and Cora, a group of us danced to records, popped caps off soft drinks, and munched on pretzels. But the Sumbergs, agitated by the drifting smoke, brought the proceedings to an abrupt halt before ten-thirty. While cleaning up, I was subjected to a lecture for associating with riffraff.

Before the Christmas break, my classmates were tripping over each other vying for jobs as temporary sales clerks at Kresge's and Woolworth's. Confident I could do better, I designed and mass-produced a season's greetings sign. The odor of the chemicals brought the Sumbergs to the cellar. In spite of their remonstrations, I quickly silk-screened one hundred sixteen-by-twenty posters in three colors.

With a batch under my arm, I entered the local barbershop. The moment the barber realized I wasn't there for the usual, his manner changed so drastically that I had trouble believing it was the same person. "I don't know

*   garment

what I'll do with it, but I suppose I'm obliged." He grudgingly reached into his pocket for a dollar. Most storekeepers were content with what they already had, a puny sign in one color sprinkled with glitter, at half of what I was charging. The proprietor of a fur store admired my artistry and didn't quibble about price, but found it too obtrusive for his window. When the stores closed, I returned home, lugging the heavy bundle.

Phil was even more upset than I was, and suggested I'd be wiser to paint signs to order. A relative of his, who had a press in his basement, provided business cards gratis — and Phil distributed them to the neighborhood stores.

One day Mrs. Sumberg answered the phone to the sound of a voice asking, "Is this Kuper Signs?" She recoiled.

Picking up the receiver and lowering my voice at least one octave, I caroled, "Kuper signs. Mr. Kuper speaking." Fifteen minutes later, I walked into a fashionable ladies' wear store.

"Kuper Signs," I said with a smile and pulled out a crumpled notebook and pencil stub from my pocket.

The lanky man furrowed his brow. "They sent you?"

"You're lucky to get anyone this time of year," I said.

When I asked for a tape to measure the windows, he took a double take. I was fretting over how I was going to construct the forty-foot sign he required for above the store, when he told me there was one languishing in the cellar. "By reusing the frame, you'll save money," I said. The smile that spread across his face made him look ten years younger.

"Mr. Kuper will call you with a price," I said on my way out and ran for the streetcar.

"This is Mr. Kuper," I said into the mouthpiece.

"Two weeks?" he hollered into my ear. "I told that stupid kid I need it immediately."

"The shop is humming like a beehive, but I'll see what I can do." I caught a glimpse of Mrs. Sumberg shaking her head in disbelief.

Everything rolled along nicely until the Sumbergs saw their prized ping-pong table stained with oil paints.

"You again?" the proprietor fumed, when I came through his door, struggling with the signs in my arms.

An employee showed me where to find the stepladder and brought me a pair of scissors and scotch tape. Soon the windows were plastered with banners, the show-cards were fastened to the racks, and the boss was summoned. While he was still in a good mood, I recruited him to help drag the old frame outside. Unfurling the new canvas, I looked for a stapler. Muttering to himself, he left, returning with one in a moment. As we knelt on the freezing pavement, he held the canvas in place while I shot staples.

"We need an extension ladder," I said sheepishly.

"It's not on your truck?" His eyes almost popped out, and he led me to the back of the building.

"You think you could borrow another from a neighbor?" I said innocently. He clenched his fists. When both ladders were leaning against his store, I smiled. "Got a hammer and a few nails?"

"What kind of a company is this?" He was steaming like a kettle. I climbed up one ladder while he lumbered up the second. I was still hammering away when I heard a voice.

"It looks great, Merv."

As I jumped to the pavement, the admirer handed me his card. "Have your boss call me."

When school resumed, the phone continued to ring. "Is this Kuper Signs?"

"They've moved," a relieved Mrs. Sumberg sighed.

One evening, when Chester sniffed his way to the deli, we found the windows blanketed. A neighbor, out for a stroll with his golden retriever, told me the concentration camp survivor had hanged himself, for no apparent reason.

Homework assignments swam before my eyes, my stomach growled, and I made my way down the back stairs into the kitchen. I could hear the Sumbergs in the library.

Except for a pickled beef tongue wrapped in cellophane on a platter, the refrigerator was almost empty. Whistling to calm my nerves, I buttered two slices of whole wheat bread and started to carve the meat when the door flew open.

"This is tomorrow's supper," Mrs. Sumberg shrieked. The knife and my eyes fell to the floor.

The next morning I left for school without setting foot in the kitchen. Afterwards, I skulked up to my room and when "supper" was hollered, I didn't respond. Cora came to plead with me, but I wouldn't budge. Phil advised me to get out before they stifled my spirit.

"You're a selfish, self-centered individual," Mr. Sumberg said sternly the next morning. "And your irresponsible behavior has brought discord into this household. I will not tolerate it. Under the circumstances, it's best you leave." My silence infuriated him more.

With fiddle and suitcase in hand, I stood on the threshold and bade Mrs. Sumberg farewell.

"Goodbye." She looked troubled. "Keep in touch."

As I was leaving for school, the postman handed me two letters. The first was from Margaret. I pictured her on roller skates with a protruding belly. Every time the doorbell rang, I was certain it was the police. In response to a letter I had sent her, she wrote about her studies, her family, and confessed that her pregnancy had been a joke. She added that she wouldn't mind if I were to father a baby for her. I exhaled with relief.

The second was a registered letter postmarked "Israel," from a woman in Tel Aviv, written in Yiddish on onionskin paper. "If you are Jankel Kuperblum from Pulawy, I am pleased to inform, that your mother, presently residing in Cernauti, is looking for you."

6

WHEN I TOLD my classmate Manny Silver that I was looking for a place to board, he suggested I move in with him. His family lived close to school in a row house on a main artery where streetcars ran, and his father, a junk dealer, was hardly ever home. Dark veneer furniture, topped with doilies and framed family photographs, cluttered the rarely used living room. Off the kitchen was an enclosed veranda, where Mrs. Silver kept old bottles, newspapers, and discards. When she smiled, which was rare, pain contorted her face.

As Manny's older brother, his sister, and her husband and child also lived in the house, there was no spare room, so I agreed to share Manny's. His mother liked me — and besides, the sixteen dollars a week the Jewish agency paid for my keep came in handy.

No longer did I look to others for handouts at school, and what a relief not to be corrected at the table every time I opened my mouth to speak. To cover my laundry, school supplies, clothing, entertainment, and incidentals, I received from the Jewish agency a weekly stipend of one dollar and seventy-nine cents.

Though I responded to the letter from Tel Aviv, I didn't expect a reply. Mama alive? Sobibor was an extermination camp. Obviously a mistake or a terrible hoax. Yet the press occasionally carried accounts of people rising from the ashes.

When I asked where Cernauti was, I was met with blank stares. Inquiries at the post office proved fruitless. I scoured the atlas, searching across continents. Three sleepless nights later, the mystery surfaced under a magnifying glass. Once part of Romania, now in the Ukraine in the Soviet Union, its name had been changed to Chernovtsy.

Surprisingly, a reply arrived, advising me that my address had been forwarded to my mother. The remainder of the woman's three-page letter concerned her family and the hardships they were enduring in "the Promised Land." In the postscript, she asked if I could ship her a refrigerator, in appreciation.

A scheme! Perhaps a trap! What if the communists are conspiring to recruit me? As I was torturing myself with these scenarios, a letter with Russian markings, addressed to me, was pushed through the Silvers' mail slot. I tore open the envelope and a photograph fell out. A chilly gust shot through my veins. There was Papa, a girl of about six, and a heavyset woman with a baby in her arms. In fractured Yiddish, the letter expressed great joy that they had finally found me. "Your father is away, but the moment he returns, he will write to you personally. In the meantime, our need is great." A list of clothing and medicines followed.

With the money I had saved while at the Sumbergs, I mailed a parcel. In reply, my stepmother Lena complained, "In future, these expenses are to be paid at your end." The duty had cost her more than the goods were worth. After three or four more exchanges, and with my suspicions growing, I threatened to disengage the contact unless I heard directly from Papa.

I had a disturbing nightmare in which I found myself in a cellar, where buried beneath the cement, was a body for which I felt responsible.

Petrified, I awakened and realized that this bad dream had haunted me since war's end.

NOW AND THEN, I'd run into some of the other orphans who had come to Canada with me. One owned a dry-cleaning store and insisted on giving me discounts. Another, a cabby, treated me to the occasional movie. Two brothers, who looked like twins, both fair-haired and lanky, would pull me into their variety store on College Street and thrust an ice-cream cone into my hand. "You're studying for all of us," they would say.

One Sunday I received a call from a friend, whose brother, visiting from London, wanted to meet some girls. I told her if he hurried he could come with me to my bowling group. He rang the doorbell and Mrs. Silver sent him up. I welcomed him, and after presenting him to Manny, I excused myself, saying I'd be back in a moment. When I returned with evidence of a hurried shave, the two were chatting amiably.

"You tell first," laughed Manny.

"Uh uh." Our guest shook his head.

Before I knew it, they were exchanging notes. Manny unfolded his, eyeing it like a poker player. The visitor read his, jumped to his feet, and was out the door. "What a jerk!" Manny smirked, tossing the note into the air.

It landed at my feet. I picked it up and read the words, in exemplary penmanship, "I ran away from home."

"And your secret?"

He shrugged.

Manny was being treated for some incurable disease, but wouldn't divulge what it was. "My mother would kill herself," he said.

When I called the English visitor, he refused to take the phone and his sister brushed me off.

FRIDAY EVENINGS, I would call Colleen O'Grady to see what she was up to. "I'm sitting by the phone waiting for your call," she replied. Not only did she fork out the seventy cents to get us into the neighborhood movie house, but afterwards she'd invite me back for her own deep apple pie, topped with scoops of vanilla ice cream. Dimming the lights, we danced to Sinatra, Tony Martin, and Johnny Ray, ending up with a necking session on the couch.

I was also aroused by a petite, vivacious Irish girl nicknamed "Sexy," but I was too shy even to talk to her let alone get close to her. Watching her walk down the school corridor wiggling like Marilyn Monroe, I would become stupefied.

Once, when I saw her at the streetcar stop, I decided to make my move. As I neared, I lost my nerve. Back home I was daydreaming about her, unable to concentrate on my homework, when Mrs. Silver summoned me to the phone.

"Hi!" It was Sexy. "My mother's drama group is staging a play and there's a part in it for you." I was tongue-tied. "If you're interested, the audition is tonight at our house."

She greeted me in a tight skirt and V-neck sweater at least two sizes too small with nothing underneath. Her mother introduced me to two neighbor women having coffee. There was vague mention of a play, and before I knew it, one of the ladies stood up. "Why don't we convene at my place and let these young people be?" They were gone as if swept away by a tempest. Sexy and I eyed each other. She was layered with fears, leading me on but unwilling to deliver. My libido pulled me on one track, but something deep within dragged me back to my roots.

One Sunday, after only a few dance steps at an upscale synagogue in the north part of town, my partner, her nose in the air, asked if I had a car. I told her it was in being repaired. For reasons I couldn't explain, I found myself calling her the following Friday, asking if she wanted to catch a film. She was offended that I assumed she'd be available on such short notice. It seemed she was booked for life, but acquiesced to go out with me a month down the road.

Surprisingly, she lived within walking distance of the Silvers, on a street of Victorian houses inhabited by working-class families. On the appointed night, a delegation awaited me in the kitchen, inspecting me from my long hair to my scruffy shoes.

"What business is your family in?" asked the grand-mother, slouching in a rocker.

"Where do you live?"

"Which Cooper are you, the dentist or furniture?"

My date finally waltzed down the stairs in a white chiffon dress, her hair curled like bed springs.

"There's a great double bill at the Christie," I said.

She made a sour face. "I prefer first runs." Then she asked, "Where did you park?"

On the crowded streetcar, she pretended she didn't know me, and in the darkened theater, when I slipped my arm around her, she jumped as if I were a leper. Later, as we surfaced onto the gyrating neon street, she pressured me into going to her favorite restaurant. All her friends were there, and she looked about the raucous room to see and be seen. Without consulting the menu, she ordered a filet mignon. I began to perspire. She took one bite, made a face, and set it aside.

Before we got to the streetcar stop, she hailed a taxi. It was worth the price to be rid of her. At her door, to punish myself further, I moved to kiss her. She slapped me, then bolted inside.

The next evening when I couldn't pay Mrs. Silver, I thought of Zygmunt, who'd grilled me about my fiddle on the train from Halifax. Later he had mocked me when finally hearing me play and had offered to buy the instrument. "Still have the fiddle?" he'd asked, when I'd run into him one day. "If you ever need a diamond, a ring, a watch, I'll give you a deal." He handed me his card.

"You still interested in the violin, Zygmunt?" I said into the mouthpiece. That rainy night, I made my way to his almost barren room, illuminated by a solitary bulb.

He examined the instrument like the jeweler he was, plucking the strings. "How much?" He tuned it.

I shook the rain from my sopping hair. "What's it worth?"

It was hard to believe the gliding of a bow and fingers dancing across the taut strings could produce such splendid music from my humble instrument. More surprising was Zygmunt's depth of musical feeling.

"Can't do a thing with it," he said, and handed it back. I left, navigating the twisted staircase.

"Wait!" he called after me. "Ten bucks." He flashed a bill.

As much as I disliked him, I now despised myself even more. Without looking at him, I handed him the instrument. The money squeezed in my hand, I rushed out and was splashed by a car. Tears trickled from my eyes as the heavenly violin strains reached me from an upper window.

UNCLE JACQUES' PEN came in handy. I corresponded with him, and later, after Uncle Shmil-Leib wrote to say how lonely he was without me, threatening to take his life unless I forgave him, I wrote to him, too. Enclosed in his next three letters were ten-dollar bills.

The money disappeared quickly, the last of it spent on a girl who had appointed me her escort at her sweet sixteen. When she attended to the colorfully packaged gifts that brought ooh's and aah's, and reached for my ninety-eight-cent bottle of cologne wrapped in brown paper, I slipped out.

I had heard nothing from Russia for many months. Then one fall day, Mrs. Silver slipped a letter under my door. When I read, "My dearest Jankele, this is Papa writing," I trembled. The letter was long and full of endearments, but before I finished, I had a growing suspicion that this writer had never set eyes upon me. Not a word, a feeling, or even a hint of a shared history. After receiving my not so friendly letter of reply, the stepmother apologized for her foolishness and in the same paragraph advised that my sister's birthday was approaching and she needed a winter coat.

Not knowing where to turn for money, I phoned my social worker and discovered I had been reassigned to a Mrs. Williams. She agreed to squeeze me into her already overloaded schedule. Plain and in her thirties, clothed in hues of gray, she opened my file and listened to my troubles. When I rejected her offer of dinner in her apartment, her nostrils flared. "If you need funds to send parcels, I suggest you find yourself an after-school job."

I responded to an ad seeking an art student. The proprietor was impressed with my female nude drawings. "This is the art department," he pointed to a desk, a taboret, and a chair. "This is what I need," he said, tossing a handful of promotional flyers on a desk. "A dollar an hour. Payday is Friday."

Before settling down, I complained about the dirt. "Dozens of artists have worked here and never a gripe," the receptionist said as she handed me a bucket of water and a rag. Afterwards, when I reached for a pencil, the only one I could find had no point. There was no sharpener, not even a knife. Brushes and nibs were caked and worn and the bottle of India ink was dry. The bulb in the lamp had burned out.

The phone rang, the typewriter pounded, and I heard the boss's screams from behind the fortress-like *Employees Only* door. At one point his wife called. "Get lost, you whore," he shouted and slammed down the phone.

Staring blankly at the Mickey Mouse watch I was to render, I thought of the dreams I had had when I'd entered art school.

"What's taking so long?" He was breathing on me.

"I'm thinking."

"For thinking, I don't pay a dollar an hour," he snapped.

Minutes later the receptionist handed me a cheque.

"I thought payday was Friday."

"For you, today is Friday."

"I'm not surprised," my social worker ranted. "It's time you faced reality." She severed my financial support, which meant that I could no longer afford to pay for my keep.

My long face brought questions from classmates, and soon the news reached the teachers. Miss McCarthy offered me room and board, and to make it more palatable, she said I could shovel her snow and cut the grass in exchange.

I was too proud. Instead I set up an appointment with Mrs. Williams' supervisor. After hearing me out, he formed a tent with his hands. "You're not at all what I'd been led to expect," he said, and I was back in the agency's books.

NO DIRECT WORD from Papa and still on a merry-go-round with his wife, I dispatched a note to Uncle Shmil-Leib. His reply was swift and emphatic and sent my head spinning. "My brother Zelik was always a hot communist, and ever since I can remember, he wanted to go to Russia to drive a tractor. Obviously he's an important man there, prohibited from corresponding with the outside world. Perhaps he's the mayor of his city, or works in defense! He might even be a general. In fact, it wouldn't surprise me if his office is in the Kremlin, next to Stalin's."

Was there a remote possibility that Papa was the person whispering into Stalin's ear? The very thought made me proud, but I couldn't share it with a soul. Nightly television featured Senator McCarthy terrorizing the continent. A classmate, Billy Smith, couldn't wait to graduate so he could enlist to kill the Reds in Korea. The press carried stories about the Rosenbergs and other alleged communists accused of spying. I trembled just thinking about what would happen to me if word leaked out about Papa.

One Saturday night, returning from a date, I found a ball of crumpled paper on the floor in my room. My curiosity got the better of me. "The doctor tells me I'm getting better, but I know I'm still a homosexual." It was Manny's handwriting. Strange, he hated "queers" with a vengeance and delighted in making fun of them.

Billy Smith could smell a queer a mile away, by his walk, his speech, a flip of the wrist. The most telling sign, he claimed, was that homos read backwards. After that I once caught myself leafing through a magazine from the back, and I froze. Didn't I have enough to contend with? I would have preferred going through life as Billy. He excelled in sports and had girls running after him.

"My mother will be heartbroken," said Manny when I told him why I was leaving. "But she will slash her wrists if you tell her why."

"HE'LL BE HOME in a month," the letters from Russia continued. But when a month had gone by, I was assured he'd be back in three months. Six months later he was still very busy and wasn't expected for a while longer.

That summer when I entered the resort deli north of the city, the cantor was overjoyed until I mentioned salary. By chance, I fell into conversation with the new owner of a hotel by the lake.

"In a week I'll have a well-paying job for you," he said, shoveling corned beef and cabbage into his mouth. "In the meantime, you can stay in one of the rooms, and whatever I eat, you eat."

Three weeks later, I was still painting, scrubbing, trimming bushes, and cutting grass. The kitchen was in disarray, with no food in the pantry or the fridge. The stove wasn't connected, we ate meals out, and when it was time to pay for them, he looked to me.

As soon as his wife got off a bus lugging two overstuffed shopping bags, it became apparent who the real boss was. One look around and she lashed into him for not having prepared the place on time.

"I hear good things about you," she said to me, handing me her deceased son's creased slacks and shirt, worn at the collar. He must have been at least three sizes larger than I.

I now sweated under her direction. As the rooms filled, I was ousted from mine. I transformed the cellar into a bedroom, decorating the walls with pin-ups, hanging a light, and throwing a mattress on the floor.

The wife cooked, several local girls were hired to be waitresses and make beds, and the husband chatted up the guests and listened to their carping. Besides being the official dishwasher, I ran errands, prepared vegetables, and doubled as a gardener and caretaker. Late afternoon, on my hour off, I'd take a walk along the main drag and enviously watch others roller-skating and amusing themselves at the pinball machines.

The wife pinched my cheek at the end of the week. "Such a wonderful boy! Hands like gold and looks like a movie star!"

The following week and the week after that, when she handed out envelopes, there was nothing for me. I stared at the floor and mumbled, "It's three weeks."

"Listen to him!" she erupted. "We feed him, clothe him, give him a beautiful room, treat him like our own, and it's not enough!"

I left and that night shared a bed with Kurt, a fellow greenhorn who worked in the kosher butcher shop on the main drag. I spent the whole night in his stifling room, listening to lectures on Marx, Lenin, and Engels. The next morning, I found no work as the season was almost at an end, so I hitched a ride out of town.

The driver was heading north, to Wasaga Beach, a larger resort area on Georgian Bay. Biting into a hamburger in a fast-food joint, I overheard the manager giving someone hell for not delivering the signs she'd been waiting for all summer. I introduced myself. It was past midnight by the time I finished lettering the ten show-cards. In the morning my strokes appeared wobbly, the letters poorly spaced. I thought about junking it all and starting over, but in a last-ditch rescue attempt, I added shadows and embellished the letters with highlights. After taking a step back for a second look, I added illustrations. I ran to deliver the barely dry cards and came away with ten dollars and an order for six more. At the end of the season, I returned to the city with several hundred dollars in my pocket.

That fall, another registered letter found me at my new address, in Toronto, on Lippincott Street, where I boarded with a warm family of immigrants from Poland. Inside the envelope was a sealed envelope. This was indeed from Papa. He wrote that he was well, that he played mandolin, read a great deal, and was particularly fond of Jack London's writings. Had I read any of his works? The pleasure he expressed about cities rising in the great frozen wilderness was puzzling, as was the absence of a return address. He advised me to correspond via Chernovtsy.

I wrote back about my life, my studies, and my dreams. I savored his letters, reading and re-reading every word, answering straightaway, waiting restlessly for the next one.

The following summer I returned to Wasaga Beach. Renting a cabin by the roadside, I painted a monkey's face on the door with "Kuper Signs" above it. Still fearful, I told those curious about my origin that I was French Canadian. From the start I was swamped with work and raising my prices hardly stemmed the tide. My only competitor had a drinking problem. What's more, not knowing better, clients viewed my work as superior. In fact, even when he was drunk, the local sign painter's stroke was surer than mine.

His beautifully formed black letters on white with no frills and nothing to overshadow or distract, could be read from a mile away.

By midsummer, he knocked on my door. I bowed my head when I saw him. "Okay, kid," he slurred. "Got any work?"

On weekends the beach was invaded by bikers. Riots, gang wars, and arrests were the norm. Some nights when it was impossible for vacationers to find a vacant bed, my cabin was filled with sleeping strangers.

Karen — a double for Sophia Loren, wearing tight pedal pushers and no shoes — stopped one day to admire my handiwork. On Saturday night I took her to the dance at the local hangout, shared a burger, and later walked with her along the white sandy beach. It wasn't till we were back in Toronto at summer's end that I told her I was Jewish. It didn't matter to her; however, when she introduced me to her Macedonian immigrant parents who owned a restaurant, she told them I was from Quebec. Even then they eyed me suspiciously.

After graduation from Central, oblivious to the dozens of established sign companies listed in the Yellow Pages, I opened a shop on Harbord Street, next door to the Harbord Bakery. This time "Kuper Signs for Better Business" was plastered across the front. Six months later, I returned the key to Mr. Kosover, the landlord.

Manny landed a job as a window dresser in a chain of ladies' wear stores. With his first paycheck, he outfitted himself from head to toe in fancy clothes. Later he sported a gold watch, and one morning checked himself into a plastic surgery clinic, coming out with a bandaged face. He lay in bed for about a week and when the dressing was removed, half his nose came with it, revealing a new one out of harmony with the rest of his features. I went to visit him. His room was dark. Suddenly a spotlight fell on an adorned and bejeweled mannequin. "What do you think of her?" he asked.

"You're his friend. What's wrong? Can't you introduce him to a nice Jewish girl?" his mother pleaded when I stuck my head in the kitchen on the way out. Thinking it would ease her pain, I spilled the beans. First she acted as if she didn't understand. But when I spelled it out, she turned on me. "It's a lie!" she said. "No child of mine . . ."

In my letters to Papa, I enclosed photographs of myself and repeatedly requested a picture of him. Finally, a black and white snapshot arrived. In place of the adjutant bedecked with medals, there was an emaciated, unshaven man with graying hair sitting on a flimsy chair, in a creased suit and misshapen shoes, a mandolin resting on his lap. His eyes stared back at me, filled with fear.

My Papa, whose life ambition had been to drive a tractor in the Workers' Paradise, was a slave in Siberia.

7

ON THE STREET WHERE I now lived in midtown Toronto, ladies of the night plied their trade. The once-proud mansion in which I roomed reeked of stale air. The landlady, a mother of three with no husband in sight, busied herself vacuuming, dusting, and washing.

My eight-dollar-a-week room featured a tarnished brass bed, a battered armoire, a hot plate, and a minuscule table with two wobbly chairs. The art-deco fixture hanging from the high ceiling discharged a shock when switched on or off. Adding to the gloom were faded floor-length curtains and a worn, dirt-infested carpet. Telephone numbers, some scribbled in lipstick, covered the walls.

An elderly couple lived next door. He was robust and short-legged with a drunkard's nose; his mate was a shriveled bundle of skin and bones with a face caked in rouge, who stuck her head out whenever she heard footsteps.

A family lived across the hall, and frequently an ambulance carted the father away in a straightjacket. He'd be gone for a couple of months, then reappear, and the cycle would repeat.

The bay window afforded me a good view of the broadcast complex with its newly built tower. It was 1952, and television was making its debut in Canada. I decided to test my luck. My letters to the art department went unanswered. Everyone told me connections were the key. Yet the one I addressed to the talent department got an instant response. I was invited to audition, and soon received a call to appear in a series called *Tales of Adventure*. I could see my name on marquees around the world until I arrived in the studio and found I was one of a dozen extras to be dressed as Indians. The director was busy with the stars, and by the third episode I had still not been introduced. His assistant shepherded us around, telling us where to stand and look, how to canoe and pow-wow around a campfire. The live show aired early evenings, and when I got home my land-lady would tell me excitedly that she had caught a glimpse of me.

Karen bragged to her friends that her boyfriend was a TV star. Home from his restaurant day shift, her father turned on the set and recognized me. To be certain his eyes were not deceiving him, he waited for the credits and saw my name roll by. "I knew he was an Indian," he raged when his daughter got home from school. Tearfully, she blurted the truth. "A Jew!" he shouted, and like a jilted lover in an opera, clutched at his heart. I was forbidden to set foot in their house.

During a rehearsal, while waiting on the sidelines, envy-ing the stars going through their paces, I followed a sign to the art department. Six or seven graphic artists were stooped over drawing boards. When I told them I was a graduate, the one in charge smiled charitably, "Bring in your samples." I ran across the street and fetched my portfolio. That night he called, offering me a job.

I longed for fans to chase after me, tearing at my clothes, but the three thousand dollar annual salary was hard to resist, measured against the thirty-five dollars per episode I was earning. Even the stars in the cafeteria line never seemed to have enough change to pay for coffee. What was there to look forward to?

It soon became apparent that I had been hired for my presumed sign painting skills, something the other artists considered beneath them. My first day on the job, when I went for coffee, I brought back extras.

"Never drink the stuff," mumbled one.

"Don't do that again," said another, and a third insisted on reimbursing me.

Eager to prove myself, I volunteered to work late, weekends, and holidays, but never recorded the extra hours, fearing someone higher up might question it.

A former member of the Wehrmacht, who persisted in calling me "Kupferblum," adding an "f" to my name the way it would be spelled in German, arrived late, took extended lunches and extra coffee breaks, yet earned more in overtime than I in salary. "Don't be so eager," he cautioned me, his eyes narrowing.

The control room fascinated me and I spent endless hours watching camera run-throughs and live on-air telecasts. Afterwards, I'd join the actors and crew at an all-night hangout. I spoke my mind about the shows. "If you know so much," an irritated scriptwriter said, turning on me, "why don't you do better?"

I took him at his word and like a prisoner of the past threw myself into preserving the memory of my family. A year later I handed in *Sun in My Eyes,* a three-act play, set in a Polish *shtetl* in 1942.

"This is 1954. It's time to forget," said the editor, supporting the rejection.

Next I submitted it to a respected TV producer. He sought the opinion of a Jewish colleague, who agreed that it would only stir up old hatreds. However, an award-winning director was touched by the story, telling me my writing was reminiscent of Chekhov. "Unfortunately," he said with regret, "it has nothing to do with Canada."

A New York Stanislavsky method type, hiding from the

"Red scare," advised me to change the play's setting to the frozen north and the characters to Eskimos.

Still another friend pointed towards New York, where he thought it would find a sympathetic ear. Rejection slips continued to pile up. "Too late, the subject has already been covered in *The Diary of Anne Frank*." I began to resent that little girl. After forcing myself to read her diary, I thought it frivolous. I couldn't understand why people wiped their eyes on the way out of the theater. The hardest for me to swallow was the last line: "In spite of everything, I still think that people are good at heart."

As a last resort, I adapted my play for radio. Within days of dropping the script off, the editor called, inviting me to dinner. Twice my age with a pockmarked face, he shared his fashionable apartment with a menagerie of cats. Born into a wealthy Anglo-Saxon family, educated in private schools, his life sounded heavenly. What he alluded to as ordeals sounded trivial to my ears.

"Sorrow is relative," he philosophized, cutting into his mushroom crêpe, "and wealth is no insurance against pain." After dessert he suggested we have coffee in the living room. Although there was no shortage of seats, he sat beside me on the couch. "Now, about your play . . ." His arm fell on my shoulder. I inched away and he followed. I sat elsewhere. He didn't give up.

He was as sly a fox as I. Shamefully I remembered the time I offered to do a drawing of a shapely girl named Bernice and ended up chasing her around her living room when her parents were away for the weekend. Though she vigorously resisted, I speculated it was an act and that she really wanted me to disrobe her. Out of breath, frightened, pinned to the ground, she said, "You can have me, only you'd better know I'll tear you to pieces. I'm a nymphomaniac. No one has ever been able to satisfy me." I let go of her wrists, and took off.

A local drama group needed someone to play the young American sailor in Tennessee Williams' *The Rose Tattoo* and they found me. The play premiered at the provincial drama festival and walked away with every award, including one for my performance. My picture and name appeared in the press, and before long I was invited to New York to audition for the film version, starring Burt Lancaster and Italy's fiery Anna Magnani.

CABBIES LINING THE exit at Grand Central Station hassled for fares. I had been warned to be on my toes, so when one reached for my suitcase, I fled. A newspaper vendor pointed me to an inexpensive hotel. Gripping the handle of my bag, I walked along, with visions of the city's monstrously tall buildings shifting from their foundations and crashing down onto my head.

In the shabby hotel in the theater district, there was no door attendant and no bellboy — only a shriveled man behind a caged window who took money and handed out keys. The elevator accommodated two persons, but it was so slow that most guests took to the stairs.

With the day to kill, I thought of Tim, from the Red Barn Theatre, with whom I'd been exchanging Christmas cards. I dialed his number and got a busy signal. Rather than wait, I set out for Greenwich Village. The streets felt less threatening now that I was not carrying luggage. Still, I repeatedly fingered the wallet in my breast pocket.

Among the battery of names in the vestibule of the brownstone where he lived, I spotted his. "Yes?" a muffled voice came through the speaker, and I heard footsteps racing down. He looked the same — apart from a few strands of grey hair. Clad only in boxer shorts, he looked me over. "Well, well, well! You must be the newspaper boy. Come right up."

"The Red Barn," I grinned.

He shook my hand vigorously. "What a pleasant surprise! What brings you to town?" The walls of his tiny place were papered with autographed glossies of movie stars. After he dressed, we grabbed a quick lunch at a stand-up deli and I went with him to see his agent.

We had barely entered when the receptionist greeted him, "You again?"

"I happened to be in the neighborhood," he smiled for effect. "What a wonderful hairdo!"

"If something comes up, we'll call." She answered the buzzing phone.

A few blocks later, we arrived at a similar office with similar results. "It takes perseverance," he said, failing to convince even himself.

"How many agents do you have?" I asked on the way to yet a third.

To keep alive he worked as a temp in the shoe department at Macy's and spent the warm months in summer stock. But other than a few bit parts off Broadway and occasional roles in TV soaps, he had little to show for all his years in the big city.

It was devastating running into people he knew, who would wink at him seeing me at his side. He had a couple of comp tickets to a play and I didn't have the heart to turn him down. Walking back from the theater that night, I worked up sufficient nerve, but before the words in my head could reach my mouth, he answered, "Yes, I'm a fag, but don't think I have designs on you. I'm engaged." He displayed a silver band.

I couldn't help laughing and immediately felt terribly ashamed. Fortunately, Tim was understanding.

"When I was a teenager, I used to double date with a friend. We'd take the girls to a local drive-in, neck, pet, and all that crap. They were teasers — they'd get us aroused, then make us take them home. Once my friend was so fired up, he jumped on me." Tim gave a measured laugh. "He's married, has a slew of kids, works for an insurance company back home, and attends church every Sunday."

The next day a doorman barred my entry to the building where the movie mogul's office was located. Only after checking with someone on the phone was I allowed to proceed to the elevator. The door with the producer's name on it was locked. After I rapped on it, it opened a crack.

"Tony Curtis," said the shrewd-eyed, fast-talking New York woman who let me in. Then she felt my muscles and asked me to remove my shirt. She was the casting director, who claimed to have discovered Burt Lancaster.

"He's cute!" said another woman, sticking her head out of a separate office.

"The problem is," the first thought out loud, "all the characters in this picture are Puerto Ricans except the sailor. I suppose we could dye your hair blond." She threw me my shirt. "Ever thought of taking up weight lifting?"

In the evening I phoned Tim to say goodbye, assuring him I would remain his friend. "Same here," he said. But when the festive season rolled around, we each crossed out the other's name from our Christmas card list.

BACK AT THE graphics department, I received a call from Sexy. We arranged to meet at my place. She still had that same allure, and when she crossed my threshold, my arms enveloped her. She stiffened, and biting her lower lip, said, "Let's go out."

In the back row of a movie house, like a kitten in search of warmth, she cuddled up to me. Afterwards we shared a meal in an out-of-the-way diner.

"I'm married," she said without passion, "a nice Irish lad my mother liked. He's a teller in a bank." They were saddled with a mortgage and instalment payments on furniture, and pinched pennies for holidays. "Mom is nagging me to start a family," she said. I listened, nodding my head, all the time plotting how to lure her into bed, but when I saw her off at the subway, I didn't expect ever to hear from her again.

Only days later, she called, inviting me to a Hallowe'en party. I asked if I could bring a date. "Come alone," she purred.

A loud pounding on my door startled me. "Shell out! Shell out or I'll break your windows out!" a voice peeped. I opened the door to find the little girl from across the hall in bride's apparel, and saw myself at a peasant's door, begging for a crust of bread. I put a ten-dollar bill into her outstretched hand. Within minutes there was another knock. It was one of her brothers, Tarzan in a loin cloth, with a knife between his teeth. I dug into my wallet and pulled out a five.

Next I was summoned by singsong threats from a chimney sweep and a little angel. I gave the sweep my last two dollars and emptied the change in my pocket into the cherub's hand.

As I was about to leave for Sexy's party, I was surprised by yet another knock. Covered in a white sheet with holes for eyes, there stood the mother. I saw Mama peddling tobacco, door to door.

"Sorry, all I have left are a couple of streetcar tickets."

An embarrassed laugh arose from under the bedsheet. "Just havin' a bit of fun."

At the party, prancing around in a French maid's get-up, complete with rosy cheeks and feathered mop in hand, Sexy left it to her husband to mix drinks, pop beer caps, change records, and greet arrivals.

He was exactly as I had pictured him: frail, with long, bony fingers, a receding hairline, and eyes staring in perpetual wonderment. The guests wore homemade disguises — unlike the penguin contraption I was upholstered in courtesy of the TV costume department.

My awkward apparel was stifling enough, but when she lured me into an upstairs closet, I thought I'd suffocate. She decapitated the penguin, unzipped the body, and let the bird fall to my feet. Pressing her loins against mine, she infused me with desire and, unlike in the past, she now attempted to guide me into forbidden territory.

"Your husband . . ."

"Don't worry." She planted her teeth into my neck.

Out of fear, a sense of decency, or possibly both, I couldn't allow myself to have my way with her.

WOULD-BE CAMERAMEN were practicing in an empty studio. Seeing an opportunity, I harnessed their energy to experiment with sets and graphics. The kinescope of my efforts somehow ended up in the hands of a producer. He was impressed with the idea of credits painted on the floor with feet walking across them and wanted me to duplicate it for a show he was producing.

"It won't work for a variety program," I told him. "It would be great for a spy story."

He sized me up. "I'll be the judge of that." We locked horns. "Do it or I'll have you fired," he said.

"I'll save you the trouble," I said, and stormed out.

He sent his studio director after me. "What do you care? Give him what he wants," he advised.

"Get someone else."

"He likes you. Because you're not a yes man!"

"It's 'The Big Revue'!" an announcer trumpeted every week at eight on the dot. The drums rolled and the title I had painted on the floor came up on the monitor. The camera dollied forward, catching the dancers' legs crisscrossing the credits and it would stop when it came upon my hand finishing the lettering: "Produced and Directed by Norman Jewison."

I flirted with the dancers and dated a few. Midway

through the season, I noticed a fresh pair of stunning legs, with a face and body to match.

"Hi, beautiful," I winked. She looked away, and when I followed that up with something just as asinine, I received a "get lost, jerk" look.

My Sophia Loren desperately wanted to get married. The mere thought of it sent me reeling, but we continued to date clandestinely until she maneuvered her parents to invite me for Christmas dinner. When I presented her father with a bottle of Crown Royal, he threw his arms around me, and with tears running down his cheeks, called me son. By summer, when the family was taking a trip to the States, the old man begged me to join them.

"Where's the *shikse*?"* the waitress at the Bagel Restaurant asked. "A good-looking boy like you could have the pick of any Jewish girl. Someone who'll put you on your feet."

I laughed, thinking of the one I once dated who found me exotic in my worn jeans and sandals. "I wouldn't mind parking my slippers under your bed!" she had said. Slender, with fried-egg-shaped breasts, she had chauffeured me in her father's Cadillac convertible to a party at her house. Her friends talked about exotic holidays, shopping sprees, and how many miles they got to the gallon. Her father matter-of-factly declared that whoever married his little darling would inherit the *shmata* factory. "I hear you're some kind of artist," he said, pointing to a gilt-framed oil painting of a wet Parisian street scene. "I paid a fortune. What do you think of it?" I didn't have the heart to tell him.

Leaving a generous tip for the waitress for her well-meant advice, I dropped in at a B'nai B'rith dance and ran into an acquaintance. While we were chatting, my eyes spotted the dancer who had snubbed me on the set of "The

* Gentile girl

Big Revue." "You see that girl over there," I gestured. "I'm going to marry her."

Terrye was seventeen and I was grateful she didn't remember me. After the dance, I asked if I could see her home and on the way we stopped in a park, where we sat under a tree, gazed at the moon, and counted the stars. She was about to join a New York ballet company.

"Forget New York," I said. "Stay here and be my girl."

It was past two in the morning by the time we got to where she lived, in a third-story walk-up above a laundry. I said I would call her.

"When?"

"Tomorrow."

"What time?"

Two minutes before the agreed hour she called me.

Classical music from an ancient radio sweetened the air of their flat. Potted plants thrived on windowsills, shelves and fire escape. The walls were covered with paintings. A few were still-lifes and *corps de ballet* scenes, but most were of Terrye, her sisters, and her mother. The eldest was married and the middle one was about to walk down the aisle. Terry's beautiful mother won me over instantly with the contents of her monstrous wheezing and sneezing fridge.

"You must try my braised steak," she said, pushing me into a chair. I had just stuffed myself on a full-course meal at the Bagel. "Just a taste," she said in a honeyed voice, and dished out a plateful. Typically, I cleaned the plate and managed the cake and tea that followed.

On my next visit, I met the artist: a walking encyclopedia, overly polite, dark complexioned, with a cultured British accent. Since he paraded about in pajamas, I concluded he was a live-in.

Saturday night, after returning from a date with my new-found love, my landlady told me Karen had phoned several times. Next morning, she was knocking on my door.

After a passionate kiss and a bear hug, she slipped a black onyx ring onto my finger; a present from Arizona.

How could I tell her that although I had lost confidence in the God of my childhood heaven, I wanted my children to sit at a *zaidy*'s table at the Passover *seder*?* And could I share with her my nightmarish scenario, in which in a moment of anger, she calls me a dirty Jew?

"I'm not ready to get married and I don't want you waiting for me," I told her. Rivulets of tears coursed from her pretty eyes.

"ENGAGED?"

"Sure," said Terrye. "How long can you go steady?"

I found myself in a jewelry store examining rings. That evening, I tossed it to her.

She gave it back. "You have to present it properly."

After her family and friends had inspected the stone, she began lobbying for a wedding date.

"Once and for all, you'd better know I'm not ready to tie the knot," I said.

Terrye's mother pleaded with her, "You're young, talented, beautiful. You can have a doctor, a lawyer. What do you see in him? He's a poor struggling artist with long hair and pointed sideburns. He'll eat you out of house and home."

"How about June?" Terrye asked coyly, nuzzling up to me.

* Passover dinner

8

"MAY I SPEAK TO the rabbi?" I asked.

Soon the rabbi was at the other end, his voice rich, cultured, his words evenly spaced and tinged with a Yiddish flavor.

I introduced myself, then said, "I want to get married."

"*Mazel tov*," he sang. "Come and bring your *kala*.* May God bless you." He hung up.

As easy as making an appointment with a dentist. Then why had I procrastinated? Having a rabbi officiate at my wedding made me feel like a hypocrite. But the thought of a city hall clerk congratulating me with a dead-fish hand-shake was worse.

The rabbi's study was on the upper floor of the temple in the part of town where the affluent Jews lived. It could easily have been mistaken for a lawyer's office. The rabbi hardly looked like the one etched in my childhood mem-ory. He didn't even have a beard.

"I believe I married your sister," said the modern sage when hearing Terrye's family name. "You have another sister. I don't remember officiating at her marriage."

"She converted."

The rabbi's smile vanished. "May God forgive her. A

* bride

daughter of Israel has strayed from the path." And he commented on the dangers of assimilation and how to guard against it. This was the same rabbi I had seen pictured in the daily press, posing with clergy of other faiths during Brotherhood Week. "You can always tell how the world is faring by the way we are treated. The Jews are the barometer." Switching gears, he said to Terrye, "I was your father's chaplain in the army."

"I haven't seen him since I was a little girl," she said. "My parents divorced when I was three."

"He still owes me the eighteen dollars I lent him on the outskirts of Amsterdam in 1945."

"The Don Jail used to be his favorite hangout. Try him there."

With a shadow of a smile, he leaned across the desk, adjusting his *yarmulke*.* "So, you want to get married."

"Nothing fancy," I said. "Not too religious."

"Much like my sister's."

"If I remember correctly, I married her in my recreation room." Pulling on the lobe of his ear, he focused on me. "I'm not familiar with your name."

I started to fill him in.

"I saw the camps with my own eyes," he intoned in measured cadence.

We set a date.

"Not to worry," he reassuringly cupped my hand in his when I asked about his fee. "Whatever you can afford will be ample."

"Not a penny more than fifteen," advised my future brother-in-law. "That's what I gave. It's just a tip. He gets paid by the province."

I rose early that June Sunday, and no sooner had I slipped into the pants of my new glen-check suit than my landlady called me to the phone.

* skullcap

"It's Hart," declared the TV producer. "Listen," he bubbled, "my wife's cousin, a very intelligent girl, is in from New York . . . and I thought you might like to show her around town."

"Sounds good," I chuckled, "only I'm getting married in a couple of hours."

He managed a *"Mazel tov!"* and hung up.

"Just keep on driving, right to the airport," I joked with my best man, Sid Furie, as we approached the rabbi's street — the same Sid who years earlier had left the farm camp after only a day's work.

"This is for the rabbi." I handed him an envelope.

I lumbered down the stairs. Meshing with the plywood paneling and the checkered floor, the assembled crowd blurred before my eyes. Not a distant relative, nor anyone who might even have known my parents or grandparents. Without a soul bearing my family name, melancholy invaded my spirits on what should have been the happiest day of my life.

We had mailed invitations to Brussels. Uncle Jacques sent greetings and Uncle Shmil-Leib regrets. June was his busiest season. We also wrote to Papa, who replied that on the day of our wedding, he would party with his comrades. In my mind's eye, I saw him raising a shot glass. "To my Jankele's and his beautiful bride's good health!" They downed the vodka and hurled glasses over their shoulders.

I stood under the *chupa** beside my radiant bride. Before I realized, I had placed the gold band on her finger, shattered a plastic glass under my foot, and we kissed. In record speed the rabbi had joined us in matrimony.

The room buzzed with *Mazel tovs!*

Where were the rabbi's inspiring words? Though critical of ritualistic platitudes, I now hungered for even a taste. Just then, from the corner of my eye I caught the rabbi's

* wedding canopy

index finger beckoning me. Holding a door ajar, he motioned me to enter. Instead of a private study, I found myself in the furnace room. It reeked of oil. And in place of the wisdom of the ancient sages, I heard, "This was a fifty-dollar wedding, but seeing you're a survivor, give me another ten and we'll call it even."

I restrained myself from leaping at his throat. As if guided by an unseen force, I reached for my wallet. "I earn sixty-five dollars a week. You, venerable rabbi, have just been paid twenty-five for a ten-minute ceremony. If in God's eyes you think I've wronged you, help yourself." I parted the billfold and held it under his nose.

Pushing it away as if it were pork hocks, with scarlet face he whisked me out of the room.

9

IT WAS HEAVENLY having our own place, a basement apartment at Eglinton and Bathurst. It had affordable rent, a telephone with our listing, and a fridge I could open without having to look over my shoulder. I also got a kick watching my bride plunge blindly into domesticity. After a run-in at the studio cafeteria, where I had ordered spaghetti and meatballs and received a few strands with a single ball the size of a dropping, Terrye had served me a bathtub full of spaghetti and enough meatballs to feed a platoon. Hardly discouraged, she marched forward, cooking and feeding whoever was around. That's how I met the postman, the milkman, the lady from the corner store, a few delivery characters, and a host of others.

Regretting that he had missed our wedding, Uncle Shmil-Leib arrived a month later, in July 1955. In anticipation, we purchased a TV set and a new Chevy. As there was no extra space, we rented a room for him at one of Terrye's sister's relatives. A few days into ferrying him back and forth, he begged to sleep on our floor, rather than return to the stifling attic where he was lodged. He ended up on a daybed in our tiny kitchen. After Terrye and I left for work, he amused himself watching TV. In the evenings and on weekends, we drove around town, visiting and showing him the sights.

When he first arrived, he had handed us an impressive cut crystal bowl with a silver-plated base. Later one day, returning from a walk, he presented us with a tablecloth from one of our local stores, and let it slip that the crystal was from his older brother. "This trip has cost me a small fortune, Jankele," he said uncomfortably. "Had I been smarter, I would have sent you the money instead."

"Having you here is the best gift of all," I said, to please his ears.

"You should see the spectacular bedroom set I bought your cousin Jacquy when he married. Handmade in Italy with inlaid olive wood."

Jacquy was far from close to Uncle, had parents, had married a wealthy girl.

From the start, Uncle wanted to see Niagara Falls, but since he had come for a month, there was no reason to hurry. Canada appealed to him. He was especially captivated by the way business was conducted at the snap of a finger. But what really sent him into orbit was how my darling wife could place the chicken in the automatic oven before leaving for work, and have it pop out ready to eat upon her return.

"The socialist government is tearing pieces off me," Uncle said one night. "Taxes in Belgium are sky high." I was the only one in the entire universe who could rescue him, he said. The money he had amassed under the table needed to be laundered.

I had mixed feelings about helping him. He had cheated and lied to me. But without him I might never have made it to Belgium. Not only that. How many uncles did I have? And so I agreed to be his washing machine. That in place, he packed his bags.

When we saw him off for his flight back to Brussels, I felt sick when he said, "I'll see Niagara Falls next time."

After his departure, I attacked a new play based on a woman who had once offered me money to take her unattractive daughter out on a date. In reality, I had refused, but in the play, I had the young man accept, only to end up falling in love with plain Jane.

Unlike my previous play, this one sailed through unhindered and I was hailed as an up-and-coming new writing talent.

About that time Terrye announced I was going to be a father. My stomach ached while hers swelled. Depleting our bank account for a down payment, we swapped our basement for two mortgages and a five-room bungalow on the northern outskirts of town, just in time for the arrival of a darling baby girl. We named our new sunshine Ellen, after Mama, and fearing I might never have another chance, added a second name, Jill, for my brother, Josele.

In a separate bank account, sitting and doing nothing, was four thousand dollars belonging to Uncle — waiting to be washed. When I proposed to borrow it to pay off our second mortgage, which, like a constrictor, had wrapped itself around my neck, he panicked. "The inspectors are coming in two weeks. Send my money immediately or you'll be visiting me in jail."

By then, the couple of dozen designers in the graphics department were under union wings, negotiating for us to go on contract. When I heard the paltry figure I was being offered, I almost fell off my chair.

"You're terribly valued, I want you to know that, and I'm certainly cognizant of your dedication and the contribution you've made to this department," the congenial cherub administrator said, in his best Oxford English.

"Then what is it?" I gulped. "Others, with less seniority and no recognition, have been offered fatter sums."

"It's a formula. We took the basic salary, added your average overtime, and tacked on a seven percent increment." Clasping his hands across his chest, he leaned back. "Our records show you hardly ever worked beyond regular hours."

A KINESCOPE OF MY plain Jane play somehow ended up in New York and a script editor of a U.S. anthology series, hired to work in Canada, phoned to inquire whether I had written anything lately.

I couldn't resist. "I've just finished a play," I said, and sent over a copy of *Sun in My Eyes*.

A few days later I received a contract and a commission to write a new work. Things were looking up.

It was chilling listening to actors portraying members of my family, mouthing their lines. And eerie walking through the propped set, staring at myself hard in the mirror of the past.

After the taping, over a drink at a chic hangout, the attractive actress who portrayed Mama announced she was leaving for Florida, as she was emotionally drained. She begged me to write a comedy for her next time.

Laudatory reviews, complimentary calls and letters followed after the airing of the production. I should have known better, yet I was shocked that life went on as if the events in the play had never happened.

"I saw it," said an actor, himself a Jew, who stopped me on the lot. "Very good . . . moving! But enough!"

A few survivors scoffed at me. "You were at a tea party." They were willing to share their harrowing experiences if I wanted to write something *really* poignant.

In my spare time, I did not allow my pen to rest, and Terrye continued to pound the typewriter. By the time our next offspring, Mark, joined us, I had handed in a one-hour play, modeled after a combination of Mrs. Silver and my mother-in-law.

"We already have one for Passover," said the editor with cool, if not chilly, indifference, after reading a few pages.

Collecting my wits, I recast the leading character into a Polish Catholic with a hard-to-pronounce name ending in ski, and made a sale.

Seeing my name on the screen, friends and family were sure we had hit the jackpot.

"Very nice. How long did it take you?"

"How much did they pay you?"

"Eight hundred dollars."

"That's all? For a year's work?"

The graphics department responded to my plays with silence — until the one who needled me with "Kupferblum" brought up *Sun in My Eyes*. "There were too many Jewish lawyers and dentists in Berlin, and all the female movie stars were marrying Jewish producers and directors. Something had to be done."

Wanting to unearth more, I invited him and his wife to dinner. As expected, the conversation wandered to the war years. My colleague spoke of his army days as a cartographer, stationed in Denmark.

The wife plucked a memory from those years. "I was in Poland entertaining our troops in a small, slovenly town, Pulawy." *My town!* "We had no idea what was going on," she said, teary-eyed.

"You were in Pulawy and didn't know what was going on?" I said. The silence was deafening.

Still trying hard not to be lumped with other hysterical survivors, I continued the relationship. When we were looking to rent a cottage, they invited me up to theirs to scout around.

It was on an island. At sunset while the husband busied himself outside, I lit the kerosene lamp and caught sight of an issue of *Life* on the coffee table picturing Eichmann in the Jerusalem prison: exercising his legs in the courtyard; eating lunch; sleeping, his slippers parked under the cot. A bundle of flesh and bones, a human being with eyes, a mouth, and a nose. No horns. A man and not a monster.

The wife, butcher knife in hand, preparing dinner, turned to me. "This Eichmann fellow they caught . . . Eichmann is a Jewish name, you know!"

When I entered the cabin where I was to sleep, I bolted the door and didn't close my eyes, waiting for their footsteps.

WITH NO REASON TO fear, I still feared. The beast was merely dormant, and in time truckloads of soldiers brandishing rifles would descend onto our suburban Toronto street, smashing doors and hollering, *"Alle Juden raus!"**

"Raus! Alle Juden raus!" Germans smashed down our door, driving us from the place we stayed in with Papa's family in Lublin, the winter of '41.

Outside, we joined others trudging in the snow and lugged only what we could carry. Mama carried Josele in one arm, a bundle in the other. *Buby* held on to me, *Zaidy* beside her.

The soldiers, armed for combat and positioned at intersections, prodded us with the butts of their rifles, like cattle being steered into a pen. Hours later we arrived at a fenced enclosure at the side of a factory on the outskirts of the city. There a teeming mass of frightened human cargo was being loaded onto trucks and hauled away. Mama pressed Josele and me against her body.

A *Judenrat*** official standing at the gate called out names of relatives of those who worked in German-designated industries, exempting them from deportation. In the chaos we heard, "Kuperblum," and standing between the official and a German with two savage dogs on a leash, we saw Uncle Mendel, who was employed in a shoe factory. We were saved!

A Toronto-born, Anglo-Saxon member of the graphics department, who had difficulty parsing a sentence, asked me, "Will you stand up for me at my wedding?" I was sure

*   All Jews out!
** Jewish Council

he had picked me over his friends because I owned a car. When I couldn't find an empty parking spot in the church lot, as all his friends *had* cars, I realized I no longer had to make my way in life as if negotiating rows of tulips.

American dollars continued to arrive folded in Uncle's letters, and I cleansed them, expediting via the bank, paying the transaction fee out of my pocket. At one point Uncle complained, "The authorities here want to know where does a Canadian come to be sending American money? Jankele, unless you want to see me behind bars, send Canadian dollars only." The American dollar was then worth ninety cents Canadian. Again, so as not to break up the round sum, I contributed the difference. Later, when the exchange favored Americans, he sent Canadian currency. I dispatched the same, and he griped that his bank would only accept American dollars. And when I then sent the exact exchange in American dollars, he complained that he had been cheated.

Though we treated ourselves to the occasional Chinese meal, we continued to watch our pennies. But when it was time to forward a parcel to the U.S.S.R., we could never send enough. Terrye scoured the stores for fashion items and ladies' accessories she herself would have loved to own. After paying for packing, carton, insurance, shipping, and prepaid duty to the company specializing in sending goods to that part of the world, the cost of the item doubled.

When Khrushchev came to power, Papa, having served eight years of his ten-year sentence, was released. Back home in Chernovtsy, he begged me to stop sending goods, claiming they were not in need. The old country charade was familiar: The famished visitor insists he's not hungry, the impoverished host declares he has too much and the food will go to waste. Whereupon the uninvited guest gorges himself on the pretext that he's doing his friend a favor.

To add to my confusion, alarming letters reached me

from Uncle Shmil-Leib. "Your father's situation is critical. He lives in an unheated cellar and barely sustains himself on stale bread and frozen potatoes. Yesterday I sent him a parcel so heavy, I needed help to lift it. Next week, I'll send another." As if the signals weren't mixed enough, out of the blue, Papa requested a silk *talis*.*

"Eat Jankele, it will make you strong." Papa nudged the plate of *shinka*** closer to me when Mama was away in Warsaw. The aroma tantalized me, but fear of the wrath of God hindered me from touching it.

A cotton or synthetic *talis* was expensive enough, but when I asked the price of a silk one, I almost keeled over. I sent a letter to Papa asking if he had returned to the fold and dispatched a note to Uncle Shmil-Leib for his opinion.

"I forbid you to spend that kind of money," wrote Uncle. "Knowing my brother, it's to be given away as a gift. Jankele, you're now a father and have a family to look after. That's your priority."

By the time Papa replied, he no longer wanted the ceremonial shawl.

Knowing what to send was always a problem, as most of the goods were to be sold to buy food for the table and coal for the stove. And what we valued in North America was not necessarily marketable at the other end. Costly items often fetched little on the Chernovtsy black market. Cash was best. But how to send it? One heard of channels and convoluted schemes via Switzerland, but they were risky and dangerous. Though it was possible to send dollars legally through the bank, Papa would have received a pittance in comparison with a tenfold increase in rubles on the black market.

By chance, I became acquainted with a journalist of White-Russian descent, who was on his way to, of all places,

---

*   prayer shawl
** smoked ham

Chernovtsy. When I proposed to give this gentle soul dollars to pass to Papa, he indignantly said he would never dream of doing anything contraband.

"I'll be working there for six months and will be paid in rubles. I can't imagine spending it all. I can leave your father the excess, and when I return, you'll reimburse me."

We shook hands and I handed him an envelope with a few snapshots to take to Papa. As he was stopping over in the Belgian capital, I gave him Uncle Shmil-Leib's address, then wired Uncle, suggesting that he too might want to send something. In his brisk reply, Uncle warned me that the scheme was fraught with peril, and he would annul it. I cabled back to let it stand.

A few weeks later I heard from him again. "Your man was here. The moment I laid eyes on him I knew he was a Russian agent. You have placed your father in mortal danger." I smiled to myself.

Papa never mentioned the journalist. He had to be prudent, sometimes writing in code.

"You should have listened to me," Uncle wrote months later without fear of censorship. "Your courier, accompanied by another, arrived at your father's. No sooner had they left than a police van pulled up and hustled your father to the station, where he was interrogated for three days. They demanded to know what was in that envelope."

Tossing and turning at night, I had visions of poor Papa, face swollen, eyes blackened, a defeated boxer on a concrete floor.

Finally the journalist resurfaced.

"How did he look?"

"Good. A good-looking man. Very fit."

"How does he live?"

"Seems content."

"Tell me about your visit."

"He invited me in and proposed a drink." I waited for more. "Unfortunately, we were in a terrible rush!"

"We?"

"On the way to my farewell dinner, when I told the mayor I had something to deliver to one of his citizens, he offered to take me."

This raised my temperature. "How much do I owe you?"

"I left your father two thousand rubles," he responded breezily.

I handed him a cheque.

"There's a zero missing," he said, as if in passing.

"Two thousand dollars?" My voice reached the high notes. "How can that be? On the black market, it's ten rubles to the dollar."

He didn't flicker an eyelid. "I thought I made it clear at the outset. I don't dip into excrement."

"YOU HAVE A BIG family in Toronto and they're dying to meet you," a woman with a Polish accent proclaimed in a high-pitched voice on the telephone. She wasn't certain how we were related, but details were unimportant. To find a soul with the same family name, or just from the same *shtetl*, was sufficient proof of claim.

"Will you come?" she coaxed. "And bring your wife."

Babysitters were not easy to come by, and they stretched our budget, so Terrye stayed home. I was greeted by a pale woman of medium height, who held me at arm's length, admiring me with her penetrating eyes. She had survived, disguised as a nun. She still called herself by her alias, Irena.

Awaiting me in the living room was a throng of people of all ages — from an infant in a mother's arms to an elderly woman with a cane. We searched for a connecting link. They hailed from Sandomierz, only kilometers from Pulawy. In the early 1900s, members of the family had fled the *shtetl* and settled in Toronto, changing their name from "Kuperblum" to "Cooper."

I felt no kinship with this legion. Over the tinkling of spoons and crunching of home-baked poppy-seed cookies, one related the family history that my young ears had heard: The family name was Herzberg or something like it, but when the three brothers running from persecution in Holland found refuge in Poland, they avoided conscription by changing their names — one to Greenberg, the other to Kuperblum.

"Kuperblum means copper flower in German," butted in a man in a sing-song voice. "The family were coppersmiths. Come to my home," he continued. "I'll show you copper pots stamped with 'K,' ones my father brought from the old country. The family prospered. Gypsies worked for them."

On my way out, I was showered with business cards. They insisted I visit their factories, stores, and offices to take advantage of their wholesale prices.

Whatever affinity I felt that day would soon have dissipated had it not been for Irena. She often got on the phone, bestowing birthday greetings, inquiring about our welfare, my work, and so forth. I answered politely, waiting for her to hang up. At other times, she would show up with a plant for Terrye or gifts for the children, and placing a kiss on my cheek, would ask, "How is my beautiful cousin Jack?"

For my thirtieth birthday, Terrye found an accordion listed for sixty-five dollars in the classified ads. The owner, a disillusioned immigrant Swede, needed extra money for his return ticket.

With fantasies still invading my rational mind, I strapped the squeeze-box to my body. Imagining I was the blind man, I fingered the keys. The discordant strains brought tears to Terrye's eyes. After that, I picked it up once or twice, then abandoned it in a cupboard. The appetite was gone.

That same month, Uncle Shmil-Leib's son, who lived in Tbilisi, Georgia, with his mother, turned sixteen. Uncle embarked on a rescue mission. "Your father and his wife are meeting me in Moscow," he wrote. "My hands are already laden with suitcases of suits, bolts of cloth, a watch, and whatever else I can stuff in. If you want to send something, I suggest money."

Immediately, I deposited five hundred dollars to Uncle's account. For my benefit, he had purchased a movie camera to film Papa, and when the film finally arrived and I threaded my eight-millimeter projector, demons conspired and all I could discern were shaky, out-of-focus images.

"On a walk in Moscow, I nudged your father, pointing to a knock-out of a girl coming towards us," Uncle penned in the accompanying letter. "I was so surprised when he reproached me, saying there is no other prettier than his wife. No disrespect, Jankele, but I never knew your father not to eye an attractive woman. Those years in Siberia have undoubtedly affected him."

Uncle promised his son the world, but as soon as they landed in Brussels, reality set in. The boy had little feeling for him and even less for Uncle's new wife. He was disinterested in study, so his father pushed him into diamond cutting.

For my part, I prodded Papa to apply for an exit visa. After he obtained clearances from his place of work, the police, and various other institutions, he was told to be patient. Fearing I would never see him again, I offered to fly to Chernovtsy to plant a bomb under the bureaucrats. I ignored Papa's cautioning and began making preparations, only to discover that this city was out of bounds to foreigners. I mounted another campaign and appealed to the Soviet Embassy in Ottawa. "We have no authorization to deal with internal matters. Address yourself to the police in the city where your relatives reside," stated the form reply.

Out of the murky depths, a glimmer of hope. Our good friend and lawyer, Muni Basman, petitioned a senator, who agreed to intervene via the Canadian Ministry of Foreign Affairs. The minister's Russian counterpart owned him a favor and he was ready to collect. It looked hopeful and we sat down to celebrate. The food was hardly digested when the stepmother wrote that my half-sister, Tamara, was getting married, and an impressive gift was in order. It was followed by one from Papa, requesting I add the groom's name to the list.

Fresh in my memory was the ordeal of an acquaintance who had miraculously unearthed an only brother in the Ukraine. Bribing a chain of shadowy officials, he had rescued the sibling with his barefoot family, billeted them in a furnished apartment, outfitted them from head to toe, and packed the fridge with food. But when the euphoria had settled, the wife pined for her parents, the children had problems adjusting, and the brother, a carpenter, could not fathom why the government did not assign him a job.

I broke out in a sweat and brought everything to a halt.

As LONG AS I didn't attack serious issues, I succeeded in selling two to three plays a year. "Television is an entertainment medium. Write books if you're bent on changing the world," a new editor offered dryly. I took his advice. Continuing to work late into the night and stealing time on weekends and holidays, I plunged into a book I was certain would knit my world back together again.

The supervisor of graphics left for greener pastures, and every member of the department vied for his job. Management wanted to know why I hadn't applied.

"It pays even less than the ten thousand I'm earning now," I answered.

"For somebody who constantly complains about what ails the department, it's an opportunity to set it straight."

I flung myself at the challenge, and after I had revamped, reorganized, improved productivity, and brought down expenses, management rubbed their hands and weighted me with the still-photography department. But there was no raise on the horizon. My category was not due for one. With a third child on the way, the voyage ahead looked stormy.

Five years after starting it, I gave birth to *Child of the Holocaust*. My New York agent refused to be discouraged by the rejection letters from publishers littering his desk. "What a shame this is coming at such a late date." "We've already done our conscience piece this year." "We might consider it if the author agreed to publish it as a novel." Every rejection added vinegar to my stomach.

Quite by accident, a copy of the manuscript ended up with a British publisher of textbooks who took it home for the weekend. His wife picked it up off the night table and in the morning told him she would divorce him if he didn't publish it.

Parallel to this event, a New York book editor who was resigning because of a disagreement over a work she felt strongly about, phoned a young Californian who was just joining Doubleday and recommended it to her. She was of Spanish descent and knew little of Jews and less of the Holocaust, but was drawn to the story and selected it as her maiden project.

With the book about to roll off the presses, I was sure that at last I'd be freed from the ties that bound me to the past. But it wasn't to be. The corpse buried in the cellar continued to invade my nights.

IN 1966, THE YEAR before Papa turned sixty, I encouraged him to come for a visit, and he applied for permission to travel abroad. Even with his wife's guarantee against his defection, again he was told to wait.

My career that year blossomed, with offers pouring in from many quarters. The keynote speaker at the awards dinner in Montreal where I was chosen Art Director of the Year was the legendary Benny Becker, the *wunderkind* of Canadian advertising — a walking dynamo who sprinkled his speech and ads with Yiddish humor.

"I owe you lunch," he said when congratulating me.

We met the following week at Toronto's posh Inn on the Park, where the maitre d' and the tailed waiters fawned on him at his favorite table. Over oysters for me, and spicy bloody Marys for him, he proposed that I join his agency.

"You can't afford me," I joked.

"A talent like you doesn't come cheap. Name your price."

"Twenty thou," rolled out of my mouth and I was astounded he didn't so much as crack a smile.

"With or without a car?"

"I have a car." I winced, fearing my bantering had gone too far.

"When can you start?" he asked, tucking the napkin into his collar.

"I need to think about it and talk it over with my wife."

"What's there to talk and what's there to think, *Bubale?*"

"It so happens I've had a feeler from educational TV, and I'm meeting with them."

He stopped in mid-bite. "If it's the car, you can have it."

The bill arrived; Becker signed. On his way out, he was thanked profusely by the army of heel-clickers, all looking forward to his next visit.

The lunch with two reps from educational TV was at a Hungarian outdoor café, in the Lothian Mews off Bloor Street.

"You'll be the creative head, and all writers, producers, and directors will report to you," stated one.

"You sure you've got the right candidate?" I asked.

"Don't think we haven't investigated. You're our man, all right."

"I hate to be crass, but what does it pay?"

They eyed each other. "If we press the minister, we think he'll cough up twelve thousand."

My eyes fell into the goulash soup.

"Think, Jack, there are kids in the far north who have never seen a subway. You could show it to them. Others who will never visit an art gallery unless you take them. Many could learn to appreciate classical music, if only someone gave them the appetite."

The bill landed on the table and sat there. After a lot of throat clearing, one looked to the other. "Do you have any money on you?"

"No, don't you?"

"We must speak to the minister about some sort of expense account."

I snatched the bill and walked to the cash register.

"Next time it's our turn," promised a voice in the back seat while I was giving my suitors a lift back to their office.

I'll have to perform twenty thousand dollars' worth of miracles, I worried. But within days, as radio-TV director of the advertising agency, I realized I had made a poor deal. Many of the creative staff with less experience were earning more.

A copywriter spent two weeks holed up in his cubicle before storming out. "Guys, I've got it!" he screamed at the top of his lungs. A stampede advanced, their mouths agape. As if dropping pearls, he mouthed, "Get together with Canada's great, light beer." The hush segued into tumultuous applause and he was lifted off his feet and carried above heads, like the groom at a wedding.

My first assignment was to produce a pool of commercials for a national appliance manufacturer at a local TV station in Winnipeg. My secretary asked how much cash I needed.

"You think they'll mind if I ask for fifty dollars?"

No sooner was she gone than Becker, known as "BB" at the agency, entered.

"Listen Bubale, I don't know how things worked in TV land, but here, to make *gelt,** you've got to spend *gelt*. Buy drinks, dinners, shows, act like a big shot. Surely I don't have to spell it out," he winked. "In a whorehouse, you can't be a virgin. Take five hundred."

Our client, the advertising manager of the appliance company, met me in the airport departure lounge. I was determined to get it right this time. The moment we boarded, I suggested a drink.

"They don't serve before we're up," he said, smiling politely.

Later, when the trolley came by and I reached for the bundle burning the hole in my breast pocket, I was told refreshments were complimentary. When we landed, I invited him to dinner.

"You go ahead," he said apologetically. "I'm going to phone home, then call it a night."

I was unpacking when the producer from the local TV station knocked at my door. Playing the big operator from the big city, I asked what he drank.

"Coke," he replied, easing into a chair.

"Coke and what?"

"Just Coke."

"Come on. Have a real drink." I imitated Robert Mitchum.

"Coke," he repeated flatly.

I dialed room service, "One Coke and one gin and tonic."

"No gin, sir," came the wheezing voice.

"Then make it vodka and orange juice."

"We can give you orange juice, but no vodka."

"How about rye?"

"No liquor allowed on Sundays, sir."

---

*   money

124

"Two Cokes then."

The visitor, eyeing me in the mirror, made me feel like a flat tire.

Breakfast came with the room and we were treated to lunch at the station cafeteria. But as dinner rolled around, I succeeded in luring the client to a glitzy restaurant with a dazzling floorshow. When I asked for the tab, I was told it had already been looked after.

THE AGENCY'S CREATIVE department was a revolving door. Writers and art directors arrived and departed with inconceivable speed. Today's genius was tomorrow's burnout. Hand on forehead, BB walked about lamenting, "We're creatively bankrupt." When an art director left in a heated frenzy, Becker came crying into my office. "*Bubale*, get one of your TV art guys over here."

It took some persuading to get a hardworking award-winning colleague to show up with his portfolio. He and Becker closeted themselves for some time, and when the applicant emerged, he reported, "I told him I wouldn't move for less than twelve thousand."

After he left, BB stuck his head into my office. "*Bubale*, I need a twenty-two thousand a year man and you send me a twelve."

It was common to be invited to lunch or dinner and to receive comps to games or the theater, provided by suppliers bidding on jobs. But I wasn't quite ready when one asked how much to build into the quote for me.

"I told you," I answered, "the agency charges the client fifteen hundred per day for my directorial services."

"I just thought a young fellow like you could use some extra bucks." His bid was high and the job went elsewhere.

Next time, over an extravagant lunch, the same supplier again proposed that he line my pockets. I suggested a game of chess. This quote was also too high.

On the third occasion, when he invited me to his office for a rematch, I accepted on condition that I bring lunch. We had barely set up the chess pieces when he began poking for ways to corrupt me.

"Don't think I'm an angel," I said. "It's just that if I win this game, I want to be certain it's on my own merit."

He opened a drawer in his file cabinet and pulled out a laundry list of familiar names. "For him," he pointed to a name, "I had to buy a car. That one, a refrigerator. Harry's girl loves to sun herself in the Bahamas in the winter. This animal makes me pay his mortgage, and still I don't get all his work." When his finger reached the last name, he looked up. "How about coming to work for me?"

Other offers came my way, each more lucrative than the last, but I didn't nod until the president of the largest commercial production house in the country slipped me a note. "How does $25,000 strike you?"

We bought a larger home in the city, at Avenue Road and Eglinton, traded in the Chevy for a Celica, acquired a dachshund, took up skiing, and increased our visits to our favorite Chinese restaurant, Sai Woo on Dundas Street. The view from the top was spectacular.

But there was a price to pay. I was not only expected to create magic on the screen, but had to attract a never-ending stream of clients. I was certainly at a disadvantage because I did not frequent bars, but it was my way of shooting from the hip and letting the chips fall where they may that distanced those who looked to have their egos massaged.

After spending an entire day auditioning noses for a sixty-second nasal spray spot, I went home with a migraine and on the day of the shoot, phoned in sick. Later that morning, I received a call from a stranger who wanted to see me. From his name, Ben-Adam, I made certain assumptions, and suggested that if he hurried, he could join us for a piece of Terrye's still warm gefilte fish.

"I don't think I've ever tasted that."

"Your mother never made it?"

"My mother?" Tittering filled my ear.

A taxi dropped him off. Swinging half a bottle of liquor, he drawled, "I brought this in case you're not a scotch drinker." He had a firm handshake, an engaging smile, thinning reddish hair combed to one side, and sapphire eyes that complemented the immaculate business suit with matching tie. He asked for a glass with ice and helped himself to a generous drink from his Chivas Regal bottle.

"Your name intrigues me," I said.

"My father's an Englishman who became an Israeli general."

"Then you *are* a Jew?"

"In a manner of speaking." He dragged on his hand-rolled Sherman's cigarillo. "My mother was an Irish-American Presbyterian from the Midwest."

The Inuit carving on the coffee table caught his eye, and he admired the Tiffany lamp. After scanning the titles of the books lining the shelves, he said, "I like what I see," and told me what was on his mind.

"I'm with one of the largest advertising agencies in the world," he said. "There's been a revolt at head office. The Young Turks have taken over and sent me to revamp the Toronto branch. The expenses here are out of reach, the morale is low, and the place hasn't attracted a new piece of business since Methuselah. If you'll come on board as creative director, together we can have the joint humming." He refilled his glass.

"There's a problem, and his name is Steve Barclay," he went on. "He was a general manager, but now has to report to me. Naturally he resents it. I was hoping he'd quit, but no such luck. Head office keeps warning me not to push him. He's convinced them that if he walks, clients will walk with him. We'll have to make inroads by doing award-winning work, so by the time he's out, their loyalty will not be in jeopardy. I've already fired the guy you're replacing, a drinking buddy of his."

A SHAPELY BLONDE woman ushered me into an enormous office on a high floor of a skyscraper in Manhattan. There I met Howard. His tie hung loosely over a white shirt with straining button holes. The fat cigar lodged between his thick lips corrupted the air.

"I'm sorry to have kept you waiting." He tried to smile. "I've been running from one meeting to another." He invited me to sit. "Can I pour you a drink?" I declined. He relit the stub, took several puffs, then leaned back, his stocking feet resting on the glass desktop. "Let me tell you a little about myself. I'm a poor boy from the Bronx. I worked here, I worked there, and somehow ended up in this shop. I wrote a few things that caught fire, and before I knew it, I was promoted to group head. You may be familiar with my 'I saw the light,' campaign," he said with pride. "After that, they made me creative director, and the rest is history." He scratched his protruding belly. "I tell you this, only to demonstrate what kind of a company this is. If I can make it to the top, I figure anyone can, especially someone as gifted as you."

"You've never even seen my work."

He blew smoke rings into the air. "We've checked you out. I understand you've got a book coming out. Ben-Adam tells me he interviewed a legion of candidates, and you're his choice. Our only concern is, can we afford you? I hear you want thirty thousand . . . that's a lot of bread for Toronto. The guy you're replacing only got seventeen."

"I'm not really interested in the job."

He squinted. "Then why are you here?"

"Because Ben-Adam begged me to at least meet with you. He said, if nothing else, I'd enjoy a few days in New York, all expenses paid."

He picked up the buzzing telephone. "Yes . . . yes . . . put him on . . ." He downed his drink. "This'll just take a minute," he said to me, then removed his hand, which was smothering the mouthpiece. "Sheldon, here's why I called. Look, several months ago I was at this party and this crazy chick corners me, telling me she's a copywriter. The next day she's sitting in my office crying, I mean begging on hands and knees. I felt sorry, and since I had a spot open on one of the accounts, I hired her. But she couldn't write. She's lazy and on dope and all that shit. I fired her. Today her lawyer calls and tells me I tried to rape her. I never so much as pinched that ugly piece of shit." He swung his feet to the floor and swayed forward. "Of course, it's the truth. Anyway, Shell, I don't want any trouble. You hear? Give her two months' salary, three months' . . . whatever. Whatever she wants, but get her off my back." He slammed the receiver down, wiped his damp head, and yielded a meek grin.

"Ben-Adam is right," he said. "Our clients will love you." He extended his hand. "Thirty thou it is." I shook it without twitching a muscle.

I couldn't wait to get home with the news, but the boy from the Bronx beat me to it by sending my wife a dozen American beauty roses with a note.

"Thirty thousand a year!" I lifted Terrye off her feet, and we fell to the floor, rolling on the carpet. But I knew that being the highest-paid creative director in the country was only an aspirin and would not cure what ailed me.

10

ON THE STORYBOARD the commercial looked simple enough: about fifty dogs of varied species, colors, and shapes, romping in an empty studio. In the pre-production meeting, I had joked with the director of photography about telephoning in my instructions on shooting day. What was to direct? All I required was some wild footage. It was at the editing stage, when images would be meshed with voice and sound, that I foresaw sleepless nights.

The production house managed to assemble the dogs from several sources. The studio floor and backdrop were painted white, and a wire fence was erected to contain the animals. A piece of cake! We'd wrap by noon and I'd take the afternoon off.

On the day of production, the animals started to chase and bite, tearing at one another, but in due time they settled down. No sooner did I holler, "Roll camera!" than too many proceeded to relieve themselves, bringing the filming to a halt. The propmen jumped in to clean up the mess, the painters touched up the floor, and we began again. By the time we broke for lunch, the crew was sweating and I was feeling the pressure from client and entourage. Eight hours later, we had shot less than one thousand feet of film of our stars urinating, defecating, and fornicating. In the midst of all this, the phone rang.

"Take a message!" I told the script girl.

"It's your wife!" She waved the receiver.

"I'll call back!"

Close to midnight, after the bleary-eyed cameraman assured me it was "all in the can," we wrapped. I lit a cigarette and called home.

Terrye could barely contain her excitement. "You received a telegram! 'Arriving Montreal, May 3rd, 1:00 P.M. Love, Papa.' He's coming for three months!"

Out of the darkness at the other end of the studio, a tall shadowy figure in a trench coat and fedora came towards me and lifted me into his arms. "Do you know who I am?" He dangled a bunch of purple grapes. I stared. "I'm your Papa," he said, and kissed me.

The train ride to Montreal was pleasant: there was ample leg room, and large windows with an unclouded view of the quilted countryside. I was armed with a book and the morning paper, but couldn't concentrate on either. I was scheduled to arrive by nine in the evening and planned to have a good night's sleep so I would be fresh to greet Papa. Booking a hotel had proved futile as the city was bursting with visitors to Expo '67. By coincidence, my friend Pierre, who worked in advertising and for whom I had directed a pool of commercials, was leaving with his wife for Europe. He'd offered me their place.

The diner car was packed with jubilant passengers chatting noisily between sips and mouthfuls. I sat at a table across from two businessmen. Their conversation revolved around commerce, then drifted to reminiscences of days together in the Canadian Armed Forces.

"The best time of my life!" exclaimed one, with shining eyes.

The other concurred, signaling the waiter for another

round. By the time their meal arrived, they were exchanging accounts of their passionate adventures in war-ravaged Europe.

I fidgeted in my seat, smoked two cigarettes, and barely touched the dinner I had ordered. The pair behaved as if my seat were vacant.

"Zelik, let's all go together," I heard Mama whisper.

"First I'll go, then you'll follow." Papa was planning to escape to Russia but didn't have enough for train fare.

"Mr. Kuperblum, we demand our rent!" an irritating voice intruded.

"Or we'll call the police," joined another.

"Please ladies, come in for a glass of tea." Papa tossed them an infectious smile.

"We don't need your tea, Mr. Kuperblum." They remained in the doorway. "You owe us two months' rent."

"My dear ladies, if I had, wouldn't I pay?"

The aging sisters flushed with anger. "We'll have you evicted!"

"You're getting upset and that, especially at your age, is not conducive to good health," Papa said. "You, good ladies, have enough wealth to last for not just one, but multiple lifetimes, if that were possible. And here you're endangering your well-being for a few measly *zloty*. How long do you imagine the Germans will tolerate two Jews occupying an entire mansion? And your money, my dear ladies, isn't much safer. Can't you see the writing on the wall? Today, one has to sleep with his suitcase packed, and even then one may not have sufficient time to take it along." Pulling up chairs he motioned for them to sit. They looked at each other, then ambled into the room.

I studied their craggy faces at close range, trying to count the gold teeth whenever they opened their mouths.

"Life offers opportunities," Papa continued, "and in your case, esteemed ladies, the time is now. There are people who are hungry with no place to rest their heads this very night. Others, who with a few niggardly *zloty*, might succeed in saving their lives. Do you see what I'm getting at?"

Numbed, the spinsters left, tight-lipped.

When next I saw them, they were wearing forced smiles and one carried a plate of raisin cookies. "Mr. Kuperblum, we need your help," they said. Recounting their sleepless nights, the elder said, "We considered our coat linings, but that's the first place they search."

"Let's see now." Papa placed his forefinger on his brow. They waited for him to spring the impregnable lock. "I think that would do it nicely," he mused at one point.

They jumped. "What? Tell us!"

He dismissed the thought with the flip of his wrist, then lit up like a lightbulb. "I've got it! Yes, that's it. No question about it. And so simple too!" The pair craned their necks like ostriches. "A large handbag with a false bottom," Papa crowed.

Nervous titters. "Do you think you could engineer such a contraption?"

"My dear ladies, you're looking at the specialist!"

"How much will it cost?" Now they were cooing like doves.

"Let's not talk of money! You'll deduct it off the rent." More titters. Mesmerizing them with his sky-blue eyes, he requested a handful of bills to determine the precise dimensions of the concealment.

IT WAS GHOSTLY being alone in Pierre's apartment. I clicked on the television, caught glimpses of the news, a late-night talk show, and the tail end of one of my commercials. Remembering where Pierre kept his liquor, I opened the Quebec pine cabinet. There was no sign of the selection I had seen there in the past. Rummaging around, I found an uncorked bottle of red wine in the kitchen and downed a large glass. It was acrid. I emptied the bottle all the same, smoked a few cigarettes, undressed, and crawled under the covers of the ornate bed. The ceiling fixture glared as if it was in an interrogation cell.

Before I knew it, I was back in my recurring nightmare. Covered in sweat, I bolted up and ran to the toilet to retch. After shoving my head under the tap and splashing my face with cold water, I faced a stranger in the mirror.

Papa's already on the plane, I thought, and went back to bed. I stared into the darkness, waiting for dawn to rescue me.

"I'll send for you, I promise," Papa whispered. I opened my eyes and saw him in a makeshift Polish army uniform, hat askew, a soldier's duffle bag hanging at his side, embracing Mama. Kneeling, he kissed Josele, asleep next to me on the floor. I closed my eyes tightly. "Take care of your mother, Jankele," he murmured, pecking my cheek. Then he tiptoed out of the cottage to face a chilly dawn.

"Papa!" I called after him, and touched my cheek where I could still feel the wet of his lips.

The Montreal traffic was heavy. A radio announcer with a barker's voice reported an accident. "Don't worry, Monsieur," the cabby said, studying me in the mirror as I peeked nervously at my watch. "I'll get you there on time." He accelerated abruptly, maneuvering between cars.

The hands on the large clock at the arrivals gate showed a few minutes past eight. The plane wasn't due for another five hours. I couldn't sit still. Every minute seemed like a lifetime. God, why can't you fast forward the time? By noon the airport resembled an oriental bazaar, with arrivals from every corner of the world.

Through clouded eyes, I discerned unsmiling, luggage-laden travelers with Slavic features emerging from behind the electronic doors and was terrified that I might have missed Papa. "Were you on the Russian plane?" I said to one. He walked by. "Are these the Aeroflot passengers?" I asked the guard. He nodded. "When did it land?"

I scrutinized the face of every passenger trickling through the door. Dear God! Let Papa be there when the doors part next. And when they did, the somber crew emerged carrying their night bags. I've missed him, or else he wasn't on board! Suddenly, I heard my name breaking through the bedlam from the loudspeakers.

"Where's the Air Canada desk?" I vaulted onto the escalator, pushing my way to the top. I jostled past the long line. "Excuse me! Excuse me! My name is Jack Kuper. You were paging me."

"We were not calling anyone by the name of Cooper," the harassed attendant replied.

"K-U-P-E-R."

"Sorry."

"But I distinctly heard," I panted. "Were you calling a Jankel Kuperblum perhaps?"

Halfway down the escalator, I spotted other passengers pouring out. "How many more have come through?" I breathed down the guard's neck.

He stabbed me with his steely gray eyes. "I don't count them."

"Are there others inside?"

"How would I know?"

"Can I look?"

"Can't you read?" He pointed to a sign.

When the doors parted, I rushed in. "Zelik Kuperblum," I pleaded with a stewardess who was stamping documents.

"Sorry, sir," she replied. "We don't have a passenger list."

In an adjoining room, more travelers were milling about. No Papa. Unexpectedly, I came face to face with Charlie Chaplin. Not the little tramp, but his creator. He had thick white hair and was clad in a trench coat. In one hand he grasped a small suitcase tied with a coarse string. In the other, a mandolin and a samovar wrapped in newspaper. The moment our eyes connected, he dropped it all and we fell into each other's arms.

11

I'D BEEN WAITING a lifetime for this moment, yet now on the flight back to Toronto, with Papa at my side, I became tongue-tied. I could only stare at him and wonder if he was real.

When the limousine pulled up to our home, Terrye, our children, and the dog, Farfel, were anxiously waiting to cast their eyes on *Zaidy*. The surrounding neighbors gaped from doorways and windows. Smiling, Papa emerged from the car, waving as if he were indeed the celebrated Chaplin. He hugged my pregnant wife, calling her by her Yiddish name, "Tobala," then turned to the little ones huddling behind their mother.

"I, *Zaidy*," beamed Papa, planting kisses. Farfel vied for attention. "Feh!" Papa kicked him and shooed him off, triggering a memory:

"Feh!" Papa scowled at the mess on the floor left by the cuddly brown puppy with droopy ears and sleepy eyes that a friend of Mama's had given me. The next morning when I awakened, my sweet dog was gone. Papa said dogs were for guarding animals in barns.

"How was your flight, Papa?" Terrye inquired.

"What is she saying, Jankele?" He looked at me.

The few words of Yiddish Terrye had learned on her *Buby*'s knee were inadequate for carrying on a conversation.

He reached out to the children — Ellen, eleven, Mark, eight, and Shaul, three — but they didn't know how to react to the man with the mouthful of stainless steel teeth, who spoke a language they could not understand. They waited for the gifts he made no move to distribute.

"Who are they for?" I inquired, when he handed me several babushka dolls.

"Do I know?" he shrugged. "My Lena packed them."

"And the samovar?"

"Probably for Tobala," he grinned.

I too waited. A grown man hungering for gestures meant for children. "Zelik, didn't you bring Jankele a present?" It was Mama's voice after Papa's trip to Warsaw.

"The mandolin," he said, "is for Mark." Yet he picked up the instrument and crossed his legs, and after asking me to close the window so as not to attract attention, he began to strum. Fingering it, often plucking the wrong string, he played disharmonious chords to accompany the Yiddish folk song he sang. Lost in his own world, he immediately segued into another tune. The children sneaked off. Terrye withdrew into the kitchen.

I feared he would break down when he saw the traditional feast my wife had spent days preparing: gefilte fish with sliced carrots, chicken soup with noodles and lima beans, roasted brisket of beef with potato pudding, and a compote of dried fruit. But when a serving of the fish was placed before him, he just stared.

"How's the gefilte fish, Zelik?" Mama called from the other room.

His head buried in the *Warsaw Yiddish Daily,* he rhapsodized, "Mmm! The best you've ever made," and groped for the fork.

"He's not eating," Terrye frowned.

The children studied their *zaidy* from the corners of their eyes. Papa fidgeted, tapping his finger on the table like a woodpecker.

"What's wrong?"

"I don't eat this."

"What? What's he saying?" Terrye poked me.

"Don't you like it, Papa?"

"I love it!" He licked his lips. "But I only eat in the morning. *Kasha.*"*

"For breakfast?" Terry grimaced.

"Just *kasha*, Papa?" I wanted to make sure I understood him correctly.

"And cabbage," he added. "Also bread, but only black." While I was still translating, he cut in, "And if it isn't too much, Jankele . . . apples."

Later, he wandered into our bedroom, crouched down, and poked his head under the bed.

"Papa, what are you looking for?" I asked.

He rose to his feet. "All the years when I dreamt of the day I would be with you, I imagined myself cleaning the lint from under your mattress. I see somebody beat me to it!"

In the dark hours of the morning I heard a movement downstairs and wondered why the dog wasn't barking. The front door squeaked open and shut. I jumped out of bed, crossed into the boys' bedroom and peered out the window. A man in briefs was skipping in the middle of the road with the agility and delight of a ten-year-old.

"I don't believe it!" I gasped.

By the time I came down, the counter was in disarray: utensils lay about, drawers and cupboards were open, and bits of food littered the floor. He had cooked a pot full of *kasha*, boiled an entire cabbage, and together with chunks of black bread, was shoveling it in, as if feeding a furnace.

---

*   buckwheat

Next he converged on the apples, peeling them with a bread knife, letting the skins land on the floor. Quartering the fruit, he speared each section with the knife, thrusting it into his mouth and spitting out the seeds, alongside the peels. Farfel wagged his tail, sniffing the offerings. "Eat, eat!" Papa pointed to the discards.

Fearing Terrye would have a coronary, I cleaned up. Soon the children teased on the quiet. "Who slurps louder? Farfel or *Zaidy*?" Keeping my cool, I gently commented on the chomping, smacking, and wolfing.

"Never mind how one eats," Papa said between smacks. "One is lucky to have something to eat."

He was napping in the backyard hammock when I came home from the office. Terrye was on the brink of tears.

"What's the matter, hon?" I asked, and held her in my arms.

"The moment you left, he started scavenging for something to do. He discovered the sticking garden gate and attacked it with this." She pointed to one of her cherished knives lying wounded on the counter.

Running my thumb along the bent blade, I tried to be philosophical. "It's only a knife."

"That's not why I'm upset," she sniffed. "Then Mr. Fix-it decided to repair the worn heels on Mark's running shoes. Guess where he got the rubber?" I was afraid to ask. "He cut off the high heels from my good winter boots and nailed them onto your son's shoes. Mark has nothing to wear to school tomorrow and the store closes in half an hour."

I promised to have a word with Papa.

"You'll have to do more than that," Terrye bristled.

On a tour of the city, as we drove through Forest Hill Village, Papa had trouble believing that the stone mansions and the vehicles parked in driveways belonged to single families.

"And those?" he pointed, when we passed a downtown parking lot. "I read in *Pravda* that in America only the big bosses drive cars. Workers go on foot." He had also read accounts of drinkers causing car accidents and was concerned for our safety.

To show off, I took him to the Royal Ontario Museum, Chinatown, and later the Art Gallery of Ontario. Our award-winning City Hall made no impression on him, and he screwed up his face at the sculpture in the square. I explained what I knew of its creator, Henry Moore, and what it had cost.

"Insanity! I wouldn't pay even a hundred dollars, if I had that much money. But if I did, I'd buy myself apples."

To balance the picture, I exposed him to the poor part of town. He convulsed with laughter looking at the rows of Victorian homes with parked cars and antennas dotting the roofs. And he was bewildered by the unkempt, long-haired youths who lounged on steps and meandered down the sidewalks in Yorkville.

"Feh! If I were president, in one, two, three," he worked his hands like cymbals, "to Siberia!"

Seeing produce displayed outside a supermarket, he said, "Amazing! People walk by without stealing." He was equally impressed at the checkout counter. "This America is really something! Back home you wait in line to pay, then with the receipt, you wait in another line to get the *kasha*. If I bring my own sack, good. Otherwise —" He indicated his jacket pocket.

AS WORD OF PAPA'S arrival spread, friends and acquaintances lined up to meet him. One of the first was a former postman, now a highly respected advertising agency executive, who in spite of his capitalist trappings, had remained a captive of his youthful indoctrination. In a silk suit and floral tie, with his hair neatly coiffed and face bearing a pungent scent of expensive aftershave, he sat on our couch, face to face with Papa, relying on me to translate.

"What kind of work do you do, Mr. Kuperblum?" he inquired between sips of a cool gin and tonic with a twist of lime.

"Until my recent retirement, I worked in a shoe factory," answered Papa, as if filling out a questionnaire. "Now I'm on pension."

"So how do you spend your days?"

Papa offered a silver grin. "Oh, I belong to a sports club where I exercise daily, run on a track, and swim in an Olympic-size pool. I also belong to a social club where we discuss literature, politics, music, and so forth. Weekends my wife and I attend the ballet, the opera, the theater, and also the cinema. There's a television set in our living room, with no shortage of fine programs. I'm also a member of a mandolin orchestra."

"Where do you live?"

"In Chernovtsy."

"I mean in a house? An apartment?"

Papa spread his arms indicating our living room. "Like this."

Twirling his manicured moustache, the former postman beamed from ear to ear. "We constantly read about long lineups, oppression, and corruption in the U.S.S.R."

Blood rushed to Papa's face. "Lies! Capitalist lies!"

"Why did you tell him such rubbish?" I asked after the visitor was gone.

"The moment he sat down," Papa giggled mischievously, "I could see what kind of customer I was dealing with. Had I told him we share a one-room cellar with mice and rats and an outhouse with a dozen families, you think he would have believed me? Besides, it's not nice to talk badly about one's country. Also, you never know how a slip of the tongue, a careless word, even a whisper can come back to haunt you. They have spies everywhere, and in three months' time when I go back, you can be sure they'll know everything I saw, did, and said here."

We were friendly with a suburban couple. The wife's parents adopted us, in a matter of speaking, inviting us for Passover *seders* and Rosh Hashanah dinners. Our children grew up calling them *Buby* Naomi and *Zaidy* Reuven. Reuven spent Sunday mornings teaching our Mark Jewish history.

Reuven was a few years older than Papa — tall, with stooping shoulders, a balding head, and thick-lensed glasses, which gave him a fish-eye appearance. Of Polish origin, Reuven in his youth had also been attracted to communism's promise of a better world and spent his life fighting for it. Khrushchev's revelations about Stalin's crimes against the Soviet peoples jolted him.

He and Papa huddled in a corner, gesturing and verbalizing. Our hosts served bagels with cream cheese and lox, sweets, coffee, and an assortment of pastries. Papa refused even a glass of water. By the time the evening came to an end, the old timers were still in deep conversation and had to be torn apart.

A few days later, our friends implored us to bring Papa back.

Papa looked baffled. "I've already met these people. I'll visit them before I go back . . . to say goodbye." Nothing could change his mind. He encouraged us to go, saying he would babysit.

Later when the refreshments appeared, the telephone rang. It was our daughter Ellen. "Come quick!"

"Where's *Zaidy*?"

She swallowed her tears. "You'll see when you get here."

Barely stopping for changing lights, we raced back, and when we reached our door, screaming voices rained from above. I charged up the stairs, with Terrye behind me. A tornado had swept through the boys' bedroom: beds had been relocated, pillows and blankets scattered, and a curtain dangled from a damaged rod. Shaul, naked, sat sobbing on the floor.

"*Zaidy* tore Mark's *mezuzah** off his neck and threw it in the garbage," tattled Ellen. "Mark started to cry and woke Shaul up."

"*Mezuzah* . . . no good . . . no good!" Mark mimicked.

The door to Papa's room was ajar. He lay in bed, his nose in a children's book.

"I'm glad you're home, Jankele," he said without looking up when I rapped on his door. "There's a word here I don't understand."

"Papa, didn't you hear anything?"

"Yes. Crying is so beautiful! I love the sound. It develops their lungs."

"They should be asleep."

"When they tire, they'll sleep."

"What's all this about the *mezuzah*?"

"Feh! Feh! Ugly. Look." He held out his hands. "No rings, no watches, no peacocks on parade." He reached for my arm and made me sit on the bed. "Symbols like the *mezuzah,* the cross with their Jesus, Hitler's swastika, and Stalin's hammer and sickle have only served to divide humanity. They have led to war and ultimately to genocide." He continued, oblivious to the volatile mixture of anger boiling within me. "You know, Jankele, we are all born the same, but indoctrination sets us apart." He cleared his throat. "You may remember the gypsies in our town. These vagabonds were an unsavory lot — mostly street musicians, pickpockets, and fortune tellers. They had so many children, and my dream at the time was to adopt one of their boys and let him grow up with you. I was curious to find out the role environment plays." He leaned over to peck my cheek. "Go to sleep, Jankele. You look tired."

I told him I still had to take Farfel for his nightly walk.

---

* a small parchment scroll inscribed with biblical verses. It is placed in a case that is nailed to the door frame. A much smaller version is worn around the neck.

"In that case, I'll go to sleep." He yawned noisily and pulled the cover over his head.

IT WAS WITH MISGIVINGS that I took him to the Sumbergs. I worried that they would be judgmental. I also feared Papa's reaction when facing strangers who had substituted for him. Papa conversed with them about composers and writers, told tales, and finally broke into song, as if auditioning for the maestro. The musician interrupted and corrected, reminding Papa that after all *he* was the connoisseur.

Papa was shown the room I once occupied and received a dissertation on the art decorating the walls. "All originals — well-known artists who are personal friends," Mr. Sumberg said. Papa nodded politely. At Papa's urging, Mr. Sumberg unveiled his prized fiddle and offered a sampling. Papa's eyes filled with admiration.

When it was time to leave, sounding like his lookalike in *Two Soldiers,* he made a speech calling the Sumbergs heroes. Mrs. Sumberg offered her cheek when Papa attempted to kiss her, while the first violinist of the second row of the Toronto Symphony Orchestra drew back, keeping the visitor at bay. "That's not necessary."

"If there hadn't been a war, things would have been different," Papa reflected on the way home. "It was lucky we didn't find each other at first. Otherwise, you might not have met these nice people. What would you have had with me?"

In a shopping mall, when I selected half a dozen pairs of briefs for him, he smiled childishly. "Why so many?"

"You came with one pair, Papa."

"So, when it's dirty, I'll wash it."

He presented similar arguments for socks, hankies, and shirts. In each instance when I asked for his preference, his face turned blank. "A shirt is to keep you warm. Does it really matter if it's blue or brown?" He also defended his shoes, refusing the salesman's efforts to measure his foot. By the time we reached the suit racks, he pleaded he had no need of a suit, that he never wore, nor desired, one. He implored I take him home.

"You're squandering your hard-earned money that would be better spent on *kasha,* apples, and black bread," he said.

I hypothesized that in typical *shtetl* fashion he was protesting, but in reality needed, wanted, and expected me to force it upon him. An inexplicable compulsion drove me to make up for twenty-eight lost years.

The salesman at a clothiers outlet assured us that every suit he tried on was just Papa. The hues and textures fused and swam before my eyes until I couldn't discern one from another.

"This is fine, Jankele." Papa tried to bring the process to an end. The eager clerk squatted to turn up the pant cuffs.

We returned three days later. "Try it on to make sure it fits," I said, pointing to a curtained cubicle.

"Jankele, for sure it fits," he said. I blocked his path as he headed towards the exit. "Such a fuss," he mumbled grudgingly when he reappeared, looking like a clown from the Korona circus. The jacket was too long and the pants were cut where the knees would normally have been. The checkered pattern didn't help. Papa could read the disappointment in my face. "Now what, Jankele?"

Forfeiting the deposit, I dragged a bewildered Papa out of the store.

"So much trouble. So many spent nerves," he mumbled to himself. "I don't need a suit . . . I never wear a suit . . . Such a headache for nothing!"

Terrye had a cousin who managed a mens wear store in a suburban plaza. It was a long ride, but the prices were hard to beat. And with the special discount cousin Ronnie offered, I seriously considered buying two suits.

Cheapskate, how many fathers do you have? How many suits have you ever bought him? How many more will you buy him? Shame on you! Your poor father languished in Siberia and you're trying to fluff him off with a cheap *shmata* made in Taiwan.

Full speed down the expressway, I proceeded to Harry Rosen's downtown. I had shopped there once and made Harry's acquaintance: a low-key, pleasant man with an easy manner and trusting smile. Harry's clientele consisted of Toronto's business movers and shakers — the crème de la crème with an appetite for fancy labels. The merchandise was the best money could buy, and the store — large, beautifully appointed with exceptionally trained salespeople — was a busy place, especially on Saturdays.

As soon as we entered, someone offered to look after us, but I insisted on the boss himself. Harry was occupied on the telephone, measuring, answering queries, waving hellos. After the dutiful salesman whispered into his ear, Harry acknowledged our presence, signaling that he'd be with us shortly. I was flattered he remembered me.

Harry offered Papa his hand. "I'm very pleased to meet you, Mr. Kuper."

"It's Kuperblum," I said. Then I mentioned that we hadn't seen each other since 1939 and that Papa had spent eight years in Siberia.

The cool, calm, collected clothier didn't even blink. "Oh really! What were you doing in Siberia, Mr. Kuperblum?"

I explained that Papa didn't speak English and asked Harry if he spoke Yiddish. Harry smiled apologetically.

"I want you to make him a suit," I said.

"Anything in particular? Does he have something in mind? Is it for everyday wear, business, or special occasions?"

"When my father goes back, I want him to be the best dressed man in Chernovtsy. Price is no object." I tried to sound like one of his regulars.

Swiveling on his heel, he led us to a bolt of cloth resting on a counter and fingered the zigzagged edge. "Feel this.

New from England. It's so fine, you'd hardly suspect it's wool. Mind you, it costs . . . but there's nothing better."

I felt the fabric and motioned Papa to do likewise.

Harry played with the measuring tape around his neck. "I also have something a little less expensive."

"Only the best!"

"Let me see if Nello is free." Harry steered us up several steps, onto a platform.

Soon Nello appeared, his vest infested with tailor pins and a measuring tape resting on his shoulders. He was shorter than Papa. Bowing politely, he threw himself into his work, measuring, checking, and double checking, while Harry committed the data onto an illustrated pad. Papa, turned this way and that way, was directed to raise his arms, put his feet together and apart, and asked where he normally wore his belt. What kind of cuffs, if any, did he fancy? How many buttons on the jacket sleeves? Did he prefer single- or double-breasted? And what about the lapels, wide or narrow? Did he favor flaps on his jacket pockets? Was he partial to hand-stitched seams? And, oh yes, would it please him if the shirt cuff showed? I translated into Yiddish, stymied for a word here and there.

Mystified at the fuss being made over him, Papa stared at the eight-sided mirror, enthralled with the many angles of himself, and left all the decisions up to me. "I never had such an examination in my life, not even from a doctor," he chuckled.

Two weeks later a postcard invited Mr. A. Z. Kuperblum for a fitting. As the Soviet visitor admired himself in the octagonal mirror, Nello, with a mouthful of pins, adjusted sleeves, ripped the basted seams, and hemmed. Papa couldn't wait for the ordeal to end. When at long last the gifted tailor was satisfied, he summoned Harry to cast his experienced eye.

On the way home, Papa battled to keep his eyelids open,

and as soon as we entered the house, he said, "You look tired, Jankele. Why don't you go and rest up a little?"

"What about the children? Who will help Tobala with dinner? And the grass needs mowing."

"In that case, *I'll* have a nap," he said, his voice fading as he mounted the stairs.

When the next notice advised that the ensemble was ready to be picked up, Papa beseeched me not to drag him along. But drag him I did, and once more he stood before the magical mirror clad in the new pants, as Harry slipped the jacket on him, pulling here, pinching there. Finally, like a conductor presenting his orchestra to the audience, Harry, with a theatrical flourish, displayed the *new* Zelik Kuperblum to the world.

Papa's hair was freshly trimmed, his face tanned. In the new attire, he looked like the president of a multinational corporation. I peeked in the mirror to see what was in his eyes. He was not admiring Nello's creation, only himself.

"So, are we finished?" he asked, heading for the change room.

I held up my hand.

"What now?"

Pointing to a bulge in the jacket, I said, "I'll get Harry."

"Oy!" he exclaimed. "Leave the poor man alone. Enough already! I can fix it myself." He unbuttoned the jacket. "See! All I have to do is move it over to here." He pulled the excess fabric tightly around his body.

"You're ready to ruin it by moving a button over, to under your arm?" My voice sounded like sandpaper.

Papa carried the suit protected in a black zippered bag with the Harry Rosen label, for all to see.

"For a while there, I thought we would have to come back yet another time. It's a good thing you insisted they fix it right there," he mused, hurling the bag onto the back seat.

I inserted the key into the ignition, started the motor, and released the brake. We were silent for some time, lost in our own thoughts. "You should understand, Jankele, whenever I thought there was the possibility of coming to you, I wanted to be sure that my legs were strong enough to carry me, and what covered them was of no consequence." After yet another long pause, he resumed, "I hope I don't hurt your feelings if I tell you the material is very thin and won't protect from the cold."

Shortly after, when we were all invited to a bar mitzvah, Papa came down dressed as if for work.

"Where's the suit? What are you saving it for?"

"To pose for pictures, before I leave."

"And back home . . . will you wear it there?"

He could barely contain his laughter. "Jankele, if my neighbors saw me in a suit like this, they would conclude I had become a black marketeer. Who needs their envy? And I can certainly do without yet another police interrogation."

"You plan to sell it then, don't you? That's what it's all about, isn't it?"

He didn't answer.

12

USING A VERBAL SALAD of Yiddish garnished with English, Terrye plunged into conversations with Papa. Praising her tenacity, he made courageous forays of his own.

"I big boy. You little boy," he teased Shaul, swinging him by his arms like a merry-go-round.

By the time I left for work, Papa had finished his daily regimen, had eaten, and was taking a cold shower. "Just like *Zaidy!*" Papa laughed, carrying a sleeping Mark into the shower stall, shoving him under the freezing water. The screams brought the entire household running.

Papa spent most days by the pool in the park around the corner, romancing the ladies. Their ears bent to his every utterance, they giggled girlishly, ogling his well-cared-for physique.

Ellen reported seeing her *zaidy* attracting an audience by splashing himself like a dolphin in the ice-cold pool shower.

While we ate dinner, he serenaded us with a repertoire of Yiddish and Russian melodies. And Sundays, when we converged for brunch, he would pull up a chair.

"Papa, taste a piece of smoked fish." Terrye never gave up.

"Don't think I'm not tempted."

When Terrye and I were sipping our coffees and the

children had scampered off, Papa opened up. "In Russia, there are three categories of people: Those who sat in jail, those who sit, and those who will sit." He slid the chair closer to the table. "In fifty-one, they were arresting Jews. A neighbor, a Jewish woman who worked with me in the factory, was picked up by the police on her way to work, taken to headquarters, and told her daughter had committed suicide. They asked if she wanted to identify the body. Naturally she did, so they ordered her to sign a document. What she had in fact notarized, was a confession accusing her co-workers, all Jews of course, I being one of them, of pilfering leather.

"The police descended and rounded us up like a herd of cattle for slaughter. At first I thought it was some clerical error, soon to be rectified. We were assigned a lawyer who did what he could, I suppose, but didn't succeed in freeing me or any of the others. During one of his infrequent visits to my cell, he whispered, 'Who do you have abroad?' I told him. He held up an envelope bearing foreign stamps. 'Your wife gave me this. You have five minutes to read it.' I began, 'My dearest Papa . . .' but I couldn't continue, the tears blurred my vision. 'I could be shot for this,' the advocate quaked."

Papa filled his lungs with air and slowly exhaled. "It was that letter that made me go on. I promised myself, no matter what, I was going to see my Jankele again."

Another Sunday, he spoke of his Siberian odyssey.

"Whenever I was sent to a new work site or transferred to another camp, invariably we would be asked who amongst us rabble was a tinsmith, a mattress maker, or an auto mechanic. Whatever was needed, I raised my hand and told them I was a specialist from Warsaw; after all, who'd ever heard of Pulawy?"

"How did you manage to perform the work?" I asked.

"There were always one or two who knew what they were doing and I would watch. Soon I caught on."

His stories were morality tales, in which he played the

central character. In one, Papa made such an impression that by the time he was being transferred, the overseer declared, "I've seen many prisoners in my time, but you, Kuperblum, are truly an exemplary citizen. I hope we meet in different circumstances."

In another narrative, he begged for a piece of bread from a fellow inmate. "What have you got in return? Vodka, cigarettes?" the other quizzed. When their paths crossed again, the scoundrel was starving and Papa was the possessor of a loaf of bread.

"What do you think I did, Jankele?" Papa paused for dramatic effect. "I broke it in two. Shamed, the poor soul cried, 'You're not a man, Kuperblum, you're an angel! No, a saint!' and fell at my feet."

Another account had Papa dumped with other prisoners in a frozen wasteland. Huddled like sacks of potatoes trying to keep warm, the motley group lamented its bitter fate. Not Papa.

"I tore off my ragged clothes and washed my entire body with pure, fresh snow. Before I knew it, Jankele, not only was I clean, but also warm. Refreshed and with renewed hope, I broke into song." He relived the moment with an aria from Bizet's *Carmen.*

"That place was so beautiful, Jankele! In the spring, when the ice melted, I became fascinated with the fossils I discovered in the nearby sea. Truly magnificent! The world is such a miraculous place!"

"The other prisoners, Papa, what were they like?"

"Swindlers, collaborators. One or two had committed crimes of passion, but the majority were as innocent as I, convenient slave labor. Diehard believers wrote to Stalin, declaring their undying zeal for communism, imploring 'The Great One' to intervene." Papa laughed sadly. "But those letters never left the camp.

"Even the best of men became demoralized, resorting to liquor, nicotine, and other vices. The food was far from good, but enough to sustain a body. Many died. Some tried to escape, got lost in the tundra, and froze or expired from hunger. That's why a pair planning a breakout would invite a third — a fat one — to have something to nourish them along the way."

Terrye gasped.

"But the majority died of aggravation. They worried where their next shot of vodka would come from. How to survive the bitter cold, having gambled away their warm underwear. Mostly, they brooded about their families. Especially the fidelity of their wives."

"And you?"

"I kept to myself as much as possible. The moment I arrived in a camp, I introduced myself to the librarian."

"So you never worried?"

"Of course, I worried. Constantly. Worried that in the middle of an absorbing book, I'd be released."

NOT LONG AFTER Papa's arrival in Toronto, he received a letter. He gave it a cursory read, then tossed it into a drawer and reached for the mandolin.

"Good news, Papa?"

At first he was evasive, but later said, "Even though your brother's marks are the highest in his class and he borders on genius, the university rejected him. They allow few Jews, and usually only those who grease the right palm."

To illustrate, he said, "A man arrives at an Odessa restaurant asking for the one in charge. 'I've come from Moscow to audit your books.' The manager invites him into his office. 'Listen, instead of spending two weeks poring over a ledger,' the manager says, 'why don't you go to the beach where there are more interesting figures to gape at? I'll provide you with a comfortable room, all the food you can eat, and when the two weeks are up, I'll stuff two thousand rubles into your pocket. What do you say?' 'You must take me for a fool', answers the inspector. 'I paid ten thousand rubles to get this job.'"

Papa waved his arm, dismissing the thought of university forever. "So Mikhail will go to the army." And in the next breath, "My Lena sent me a list. They need a parcel. A headache!" He took his voice through the scales.

"I once sent a man to visit you. Do you remember him?"

"Yes, yes," he bubbled. "The journalist."

"What happened there with the police?"

"The police?" His face drew a blank.

"Was the money of help?"

"Yes, yes."

"How?"

"I think I bought a pair of shoes."

Then I asked about the *talis*. At first he didn't know what I was alluding to, then he recalled. "A religious neighbor promised Lena a fortune for a silk prayer shawl. Feh!" He discarded the memory and began to strum.

"Did you get the money I sent with Uncle Shmil-Leib?"

"I think so. I seem to recall something."

"God! I sent you five hundred American dollars and you can't even remember?"

It slipped off him like an oversized jacket. "Don't upset yourself," he said. "It's bad for your nerves." Touching me, he said, "I'm reluctant to tell you this, Jankele, but I might as well . . . since you're asking." My ears perked up. "Your uncle is not the same man I once knew. When I saw him in Moscow he was overfed, bragged a lot, and told embarrassing, smutty tales. I couldn't believe my ears. Feh! But the worst was, he had become so cold, distant! For example, he booked two rooms. One for Lena and me, and another just for himself. I ask you, why does a brother, whom I hadn't seen in so many years, seclude himself like a stranger? There he was, locked in his own cage, guarding his swelling suitcases, for fear that, God forbid, I should steal anything from him, I suppose. It was ugly!"

"What would you have preferred?"

"Couldn't we all have slept in one room? If need be, even the same bed. Just like in the old days, reminiscing about our youth, our parents, our brothers, and sister."

"What did Uncle bring you?"

"Who can remember? Maybe he did give me something. Now that I think of it, it may have been a suit."

I gasped. "You mean he never gave you my five hundred?"

"Do I know? Lena looks after these things. Calm yourself, Jankele. After all, what is it? Only money. Hardly worth getting upset over."

"I can't believe this!" I fumed. "He swore he left you two suits, a watch, and a host of other presents, together with my money."

"Maybe! Let's not talk about it anymore."

"What kind of person are you? I sent five hundred dollars and you don't know or give a damn if you ever got it?"

He stared at his feet, drumming his finger.

"I had to borrow it," I said. He elected not to hear. "Don't you care?"

"You want the truth?" He let down his guard. "I'll tell you the truth. Your uncle needed money for a lawyer to pay off the judges, and God only knows who else in order to get his son out. Trouble was, he couldn't find a buyer for the suits and lengths of cloth he brought. He was desperate and offered me the two suits in exchange for the money. Did I care? But Lena wouldn't let me. And so we came home with a watch and your money."

"What did you do with it?"

"You know, I have no use for trinkets, so I gave the watch to a friend."

"No, the money! What did you do with my five hundred dollars?"

"I bought your brother an accordion." He looked relieved.
"Does he play well?"

"I paid for lessons but he doesn't practice."

"Where's the accordion now?"

"In a corner, collecting dust." He gave me a lingering look and asked, "Jankele, why is the truth so important to you?"

"Jankele, the truth!" It was Mama's voice. "I'm *telling* the truth," I cried. "The red dot on your forehead shows me you're lying."

"Even as a child you were obsessed with the truth," said Papa. "I remember taking you for a walk in the park where I ran into someone I knew. You played and I sat down to chat with her. Though I begged you not to mention it to your mother, as soon as we got home you blurted, 'Papa sat with a woman.' Your mother was a jealous soul and didn't speak to me for the rest of the day. The truth, Jankele, isn't always conducive to happiness."

At night I lay awake. Who is this man? He's not the father I daydreamed about, nor would I have cast him for the role.

Terrye tried to ease my anguish. "What you see is what you've got. Stop torturing yourself."

WORD OF PAPA'S presence spread and eventually a *landsman**** that Papa had known in his youth showed up. A survivor of a concentration camp, he had arrived penniless in Canada but was now on his way to making his first million. He bragged about his lavish home, his fancy car, his bank account. To complete the picture, he showed off "the little wife," bedecked in finery. The biggest problem facing the shoe manufacturer was finding craftsmen.

"That's my specialty!" Papa spread his arms.

"Legally, you're not allowed to work here, Zelik," advised his old acquaintance. "But we'll work something out."

Early the next morning a honking car horn disturbed me. I gazed out the bathroom window, and there was Papa

*   countryman

entering the glitzy Cadillac that had blocked our driveway the previous evening.

Before dusk, Papa shuffled in with a box tucked under his arm and lumbered up the stairs. "At least a hundred people work in his factory, maybe even more," he recounted, resting in bed. "Such a busy place! Everything by machine. People work like robots. I wonder how they manage day after day."

"I forbid you to go back there," I said. "You didn't come here to work."

"For you," Papa pointed to the box on the dresser.

I took off the lid and withdrew a pair of leather slippers. As I leaned over to kiss him, he grabbed me, embracing the little Jankele he had left in Pulawy in 1939.

At last, something from Papa. I romped around the house proudly displaying the footwear.

"How's your father? Why doesn't he call?" asked the *landsman* when I bumped into him at the Bagel Restaurant. "Too bad he couldn't keep pace. What do they know from work in Russia, eh?" He bit into a sour pickle and mopped the juice that squirted his cheeks. He had already paid and was opening the door to leave when he turned around and called, "The slippers I sent for you, were they the right size?"

The episode with Uncle Shmil-Leib still fresh in my mind, I insisted on taking Papa to Niagara Falls. He was less than enthusiastic. After a two-hour drive through vineyard country, he took one look at the world wonder and said, "Now I can tell everyone in Chernovtsy I was here," and headed for the car.

Similarly, at the mention of Expo '67, his reaction was bereft of emotion.

"I don't know what to make of him," I said to Terrye. "Perhaps we should forget about it!"

"Too late. The hotel's been paid for and the children would never forgive you if you canceled."

As we were packing for the trip to Montreal, and I asked Papa to do likewise, he was bewildered. "What do I need? You told me there's a pool in the hotel, so I'll bring this." He displayed his swimming trunks.

Terrye, seven months' pregnant, remained at home with Shaul, while Papa, Mark, Ellen and I, our friends, their children, *Buby* Naomi and *Zaidy* Reuven, headed for Montreal.

The train was packed with noisy vacationers. Though I tried to seat Papa with *Zaidy* Reuven, he maneuvered himself next to me. He paid no attention to the ever-changing landscape and ignored the children.

From the minute we had first embraced at the Montreal airport, he talked of a *dombra*.

"What is it, Papa?" I had asked.

"A kind of mandolin. Maybe you can find one for me."

After inquiring at several music stores and reporting failure, the dream still radiated in his eyes. "Try others." I called every store listed in the city's Yellow Pages, and came up with zero.

"In America?" he said.

My search led me to the Toronto Conservatory of Music, and from there to a professor who suggested I contact Ivan Romanoff, an authority on Russian musicology. "As far as I know, the instrument is popular in Russia and one or two countries in Europe," he said.

As the train raced towards Montreal, Papa inflated himself with new hope.

"If it's unavailable in Toronto, what makes you think they'll have it in Montreal?" I asked.

"You'll see," he beamed, the sun reflecting off his face.

"Why didn't you buy one back home?"

"A worker like me? Hah! Only the *apparatchiks** have special stores where they get whatever their hearts desire."

---

*   unquestioningly loyal subordinates of the communist leadership

For months we had read about the avant-garde film presentations, the "not to be missed" American pavilion, the Bell Telephone cinema in the round, the Chinese extravaganza, and the architectural wonder, Habitat, designed by an Israeli architect. We were advised to book a minimum of five days to catch even just the highlights.

Once through the turnstiles, our friends followed their own agenda. Ellen and Mark pulled me one way, but Papa couldn't wait to get inside the Russian pavilion, darting up the many steps to the information counter. *"Dombras,"* I heard him say. In a moment he was back at my side, his face drained of color.

The grounds were already crowded with long lineups everywhere. The queue at the American pavilion snaked around the impressive structure, moving at a snail's pace. But we were determined not to miss it. Papa followed, staring blankly at the giant Pop Art paintings of Elvis Presley, Marilyn Monroe, Ketchup bottles, Campbell's soup cans, and hamburgers. He was just as impervious to the other attractions, and by early afternoon begged to go back for his nap. In spite of my children's vigorous objections, we returned to the Holiday Inn on the outskirts of the city.

In the evening, when our friends' children shared the thrills of their full day, mine looked accusingly at me.

The next morning, I urged Papa to hurry so we would not miss the bus.

"Weren't we there already?" he asked.

I wilted under his gaze. "There's much more to see, Papa."

"I saw everything I wanted to."

So in the mornings, we left him paddling like a puppy in the swimming pool, and upon our return, found him lounging in a chair scrutinizing the hotel guests.

"Suitcases! So many suitcases." He rocked with laughter. "As if they intended to be away for a lifetime. Every few hours a different costume. Sometimes it's hard to know it's the same person. You should see what they put into their stomachs. Small wonder they look like overstuffed sausages. And sick with worry that while they're here, they're missing out on something better elsewhere."

I did everything to involve him with our friends, but he kept his distance.

"I don't like getting close to those kinds of people," he confided. "Ever notice the couple? Look at them . . . old before their time. Walking around as if the world's problems were on their shoulders. And their children, have you studied their expressions? And when the time comes and they'll have children, how do you think they will behave? That's their legacy. The *zaidy* never smiles. For sure you'll never hear him sing. A truly sad individual! His wife is no different. Behaves as if she's in mourning."

"She is. They lost their only son in an accident." It didn't make a dent.

"Life is for the living," he expounded. "You cannot bring back the dead by torturing yourself."

BACK HOME, WHEN I returned from the office, Papa wasn't around.

"He's not well," Terrye informed me. "Has a fever. I tried to give him an aspirin."

I scaled the stairs.

"It's nothing, Jankele. It will pass. You'll see."

"I'm calling the doctor."

He giggled. "Let me tell you about doctors. I was a shoemaker's apprentice in Warsaw earning some twenty *zloty* a week. I lived in a windowless garret and ate in restaurants. Even though I was young and my intestines were strong, I developed a terrible pain in my stomach. I thought for sure it was the end. Naturally, I rushed to a doctor. He examined me, took my temperature, looked down my throat, inspected my ears and all the other places doctors like to look in. He demanded twenty *zloty*, gave me a prescription, and instructed me to return in a week.

"I had worked maybe fifty, sixty hours for that money, and he was relieving me of it for less than half an hour of his time. Nevertheless, a doctor had to be respected. He'd gone to *gymnasium** and university, and knew a thing or two. I spent several more *zloty* on the pills he had prescribed and followed the directions. The next week I returned, complaining of the same pain. This time he asked that I only unbutton my shirt, and with his fingers, he proceeded to knead my stomach as if it were dough. 'Continue with the medication,' he advised, 'and I'll see you next week.' That's how he swindled me out of another twenty *zloty*.

"I was walking along Nalewki Street, worrying how I was going to pay my rent and decided that I should be able to control my body the way a coachman governs his horses. I never went back to him, nor to any physician since. By experimenting with diet, I discovered that by abstaining from certain foods, my stomach cramps vanished."

"Is that when you became a vegetarian?"

"That happened later, in Siberia. Meat was scarce and we were fed gruel. Although many complained of listlessness, I was rejuvenated. There and then, I resolved never to eat flesh again. By accident, I discovered that if I didn't eat at night, I slept better. So gradually I developed some theories, which slowly evolved into my present habits."

In conversation with friends, one internist was highly recommended to me. When I called requesting an appointment for Papa, I was told the doctor was booked for the next two months. Only after explaining that the patient hadn't had a medical consultation for over forty years did the receptionist allow me to speak to the doctor. The physician

* high school

was sympathetic, agreeing to squeeze the deviant patient into his overloaded schedule.

"You're wasting your money," Papa protested strenuously. "Better you buy me a kilo of apples."

I bought apples on the way to the medical building. The foyer was upholstered in marble and the four elevators hummed, swallowing and spewing passengers at a brisk pace. In the waiting room, programmed music was interrupted by the ringing of a busy telephone. Half a dozen patients had their heads buried in out-of-date magazines.

Papa eased himself into a chair, crossed his legs, and tapped on his knee. When he was summoned, I was prevented from accompanying him, as the doctor was looking forward to polishing his rusty Yiddish. Papa was gone for quite some time, and when he emerged, it was with a requisition for blood and urine samples and for X-rays to be taken in the laboratory on a lower level. He laughed all the way home.

Days later when the doctor summoned me, I feared the worst. The specialist examined a set of X-rays while sucking on a pipe.

"Well, doctor?" I said, my voice quivering.

He exhaled puffs of smoke. "We should all be this healthy!"

I sighed. "What do you make of his bizarre eating habits?"

"It's crazy, but if it works for him, leave him alone."

I settled the hefty fee at the front desk and headed home with the good news.

Papa was blasé. "The doctor is overweight, his eyes are clouded, he is pale and short of breath. Still he smokes. Those poor unfortunates waiting to see him! How can he help them if he can't even help himself?"

TO PRESERVE MEMORIES of the past, survivors published remembrance books of their *shtetls*. A book in Yiddish from the Pulawy Memorial Society in New York City, together with an invoice for ten dollars, once landed in my lap. It was an amalgam of family photographs, reminiscences, snatches of history, and first-hand accounts of Nazi brutality — all of little literary value. But in the absence of a cemetery, headstones, and flowers, it had to suffice. The faces of those posing so optimistically were unfamiliar, yet collectively they were embedded in my memory.

One caption, under a picture of a portly man surrounded by a classroom of students, read: "Henryk Adler, the beloved principal of the Pulawy Public School, whom the Germans shot in cold blood the day they occupied the town." It was heartbreaking to read the names of my paternal grandparents, uncles, aunts, and cousins, listed in alphabetical order among the victims. But I became unhinged when in the same column, I spotted Aaron Zelik Kuperblum, his wife, and children.

Thinking Papa would find the book riveting, I plucked it from my shelf. After a glance at the cover, he placed it on his night table, and there it lay until weeks later, when I found him in the backyard hammock, absentmindedly leafing through its pages.

"Old things," he said dismissively, as if brushing away a mosquito. "These survivors live in the past." The words chilled me.

"Do you recognize anyone, Papa?"

"One account is by someone I knew quite well. We belonged to the same club where I learned mandolin. He left for America in '32, the year you were born. I see he became a writer . . . always dreamed of being one."

"How exciting! You must get in touch with him."

"For what?"

"He'd be thrilled."

"Do I know where he lives?" He raised his shoulders.

"I'll find him for you."

He considered it for a blink, then said, "It's best to let the past sleep. Once you start digging, God only knows what you may unearth!" But to appease me, he scribbled a note, and within a week received a reply, and a Yiddish book.

"A tragedy," reported Papa. "Never married, no children, he's sick, and lives in a seedy hotel in New York. He's written at least a dozen novels and if I send ten dollars for this one, he'll send me another. Clearly, he's looking to attach himself."

Catching him flipping the pages, I asked about it. "A silly story!" He opened an envelope and said, "Be so good, Jankele, and throw in the ten dollars. I wrote him that my visit is up and gave him my brother Jankel's address in Brussels." Papa laughed. "Let him bother him."

"HOW COME YOU didn't let me know your father was here?" Irena complained on the phone, and proposed another family get together. Seven years had elapsed since the first meeting, and I could have sworn this was a new contingent. They slapped my back and shook my hand. It was embarrassing not to remember most of their names. Fortunately, the attention was on Papa.

Once he heard that this family stemmed from Sandomierz, he clapped his hands and muffled the babble with his stare. "It was a holiday," he began slowly, baiting the audience. "My brother Mendel and I rented a rowboat and by noon, ended up across the Vistula River in Sandomierz. We walked around town, looked about the streets, and all of a sudden, it started to pour. While waiting under the canopy of a shoe repair shop for the rain to subside, a young man invited us inside. 'Where are you boys from?' he asked. 'Pulawy!' he said. ' We have relatives there. Perhaps you know them? They're bakers and such paupers, I doubt they can scrape enough together for a *Shabbat* meal.' 'What is their name?' asked my brother. 'Same as ours, Kuperblum.' Mendel and I glanced at each other. 'Then we are family!' Naturally, they insisted we stay to share their *cholent*."*

The audience was transfixed, their eyes on the story-teller. Papa sat back, wiping his brow.

"That was our young brother," sighed one. "Had we succeeded in getting papers for him, he'd be alive today." He rubbed his eyes.

Evidently, we were from the same lineage, but finding the couplings to the roots was complicated. The furthest ancestor Papa could pinpoint was his great-great-grandfather, Jankel Kuperblum, my namesake. Orphaned early in life, abducted into the army at age twelve, he spent the next twenty-five years serving the Czar. Conceivably he had a brother, and the Sandomierz Kuperblums were the siblings' descendants.

"You know there's another Kuperblum family in Toronto," someone said, dialing a number. "Nobody's home at Abe Cooper's. I'll try his brother."

Soon a man in his late fifties, with horn-rimmed glasses and a bushy head of graying hair, walked through the door. Straining his eyes, he focused on Papa. Papa squinted, sizing up the stranger, then rose to his feet. "Hershele!"

"Zelik!" responded the other, and they charged at each other. "We're second cousins!" choked Harry. "Always played together. Just little boys when I left Poland!"

"Hershele! Hershele!" Papa kept repeating. "Who would imagine we would ever see each other again?"

Harry Cooper was a fur cutter. After work, he frequently dropped by, armed with sweets for our children, with whom he developed a rapport, and the latest joke making the rounds on "the Avenue" — Spadina Avenue. Often he took Papa to visit his brother Abe or his own children.

Senior and retired, Abe lived with his second wife in a quaint house on Borden Street, the part of town where

* a stew served on the Sabbath

Toronto's Jewish community once pulsated. He was a giant, with a raspy voice and naked head. Over almond cookies, grapes, and endless glasses of steaming tea with lemon, Abe, whom Papa called Avrom, reminisced of the time he went from Poland to Cuba, and from there to Canada, where he arranged for his half-brother, Harry, as well as a sister to follow. Reflecting on his days in Toronto's sweatshops, he could recall the exact number of garments he had pressed and the meager salary it had earned him. He would repeat the stories and give an update on his five children, all married with families.

"My Sydney just won a multimillion dollar contract to build a bridge. You know where?" his voice boomed. "In Alaska, that's where. Ten companies bid, but my Sydney got it!" It didn't take much prodding for Abe to catalog how many men Syd's company employed or how much money his eldest had spent for the house he had just moved into. Without fail, he would remind us that the same Sydney had built the superhighway linking Montreal to Toronto.

Listening to him, I couldn't help thinking of the three brothers from Holland running for their lives through a muddy birch forest, and wondered if they had ever envisaged one of their descendants becoming a successful engineer in the new world.

Invitations for the long-lost cousin came flying from every direction. Most were casual events with coffee and dessert — none of which Papa ever touched.

The entire clan was invited to Sydney's, where he lived with his family in a stately mansion in Toronto's Forest Hill Village. A butler would not have been out of place. Instead, a uniformed maid floated about, offering tasty appetizers from a silver tray.

Some thirty people sat around the dining-room table. Candles glowed, and liquor, wine, and champagne flowed. The host toasted Papa. The honored guest, an empty glass in his hand, rose, proclaiming that in his wildest dreams, he could never have envisioned this moment.

While the assembled guests devoured an assortment of delicacies, exquisitely prepared and served on the finest china, Papa sat imprisoned in his chair, his eyes dancing on the crystal chandelier.

"Well, Zelik," asked Abe through a mouthful of food, indicating the lavish feast. "What do you think?"

The former *gulag* inmate considered for a moment. "I feel sorry for everyone here, eating so late at night."

Coffee cups in hand, the guests retired to the magnificent living room before beginning to disperse. Bidding Papa adieu, several discreetly pressed bills into Papa's hands. I felt a sting of shame watching him pocket the charity without so much as a thank you.

"What is this tank-you, tank-you, Tobala?" he had asked. "Everywhere I hear tank-you."

"Papa, when you give a child a sweet, what do you expect?"

"That he should eat it."

My wife laughed. "What about a thank you?"

Papa chuckled. "I'm pleased if he eats it."

"People like to be thanked."

"Foolish! Those who have should be happy to give without expecting anything in return."

Sydney's mother-in-law, a petite woman with a bird-like voice, held a letter received years earlier from relatives in the Soviet Union. Correspondence had been returned unopened, and she wondered if Papa could make inquiries.

"What a question! Of course, I'll look after it the moment I get off the plane."

Her hands trembled as she gave him the precious envelope with the return address scribbled in Russian.

Several days later, taking the garbage cans to the curb, I stopped dead in my tracks. "How could you do this?" I waved the envelope, yellowed with age and now crumpled, under Papa's nose.

"Where would I look?" he said after a long silence. "No doubt these people have probably been murdered. The moment I start making inquiries, the authorities will start asking questions of their own."

"Why didn't you tell her that?"

"Jankele, what harm is there in dispensing a little hope?"

Disturbing Papa's peace were the letters arriving from Chernovtsy — one after the other. "Take me to that store, Jankele," he said wearily.

With the money he'd been given at Syd's bulging in his breast pocket, we set out to the once-Jewish Kensington market. In a haberdashery store filled to the ceiling with cheap goods from Taiwan and Hong Kong, Papa selected a dozen men's nylon shirts, in varied sizes. I pointed out that although they were inexpensive, they were of poor quality.

"Good enough," he said, adding several more to the pile.

Grabbing ladies' stockings, girdles, brassieres, and other goods from bins, he mounded his pickings onto the counter. The proprietor punched in the sale on the ancient cash register and ripped off the tape. I turned to hand it to Papa, but he was already on the street. I reached for my credit card.

When I emerged from the shop with the bundles under my arm, I sighted Papa a few doors down, peering into another establishment. As he saw me approaching, he disappeared inside, where he began afresh, leaving me to take care of another bill. With minor variation, he played the same game at other stops.

At the shipping bureau, a Slavic woman examined each article carefully, recording the item, description, and value in triplicate. She tabulated the charges, then thrust the invoice at me. Out of the corner of my eye, I spied Papa leafing through a Russian journal.

*"Kompinator!"** Mama's voice rumbled. The audience at the Korona Circus roared with laughter. They were laughing at me.

At home when I checked the carbon copy of the shipping bill, the numbers didn't tally. Not listed was a sweater for Tamara. In a letter Papa had received was a photograph of Tamara with a friend. My sister wanted a sweater just like the one her companion wore, and Terrye had spent days tracking it down. I phoned to report the discrepancy and was informed that the sweater had been found lying on the floor and could not be included in the shipment unless the tariff was paid.

"Papa, we've got to go back," I told him when he got up from his afternoon nap.

"Let the parcel go without."

"And disappoint Tamara?"

"It's not the end of the world. Such a headache! Her friend has a sweater, so she must have one," he complained. "This friend came to my fifty-fifth birthday with a set of dishes. I don't know what for. We have dishes. When it was her father's birthday, Tamara came crying, 'I need money for a set of dishes.' Dishes here, dishes there. I gave her money, but warned, 'From now on, no more birthdays.'"

"Kompinator! Kompinator!" Mama's voice rang in my ears all the way to the shipping bureau and back.

Seething inside, I confronted Papa. "You think only of yourself."

He sought sanctuary in a story. "When the Titanic was sinking and people were scurrying around trying to save themselves, a woman noticing her husband walking calmly along the deck, screamed, 'How can you be so calm with your hands in your pockets while everyone else is tearing their hair out?' And he answered, 'What makes you think I'm not tearing my hair out?'"

* con-man

13

"IT SEEMS YOU ARRIVED only yesterday and already you're leaving," I said sadly as Papa's departure neared.

He closed his eyes. "Oh, what I wouldn't give to stay!"

My heart shifted into higher gear. Terrye contacted Canadian Immigration and I contacted my friend and lawyer Muni Basman. Papa's visa was extended for another three months.

In the fall of 1967, *Child of the Holocaust* hit the book stores. People talked about it. I appeared on radio and television shows. Journalists wrote about me; reviewers wrote about the book. Suddenly I was a celebrity, sought after for speaking engagements. What fascinated the public was that I had managed to come through Hitler's inferno relatively unscathed.

Of the many letters I received, one was from a psychiatrist marveling at the dearth of hatred in my life. Reviewers shared his sentiment. However, one comment perplexed me: "The only time Kuper lapses into cliché is when talking about his parents. They alone have been transformed by nostalgia into people who could do no wrong."

Following a published interview, in which I asked where God had hidden during the Holocaust, I received an offer to lead a Humanist congregation.

"We have about fifty members, but with you at the lead, we could attract other followers."

"And we'll kill those who refuse to join. Right?"

My new celebrity status took me to places like Cincinnati, Ohio. At the airport I was met by a publicity rep from Doubleday. He looked more like a tie salesman than someone who could tempt any reader, let alone a reader for a book on the Holocaust. As we approached the city, I asked what had drawn him to the profession.

"PR is just a small part of my job. You could say I'm Doubleday in this part of the country. I even deliver the books to the stores."

"How's my book selling here?" I leaned back in his beat up Volkswagen.

He maneuvered the wheel, his eyes on the road. "What's the name of it?"

Suddenly I felt a few inches shorter.

"Let's see," he reached for the list on the dashboard. "*Hotel* by Arthur Hailey is number one, at more than two hundred and seventy-five thousand copies. Only been out for a few weeks." He risked a quick glance down the printout. "We only get the first hundred selling titles. I don't see yours."

I sank deeper.

After a lackluster interview with a local reporter, I was hustled to the book section of a department store. Anticipating a lineup, I began to sign the stacked copies.

"Was it advertised anywhere?" I inquired when no one showed.

My contact pointed to a showcard bearing my name.

"Oh, what the heck, I'll buy one for my daughter." The manageress picked up a signed copy out of pity. "She'll read anything!"

A hot-dog-stand lunch later, I was rushed to a TV studio. The host was in the make-up room. "You can't be Jack Kuper," he said eyeing me in the mirror. "You look like a regular guy. Read your book in less than an hour." Judging by the interview, he was telling the truth.

Witnessing all the frenzy, Papa was anxious to know what the book contained. "Now for sure, I must learn English." He stroked the copy I had autographed for him, as if it were the *Torah*.

I escorted him to Central Tech, my old school, where there was a summer course for immigrants.

"Normally a father takes his offspring," he mused. "But in our case, it's the other way around."

Papa sat at the kitchen table practicing. "Ten, twenchy, thirchy, forchy, fifchy, sixchy." He cocked his ear at the hypnotic sound of raindrops against the windowpanes. "Reminds me of spring '44 in the Worker's Brigade, when I slept in a tent. Drops of rain trickled in through a tear in the top. Drip, drop! Drip, drop! I lay back listening. It was so beautiful! Then I heard birds chirping outside. Ah!"

A bomb exploded, littering the mired road with carcasses. Uzbek soldiers, with machine guns strapped to their chests, thundered through the village on horseback, pursing the enemy. "Where's my Papa?" my voice echoed, running after the liberators. They headed into the horizon, leaving only hoof marks.

When next I saw Papa, happy and content, rotating his tanned body with the sun, the memory of Mama's large dark eyes glistening with tears tormented me. "Your father ran away and left me holding the bag." A disturbing thought sprouted in my head: I should kill him.

Sensing something was amiss, Papa suggested I join him in a morning run and a cold shower. When I ignored him, he asked, "What is it you want of me?" The words coming from his mouth appeared out of sync with his lips.

"What kind of a human being are you?" I tore into him.

"Jankele, the apple doesn't fall far from the tree. Whatever you see in me, you'll eventually find in yourself."

In the Warsaw Ghetto Aunt Miriam carefully apportioned the week's allotment of bread, spreading margarine in miserly fashion over the slices. I flipped my piece over and stood in line once more. Transferring it onto her own hand, she sensed the grease and skewered me with "*Kompinator!* Just like your father!"

It's all a big mistake, I was sure. He's someone else's progenitor. If babies can be switched at birth, why not parents?

"Jankele, tell your good-for-nothing father his dinner is on the table." Mama faced the stove.

"Jankele, tell her she can eat it herself. I'm not hungry," Papa said to the wall.

"Of course he's not hungry. You know why, Jankele? Because for sure he stopped at his mother's to fill himself on soup." She mimicked Papa. "Nobody makes a *krupnik** like my mother!"

Resorting to silence, Papa and I avoided each other.

"Bury the hatchet," Terrye implored me. "He's your father and after he leaves in September, you may never see him again."

Terrye's pregnancy was preoccupying me at that point. But by the time she gave birth, to Simca, Papa and I found our tongues and wished each other *mazel tov*.

"You must name her after my father's mother, Chana," said Papa, recounting how as a boy he was sent to live with his *buby* and *zaidy* in Josefow, only kilometers from Pulawy. "My parents worked their fingers to the bone, yet could barely feed or clothe their eight children. So when my grandparents offered to take one, my mother picked me. I suspect I was her least favorite.

"After the First World War, Josefow lay burned to the ground, and *Zaidy* faced the task of rebuilding the house. We excavated the basement by hand, built the walls with

*   barley soup

stones from the rubble, and constructed a straw roof. There was no money for a floor, so we covered the ground with sand.

"*Zaidy* Josef was honest and pious. When customers neglected to pay him for fixing their locks or shoeing their horses, it was against his nature to remind them. Yet whenever anyone came to his door, they never left empty-handed.

"No one cooked a better *borscht* than my *Buby* Chana. She always made sure my clothes were laundered and in good repair, and she tucked me into bed with her finest goose eiderdown. Those were the best years of my life.

"Three years later, on my fifteenth birthday, when I got homesick and decided to return, my family hardly knew me, nor I, them."

As Terrye also had a favorite *buby,* Simca, we named our precious jewel Simca Chana. Papa, jesting that his mission was accomplished, said he was ready to return to Russia. But when that time approached, he latched onto me like a child.

"I don't want to go back, Jankele! My place is here with you, where I feel at home. There, I'm a total stranger."

Paradoxically, in place of compassion, I felt shame, and identified with his family at the other end of the world. Having failed to elicit my sympathy, he turned the chessboard around, begging I do everything in my power to liberate them from their hell.

"You should never have allowed Tamara to get married," I lectured, masking my guilt. "She could have found a husband here. Now there's a child as well."

"Does a father have the right to intervene? She would never have forgiven me."

I gritted my teeth. "Goddamn it! You want me to shoulder everything!"

"What's your worry, Jankele? These are young people, not afraid of work. On the contrary, life will be better for you if we're all together. You'll have family to visit, to celebrate with. Your children will have a *buby,* a *zaidy,* an aunt, uncle, and cousins. Trust me, you'll profit, and your efforts will be repaid a hundredfold with happiness."

It sounded reasonable, enticing, and it placated my conscience. Still, I looked for excuses. "Where would I put everyone?"

He pointed to our living room. "You'll throw a few mattresses on the floor."

"And food, clothing, doctor's bills, a car, insurance?"

He magnetized me with a smile. "When your mother and I were planning to get married, we had friends who wanted to do the same. But they worried: Where will we get furniture? How will we afford the rent? What if children come? And so forth and so on. On the other hand, your mother and I married, managed to rent an apartment, furnish it, and somehow provide food for the table. You came along, then Josele, and we didn't go hungry. The war broke out and our friends were obliterated, never having experienced the joys of matrimony nor the bliss of parenthood."

Feeling the heat in my cheeks, I asked him about the status of his exit papers.

"May the devil take those anti-Semites! Every time I go to the officials, they sip tea and laugh under their breaths. The last time, everything was in order, but the boss was busy, and I was told to come back the next day." He clenched his fist. "To hell with them! I refused."

"How do others get out? How do they do it?"

"Speculators, thieves, black marketeers!" He spat the words out. "They grease!"

"To survive, sometimes one has to do what one has to do."

His face contorted. "Me? Never!"

"If I can pull it off, fine, as long as it doesn't inconvenience you! Eh, Papa?"

"We won't talk about it anymore, Jankele!" he said, and launched into an aria from *Tosca.*

Once more Papa asked me to drive him to Kensington Market. "When you return from a trip, people expect something," he said, as he haphazardly selected cheap trinkets from a street vendor. "The lighter is for my old boss, I want to remain in his good books. The wallet, for the friend I jog with every morning. We tell each other things from the heart. And this wind-up toy, for Tamara's son."

"Those are made in Japan and will fall apart. Come, I'll show you where to find something better."

"Feh! As long as they get me through the door, what do I care?"

Our house was packed with people. Papa, wearing his new suit, posed for photographs. After refreshments, he raised a hand to hush the crowd and made a stoic farewell speech. The guests had arrived bearing gifts, and when they left wishing him *"bon voyage,"* one sensed they didn't expect to see him again.

"One day, Jankele, when you find a little patience, you may want to read this." Papa handed me the hardbound notebook I had given him months earlier when he had asked for something to write in. I placed it in my desk drawer. In lieu of the elusive *dombra*, I presented him with a choice mandolin and handed him six hundred American dollars.

When he was getting ready for bed, I entered his room. "Your plane leaves at nine in the morning," I said. He nodded. "That means we must be there by seven," I said. "I guess we'd better leave the house by six."

"Good."

"Are you ready?"

He returned my smile. "What's there to be ready?"

"How do you propose to carry all your things?"

"Do I know?" he shrugged, refusing to be dislodged from his complacency. "No doubt Tobala will figure it out."

In the morning Papa pecked each one of our children and tiptoed down the stairs. He hugged Terrye, calling her "the best wife on earth." She concurred and wished him a safe journey. As she closed the door behind us, I saw tears running down her cheeks.

Neighbors peered out windows, watching Papa enter the car. I backed out, and pressing on the accelerator, raced towards the airport.

Zaidy Reuven was waiting at the check-in counter.

I helped Papa check in and select his seat, and watched his suitcases disappear along the conveyer belt. As the plane was not yet boarding, I suggested we converse a little longer. Papa was impatient. He offered his hand to Reuven, said a few parting words, then spun around. We embraced and kissed, but the wall between us refused to melt. The mandolin in one hand, the boarding pass in the other, he marched like a soldier to the departure gate. I waited for a last glimpse, but he didn't look back.

Removing his myopic-lensed glasses, *Zaidy* Reuven disclosed teary eyes. "Imagine those bastards sending that poor man to Siberia just because he wrote letters all over the world in search of you!"

"Papa!" I yelled, but he had turned the corner. Just like years earlier, he vanished from sight.

A library silence reigned at home. It was lonely without him. I also missed Farfel, whom Papa had persuaded me to get rid of. I ran my fingers across the strings of the mandolin he had brought with him, then plucked the notebook from the drawer and flipped it open. On the first page, in painstakingly formed Yiddish script, he had written, "Jankele, when I'm no longer on this earth, don't forget your family in Russia." I slammed it shut.

14

ON HIS WAY back to Russia, Papa stopped in Brussels to see his brothers. Uncle Shmil-Leib had kept the rubles left over from his rescue mission in Russia in the corner of a drawer. He purged himself of the currency by stuffing it into Papa's luggage. But when Papa landed in Moscow, either his demeanor or his undeviating misfortune betrayed him. He was stripped, interrogated, robbed, and threatened with prison for trying to smuggle rubles into the country. He detrained in Chernovtsy with only a mandolin and the inscribed copy of *Child of the Holocaust*.

Commenting on Papa's visit, Uncle Jacques reported, "When I asked your father what you gave him, he replied, nothing."

In the same vein, Papa wrote that he had refused his elder brother's offer of a moth-eaten sweater.

Unable to sustain himself on his pension, Papa went back to work. He enrolled in night classes to continue his English and wouldn't rest until he was able to read my memoir. "Your book is the most meaningful gift. I never realized what you went through," he wrote. "People beg to borrow it, but it's fused to my hands."

To my surprise and delight, he launched a search for the

peasants who had sheltered me. I was astonished when he sent me snapshots of himself posing with a half-bent Mrs. Paizak leaning on a cane. She had desperately tried to save me. After Papa invited her to visit him, her neighbors warned her against it, saying it was a trap to kill her for having booted me out in the end.

Prospecting for people had become my own addiction. Every time I checked into a hotel, anywhere in the world, I'd scour the telephone directory. Terrye joined me in my quest, leafing through documents and scrutinizing indexes. We wrote letters to the Red Cross, to Simon Weisenthal's Documentation Centre, to Yad Vashem in Jerusalem, and to various tracing agencies.

In New York, I sniffed out a David Kuperblum, a concentration camp survivor from Lodz. The moment our eyes connected, we were drawn by an invisible bond. There were physical similarities, and in addition, we were both chasing ghosts.

Once, when I called home from a film location in the Laurentians, Terrye said, "Hurry back, Jack, a surprise guest is waiting for you in our living room."

When my plane touched down in Toronto, I promised the cabbie a generous tip if he pressed a heavy foot on the accelerator.

A tall, emaciated figure, half-sitting, half-reclining on our couch, extended a hand. "I would never have recognized you, Jankele!" In place of a thumb, I felt a cauliflower-like stump. "This calls for a celebration!" he slurred, attempting to rise to his feet.

His cheap toupee, deep-set eyes, and hollow cheeks repulsed me. "Who are you?"

He grinned, exposing wide gaps between teeth. "I suppose the years have changed us both. After all, you were just a child. As for me, I still had my looks, my health, and my thick black hair."

A chill ripped through me. "Kisel?" My last glimpse of

him was in our courtyard on Pawia Street in Warsaw, when with three others he performed "Brother Can You Spare a Dime?" in Yiddish.

"That's when I had a voice!" He displayed an empty glass. "If you don't give me a drink, I'll pass out! And if I do, I won't be able to drink."

"Finished everything we had: the vodka, the gin, whatever," whispered Terrye.

I scrounged a bottle from a neighbor. Kisel took a gulp and sighed with relief. He had fought in the Red Army and the Polish exile army, was wounded in Monte Casino and ended up in Palestine, toting a machine gun for the Zionist cause. Now living in New York City, he was married to a German gemologist.

"She's a *Jekke*,* but she doesn't have one mean bone in her entire delectable body," he said.

I refilled his glass. "How did you ever find me?"

"My sister in Los Angeles read your book and called me when she came across my name. I'm attending a bar mitzvah here, so I came a day earlier just to look you up." His eyes clouded over. "I often think of the evenings when my mandolin accompanied your mother's golden voice, and I can still taste her delicious *latkes.*"**

"You don't happen to have a photograph of her, do you?"

"No, but I see the entire Huen family before my eyes."

"Chuen!" I corrected him.

"You're telling me?" he reached for the bottle. "The name is Huen! Believe me! It's German for rooster."

"No wonder!" I hit my forehead.

Terrye rushed to the phone book but could not spot a Huen. However, my heart skipped more than a beat when the Montreal directory unearthed one. I was tempted to call, but the hour was late.

---

*   German
**   potato pancakes

We drove Kisel to his hotel and literally carried him to his room. His trousers were soaked in urine.

I contacted T. Huen by mail. Weeks later, one of my children called me to the phone. "Daddy, it's for you."

"Who is it, darling?"

"A funny accent."

Taking a gulp of coffee and throwing the butt of my cigarette into the cup, I snatched the receiver. "Hello!"

"This is cousin Tommy Huen," sang the voice. "You Chinese too?"

I was tempted to fall to the floor. "No, I'm Jewish!"

"That's good, too," said cousin Tommy, wondering where and when we could meet.

"I'll call you next time I'm in Montreal," I said. "If you're coming to Toronto, give me a shout."

I didn't hear from him, but when I was in Montreal, I inquired at the Chinese restaurant where he was employed and was told he was no longer there.

AN AD IN THE PAPER alerted Terrye to a rundown century farm, less than an hour's drive northwest of Toronto. The house needed extensive work, but Terrye swore she'd be happy with just a fresh coat of paint. As soon as we took possession, I took pencil to sketch pad and started redesigning. The property gave us much satisfaction and certainly occupied our weekends. No sooner was the septic tank replaced, than the electricity would fail, causing the water pipes to freeze, resulting in a flood. The roof leaked, the chimney became plugged, and the fireplace smoked. A bottomless pit! Against all odds, we persevered.

Attending auctions and browsing in antique stores, we furnished the place with the inheritance of others culled from neglected attics and damp basements. In the belfry, we installed a brass bell from a church in Quebec. From wrecking yards, I lugged solid cedar doors with hand-wrought hinges, stained-glass windows, staircases, balusters, and lighting fixtures from yesteryear. The restored cast-iron wood-burning stove kept us warm in ski season and gave the house a beautiful aroma.

As good as they were, these dream-like weekends were too short, and we regretted facing life in the city when Sunday night rolled around.

AT WORK, AGENCY STAFF changed, the offices were spruced up, efficiency improved, and it was no longer necessary for five or six bodies to fly in from New York to take a client's pulse. The competition in Toronto was beginning to take note, and writers and art directors wanted to exercise their talents for us. Yet no new business came our way.

The offices of Ben-Adam and Barclay were at opposite ends of the floor. They did everything to avoid each other. Ben-Adam kept feeding his opponent as much rope as possible, in the hope that he would hang himself.

"Any day now, New York will spring the trap," he said, salivating, behind closed doors.

A year later, Barclay was still with us.

Every Friday afternoon he opened the bar in his office. Under the guise of winning a client, the possible acquisition of a new account, the hiring of a secretary, someone's birthday, engagement, anniversary, or divorce, a party would convene. Once it was to honor an account-executive who had outlived his usefulness. Everyone pretended he had resigned for a better position, more money, a larger agency. Toast after toast reminded him of the valuable contribution he had made, how much he would be missed, and how difficult it would be to replace him.

In the process of bringing his wife up from New York, Ben-Adam engaged a flamboyant decorator to transform his luxury penthouse into a showcase. The decorator hurled himself into the assignment and the bills came flying into the office, together with ones for lavish parties and nights on the town.

The Young Turks eventually woke up and summoned Ben-Adam to New York. On his return to Toronto he invited me out. In measured tones, between sips of Chivas Regal, he told me he was leaving the agency. "But you've got to stay on," he said.

I laughed. "Barclay will eat me for breakfast."

"What do you want? Share your dreams."

I was drafting my resignation when Howard, the big cheese with the fat cigar, got me on the line, inviting Terrye and me to New York for the weekend.

A vase of red roses, along with two choice seats for a hit Broadway play, awaited us at the Pierre. Early Sunday, we boarded a train for upstate New York, where our host, his wife, their shaggy dog, and Ford Fairlane station wagon met us.

Over a hardy brunch, Howard worried about his son's bar mitzvah. They were not religious and did not belong to a synagogue, yet something was knocking on his conscience.

It slipped out that he had had several heart attacks and was suffering from an ulcer, which explained the myriad pills he was popping.

"Let the boys talk shop," suggested his wife, pulling Terrye to the garden.

Howard lit a fresh cigar. "If you play your cards right," he said, "my job can be yours one day."

By the time we boarded the train back to New York, he had sweetened me up. To celebrate the five-thousand-dollar raise and vice presidency, we called Ruth and Trevor — actor friends from Toronto who were living in New York, waiting for the big break.

"Let's have a drink," I proposed after we settled in the restaurant of their choice.

"Good idea," said Trevor, ordering one. "To the VP." He

took a long gulp, emptied the glass and signaled the waiter. "You know, when we first got here, my agent sent me to audition for a soap commercial. It paid triple scale and a bundle in residuals. I'm an actor, I told that flesh peddler, not a soap salesman."

I adjusted my tie and sipped my drink. "Some of the biggest names in the business are doing commercials these days," I said.

"Prostitutes!" he spat.

"A Montreal actor I know makes about a hundred thou a year in voice-overs alone. What do you say to that?"

"I say shit on him," he fumed.

Ruth toyed with the glass of vermouth in her dainty hands. "I'm working in a bookstore, but get time off for auditions," she said.

Terrye brought them up to date on our children, showing photos.

The appetizers arrived, followed by pasta fagioli, then the main course. After desserts and multiple coffees, Trevor, mellowed, leaned across the table. "What do you say to a little after-dinner drink?"

"Why not!"

"Cognac all around," he snapped. He drained the glass and asked permission for another.

"I think you've had quite enough," Ruth said.

"We're celebrating!"

After yet another cognac, I paid and we left. Arms intertwined, we staggered through the moonlit neighborhood, our voices raised in song.

Without warning, Trevor grabbed me by the lapels. "What are you doing making goddamn commercials? You, of all people!" He lifted me off my feet.

"Did you enjoy the meal?" I asked.

"Haven't eaten this well in I can't remember how long."

"The goddamn commercials paid for it."

"What will you tell your children when they grow up and

ask what you did with your life? I survived the Holocaust to make commercials?"

"Stupid son-of-a-bitch," I flared, but I wasn't sure who I meant.

WITH THE ASSISTANCE of a headhunter, Ben-Adam replaced himself with a young, self-assured executive with impressive credentials. The candidate, Scot Cottingham, was whisked to New York and promptly anointed.

Before moving in, the new general manager had the broadloom replaced, the office redecorated in colors of his choice, and a more majestic desk installed. Naturally, Barclay threw a party for the departing and incoming general managers. He poured drinks, cracked jokes and slapped backs, pledging allegiance. Having been alerted to the situation by both Ben-Adam and New York, the new chief was cautious.

"I'm going to turn this place around, and I need your help, Jack," he said. For the next while, I hardly saw him, though occasionally I heard his voice. I ran into him on the elevator and he suggested we go for a drink.

"Sorry, my wife, children, and dinner are waiting," I said.

He studied me curiously.

For months, I didn't even hear his voice from afar. The door to his office seemed to be permanently locked. When he surfaced some time later, he took me to lunch.

It started in the watering hole of the Celebrity Club, where he was a member and fussed over by the bartender. He leaned on the English-style bar, downing one drink after another and encouraging me to get on with mine so he could buy me a refill. We were still making small talk when a waiter told him, "Mr. Cottingham's table is ready." Scot ordered a bottle of rare wine, and when I commented on the outrageous price, he sloughed it off. By the time we got to the cappuccinos, he proposed a liqueur to finish off.

I glanced at my watch. "My God, it's almost three!"

He pushed me back into my seat. "Relax. Work won't run away, and this is a swell place to make business contacts."

I was in Quebec City shooting a commercial when I received a call to drop everything and report to New York. At head office I was confronted by a pacing Barclay.

"What are you doing here?" he said, his cigarette trembling between fingers. We tried to make conversation, but ended up staring at each other. Howard's showpiece in the tight-knit skirt broke the hush. She asked Barclay to follow her.

I picked up a magazine and was scanning the pages when Scot Cottingham crossed the threshold looking sallow. "What's going on?" he asked.

The secretary reappeared and led me into the boardroom. Howard and two associates were at the long table.

"We hear stories, get bills, and have our suspicions," Howard said. "Cottingham has spent a small fortune without landing so much as a sardine. He's been running around desperate for receipts. But still, he can't account for some four thousand dollars."

"As vice president," piped up one of the two henchmen, "it's your duty to tell us everything you know."

"I wasn't hired to be a quisling." I got up to leave.

"Wait out there," Howard ordered. Cottingham was next.

Barclay was in the waiting room fluttering his arms, as if readying for flight. "Boy, those guys are out for blood." He lit a cigarette while one still dangled from his lips.

Soon the two of us were summoned.

"We've just fired Cottingham," Howard smiled devilishly, and the others mimicked him. "And we've reinstated Barclay as general manager. Can the two of you work together?"

Barclay slapped my back. "I always got along with Jack."

"I can work with anybody." The voice was mine but I didn't recognize the words.

"Good!" Howard said. A round of handshakes ensued.

In Toronto there was the to-be-expected Friday party. At two in the morning, music was still blaring and beer caps were popping.

"You and I got to get to know each other a little better," said Barclay, throwing a limp arm around me.

Several Fridays later, as the festivities were getting started, he sauntered into my office with a handful of dockets. "We need storyboards, copy, first thing Monday in Montreal."

"Are they crazy? On such short notice?"

"Client called a week ago. I forgot to tell you."

"I'm taking my kids skiing tomorrow."

"If you can't do it, just say so," he said slyly. "I'll get a freelancer."

"Can't you ask for an extension?"

"I'll call New York, tell them you're busy with your family, and see what they suggest." The vice tightened.

I closeted myself with two of my staff, and by the time the party had subsided, we were still tossing ideas around. The cleaning crew arrived for the night round, but it didn't take long for the wastebaskets to be replenished.

Bleary-eyed and unshaven, we trudged back into the offices Saturday morning, littering the floor with dough-nut cartons, foam cups, and crumpled balls of paper. By nightfall, when the street below began to hum, we had broken the back of the assignment. By noon on Sunday, the full package had popped out of the oven.

On the flight to Montreal, Barclay entertained me with accounts of his exploits. The instant we checked into our posh hotel, a waiter entered Barclay's room carrying a tray of drinks. For dinner, he led me to a raucous spot where young leather-clad girls in tight outfits danced with each other. The star of the floorshow was a drag queen, a Marlene Dietrich lookalike in a long, slinky, sequined gown.

At one point, two women joined us. The younger one giggled and chattered while her companion hardly opened her mouth. Barclay jabbed me in the ribs when they excused themselves, walking arm in arm to the washroom. "A mother-and-daughter act," he said.

The next morning, the advertising manager was late, and when he did show, it was without the expected committee. Unsmiling, he eased himself into a chair and signaled us to proceed.

Barclay made the routine preamble, stumbling over his words. Unveiling the storyboards, I walked them through, frame by frame, explaining the camera moves, music, special effects. I was still reading the voice-over when the salt-and-pepper-haired client consulted his Timex.

"It's brilliant, Jack," he said. He motioned to Barclay, and the two of them vanished.

Wasn't advertising the art of our time? If Shakespeare and Michelangelo were my contemporaries, wouldn't they be creating TV commercials? My musings were interrupted by the phone.

"Ya pulled it off, you son of a bitch! Get your ass up here for a drinky-poo."

He wasn't such a bad guy after all!

Rushing up on the elevator, I knocked on his door. He opened it, wearing only his briefs. A glass full of ice cubes in hand and a cigarette dangling from his mouth, he moved to pour me a drink.

Our client, also in underwear, saluted me with a raised glass. "To the creative genius!"

Giggling sounds preceded the entrance of the mother-and-daughter act. Both were nude. "Come on girls, show Jack what you can do," said the client with a flourish.

I ran.

THE MORNING PAPER folded under my arm, the weed between my lips, I waited for the subway doors to open. At the station, I lit the cigarette and, sandwiched in the throng, made my way up the stairs, the smoke irritating my throat and nostrils.

I should really give it up. Especially now with all this talk of cancer. I'd promised Papa I would. Even though I never inhaled, I craved the nicotine and felt lost without the Benson and Hedges package. Was it the amusing commercial that had persuaded me to switch to that brand?

I must join the Y, I resolved, out of breath, climbing to the street above. In a few months, I'll be thirty-eight. I'm turning gray. I should go on a diet. Where did the years go? Another two and I'll be forty. I don't feel that old. Have I changed that much? It's the hair that gives me away.

"Why not darken it?" my barber had suggested.

I would have welcomed the idea, had he been more discreet.

I stepped onto the sidewalk.

"Jack!"

I turned. For a moment I couldn't remember the columnist's name.

"What a miserable day," I said, scanning the gray sky. "Suicidal weather. Every year at this time I promise myself to flee this bloody country, and here we are, 1970."

The columnist hid any problems he might have had behind a cheerful facade. "Where would you go?" he asked.

"What I wouldn't give to be a simple fisherman in Puerto Vallarta right now!"

Waving goodbye, he dashed down the same set of stairs I had scaled.

"Hello," I greeted the buxom receptionist resplendent under our agency's gold logo and roster of offices across the globe. How different was this day going to be?

No sooner had I entered my office than Bridgette, my cockney secretary, placed my Campbell's soup mug of coffee in front of me. I remembered clipping out the coupon for the mug. What was the attraction? What did I find in the construction barrier with a blinking light and CAUTION stenciled across the top, displayed in my office?

A distant voice tried to be heard. "Jankele Kuperblum, where are you?" I reached for the phone, but stopped midway. Tomorrow. Next week. I knew only too well that nothing would change in that time. I lit a cigarette and through the brooding clouds of smoke gazed at the congregation of awards on the wall. I had set out to accomplish something of value, but couldn't remember what it was. I was a messenger who'd got off at the wrong station and forgotten the message I was to deliver.

Bridgette poked her head in the door. "Is there anything you'd like me to do before I take lunch?"

"Enjoy!"

"You too, boss."

What have I been doing for the last few days, weeks, months? I haven't written a line, held a meeting, or come up with a single idea. What was my last assignment?

"I'm out to lunch," I told the receptionist, and ran down the back stairs, relieved not to have to stuff and drown myself with a client.

I longed for the thousand and one aromas of the Bagel Restaurant, but it was too far away. I meant to go to the salad bar around the corner, but ended up at the Crippled Civilians bargain center. Immigrant women rummaged through cartons of ladies' wear. Winos were trying on coats from racks along a wall. What's he doing here? their stares demanded, as they noted my pristine pressed blue suit and polished shoes. I wondered the same.

As was my habit, I headed for the cellar, where there were ranges, bicycles, scales, dishes, television sets with burned-out tubes, torn mattresses, and rusty barbecues: remnants of entire lives begging for another go in the real world. I looked at a crib and could hear the infant's cry and the mother's lullaby. Where is that baby now? Did it grow up to be a derelict? Is he upstairs at this very moment trying on a coat? Or is he a creative director in an advertising agency?

On the second floor I gave a few rooming-house discards a cursory scan, flipped a price tag or two, and edged my way back to the street. I flagged a taxi, bringing it to a screeching halt.

"Where to?" asked the cabbie.

"Keewatin Avenue," I said, sliding in beside him.

"Over One Hundred Homes Being Wrecked. Everything for Sale," I had read in the morning paper.

Workers in protective gear were smashing away. Rubble littered the street. Solid mahogany doors, dislodged from their hinges, leaned against a wall.

"That stained-glass window," I said. The foreman took it out with a crowbar and pocketed the five-dollar bill. I carried the prize along the street and onto the subway. It was past four when I arrived back at my office. I lit a cigarette and tossed the empty package into the garbage. I was about to summon Bridgette to fetch me a fresh one when she buzzed me.

"New York."

I inhaled on the cigarette and pressed the connecting button.

"How are things in Toronto?" Howard sounded tired.

Here's your chance, a voice gnawed. Tell the bald-headed shmuck what he can do with this job.

"I understand there are problems. Why don't you fly down for the weekend?" he said.

"No," I said, more to myself than to him, and hung up.

If only I had wings, I'd open the window and disappear. Mirthful laughter traveled down the hall from the party that was already in progress.

The street teemed with traffic. I stood outside like an evicted tenant. What if someone sees me on the curb with my awards and stained-glass window? Of all the times to have left the car for Terrye! I waved my arms. "Taxi!"

15

I PACED AROUND the house, poking here and there. Whenever anyone consulted a watch, I envied them for having somewhere to go. Guarded words and looks made me feel insignificant. "What do you plan to do?" people asked me. My replies distanced most, and eventually the phone stopped ringing. Not so my good pal and lawyer Muni. He came with a bottle of champagne and a jar of caviar.

Trevor was also encouraging. He wrote from New York: "I never thought you outfoxed Hitler to peddle garbage. Welcome to the camp of those who stand for something, even if it's only to say no!"

I thought of my Zionist comrades enshrined in the pages of my photo album. Their memory haunted me like a grim shadow. I felt as if every terrorist bullet that snuffed out a life was meant for me. Yet I made no move to set foot in the Jewish state, whose mere mention made me feel a foot taller. We were planning a trip to Spain when something pricked my conscience and made me change plans.

Landing in Tel Aviv with Terrye, I expected to see my friends at the airport dancing the hora. The breathtaking land tugged me and powerful hands sprouting from the ancient soil gripped my ankles. Stay, Jankele. This is where you belong.

How liberating it felt to shed the false front, the insecure role I had adopted! How wise was it to be casting my offspring's lives from the same mould?

Back in Toronto two weeks later, we sold our car and rented our house and farm. My mother-in-law implored me to reconsider, but Terrye stood by me. Fourteen-year-old Ellen called us Zionists. Neighbors were baffled. "Why are you going? This is your country."

During the five-hour delay at LaGuardia, our actor friends, Ruth and Trevor, came to the airport. Trevor threw me a mock punch. "You're sure doing the right things these days. I'm not Jewish, but I've always dreamt of living on a kibbutz."

In the wee hours of the morning, the children dozed in our laps and Trevor nursed a beer. We gazed at each other bleary-eyed.

"I have something to tell you," said Ruth. "I'm pregnant."

"That's wonderful!" Terrye kissed her.

"Congratulations!" I added.

Ruth poked her husband. "Trev, don't you also have something to tell?" Trevor stared into his glass. "Trevor did his first commercial yesterday . . . a voice-over," Ruth said.

FOLLOWING A GRUELING baggage search, the El Al plane took off, and when it landed some twelve hours later, there was no sign of Golda Meir running towards us with bouquets of flowers.

Speaking neither English nor Yiddish, the Moroccan-born cabbie had trouble locating the immigrant center in Jerusalem's Katamon district. The city slumbered; not a soul was in sight. Swearing and cussing in Arabic, the cabbie found the dimly lit street, dumped our luggage in the middle of the road, and sped off.

A half-asleep man handed me a key and pointed to the top floor. When I asked for the elevator, he raised his eyebrows and vanished. The lights went out. Groping our way in the dark, Mark found the timing device. No sooner had we reached the first-floor landing than it all went black again. By the time we dragged our way to the fourth floor, there was little left of the night.

The confining apartment was equipped with cots, dressers, a small table, and four chairs. A far cry from East Jerusalem's American Colony Hotel, where as tourists we had only months earlier sipped cool drinks, shaded under a lemon tree in the courtyard.

I embraced Terrye before collapsing onto the bed. "Let's not unpack," I said. "We're going back in the morning."

Hunger drove us the next morning to a nearby grocery, where our hands proved more useful than our tongues. Without a word of complaint, Terrye quickly threw together a meal on the single burner. Our stomachs were full, the sun was shining, and children's happy voices reached us from the street. I extended our stay for a week. We emptied our suitcases, enrolled our children in schools and signed ourselves up for Hebrew classes.

To pick up a registered letter from the post office could take almost a day, but one made friends in lineups, of which there was no shortage. Where I raged and exploded, Terrye saw only the humor of the situation.

Within a short time, the Jewish postman, the Jewish bank teller, the Jewish policeman, and the Jewish caretaker were not my brothers and sisters — just people with human frailties.

Our savings dwindling by the day, I had trouble concentrating on my Hebrew lessons. Prodded by my agent and encouraged by my editor at Doubleday, I made a stab at a new book. I sat at our kitchen table filling notebooks, while Terrye and the children were at school. I could hear explosions echoing from Jordan, where Hussein's soldiers were expelling Palestinians from the kingdom.

One day I received a postcard from a Tel Aviv advertising

agency, written in tiny, fastidious script. "It has come to my attention that you are now residing in our land. Hooray! Call me at your earliest convenience." I phoned, asking what it was all about, but the writer insisted we meet in person. I promised to call when my book was finished.

New friends extended themselves, giving advice, hospitality, and offering to help in any way they could, but I wasn't easy to please. Local film producers survived by providing TV networks with news coverage of skirmishes and documentaries of Christian concern. They embraced me in the naïve hope that I was an established producer who could provide badly needed financing and North American contacts.

At the other end of the spectrum, a young Indian Jew who had studied cinema at UCLA and was now living in a cellar in Tel Aviv, screened for me a short of himself masturbating in bed, his eyes on a snapshot of his girlfriend.

I was also introduced to Amos Kollek, the son of Jerusalem's mayor. "Where are you from?" asked the young writer-filmmaker.

"Canada."

"Canada? Why would you want to live in such a cold climate? Besides, nothing ever happens there!"

A message in our mail slot requested that I report to the Histadrut, the country's powerful labor union. Wondering what it was about, I jumped on a bus and made my way to the designated address, where naturally I fell into queue. When it was my turn, I faced a man with a merry little smile.

"You're finally here, Jankel," he bobbed his head in admiration. Apart from the battered desk with two chairs, the dismal office with the terrazzo floor was bare. Leaning across the table and breathing on me, he inquired, "Did you bring the *apparat?*" My blank expression prompted him to bring his right fist to his temple, in mock cranking.

"I'm not a cameraman."

"With an *apparat,* I could hire you to screen films at our meetings." His eyes danced gleefully. I got up to leave. "What can we do to help you?" he shouted after me. "After all, you have a wife and four children. You must earn a living."

I turned to him. "I'm lost without a telephone."

"You don't have a phone?"

"There's a three-year wait."

"Feel free to use mine anytime." He pointed to the one on his desk.

"More important for you to be absorbed into the country is a car," advised a journalist friend.

So we bought one and explored on weekends.

"To plant roots," the journalist exhorted, "get into a residence where you'll come in contact with Israelis, not disgruntled immigrants."

We scoured the real estate ads, and after using up a few tankfuls of gas, fell in love with an Arab stone house in the Katamon area. Redesigning it in my imagination, I created a garden on the flat roof. The couple who owned it were devout; his head was topped with an embroidered *yarmulke,* hers was encased in a wig. They had one child. The asking price was sixty thousand American dollars and I offered five thousand less. The haggling went on for weeks. Finally, encouraged by our journalist friend to get on with our lives, I caved in.

"I'll have to consult my father," said the vendor. Then he reported back, "My father says it's worth sixty-five."

After a brooding interlude of a few weeks, I showed up at the man's door with the offer in hand. The price had escalated again. My last offer, for eighty thousand, was also rejected. Months later I spied the ad. The asking price had escalated to ninety-five thousand.

In the German Colony quarter, I chanced upon a similar property, with a combed garden and exotic trees. It was a rental. Whatever was wanting, a coat of paint could easily have corrected. Then my eyes fell on a cable running horizontally along the wall connecting the television set.

"What butcher installed this?" I asked.

"Never even noticed it," the pensioner replied benignly.

"And that?" I pointed to a pair of unaligned electric receptacles.

He stared, flabbergasted at my malaise.

"Is that your son?" I pointed to a photograph on a dresser.

"Was," he replied, looking as if hope had been sapped from his life. "He was on that submarine that disappeared off the coast of France."

Real estate hustlers sniffed us out and came running with bargains. One enticed us with a penthouse still under construction. When I criticized the shoddy workmanship, he replied, "What do you expect from Arab labor?"

"The Arab houses are beautiful. A lot of character."

"You Americans are spoiled. In the twenties, when my parents came here, they lived in a tent."

"Yes, but the tent didn't cost a hundred thousand!"

THE CAR WAS also a help when searching for my former comrades. One inquiry led to another until I was directed to a kibbutz on the Mediterranean shore. One blistering Saturday, we piled into the car and I steered our Opel to Maanit.

"Do you know who I am?" I smiled at the familiar face of the man who opened the cottage door. He sized me up. "Show me your photographs," I said. A woman looked up when we entered. I recognized her as well. He reached up to fetch a dust-covered album from the top of a bureau. The focus of the first page was a photo of me in Russian army gear, a pistol tucked in my belt, posing with two others, also brandishing weapons. An unfurled Yiddish banner proclaimed, "Our Future." I pointed to myself.

"You're Jaakov?" His gasp tore his wife away from the sewing machine.

"You're the one who wanted to play accordion," she said.

The first pages of the album could easily have been mistaken for my own, but what followed was radically different: land being cleared, foundations poured, housing, tanks in the desert, the crossing of the Suez Canal, and the liberation of the wailing wall.

Over lunch in the clamorous communal hall, I encountered others from my group. They shook my hand with fogged eyes. I introduced Terrye, my children.

"What happened to you? Where have you been?" they asked.

An older version of the fellow orphan we had called Professor, now in overalls and rubber boots and in charge of livestock, was summoned to our table.

Rabbit, now a mathematics instructor with the same almond eyes, told us, "Motel the partisan is a big business man in Haifa. He sells tractors."

Several were no longer alive; one had been murdered in an ambush, another had stepped on a mine.

"I always felt guilty for deserting," I confessed privately to Rabbit. "Your silence has pursued me through life."

He swung an arm around my shoulders, pulling me towards him. "Don't you realize what that was all about, Jaakov? You found family and we were jealous."

On another weekend, we visited a kibbutz by the Sea of Galilee. On Friday night there were no Sabbath candles, no benedictions, and the meal was dispensed with as quickly as a bite at a fast-food joint. The tables were removed, the chairs rearranged, a screen shot up, and a projector wheeled out. A jet pilot, a member of the kibbutz who was home for the Sabbath, introduced the McDonnell Douglas film on aeronautics. Afterwards, he invited questions from the attentive audience.

Thinking back to the Friday nights in Lodz when we

danced the hora, discussed Yiddish poets, and dreamed of Zion, I grieved.

"It takes at least three months to integrate," our journalist friend had said. We visited him towards the end of that time, and I was still grumbling. "If after six months you still feel the same," he said, "I'll personally drive you to the airport. But statistically, immigrants who stay half a year are here for life."

The Chassidic songs on the radio encouraged my dreaming until his eighteen-year-old daughter stomped over and switched to Elvis Presley belting out "Heartbreak Hotel." Other guests arrived, filling the apartment with laughter and noise. I danced with one I had met before.

"I hear you're thinking of returning to Canada. Too bad! We desperately need immigrants like you."

"You mean people in the arts?"

Puzzlement clouded her delicate features. "Without the influx of North Americans," she said, "the Sephardim will soon outnumber us."

Sephardim, Ashkenazim, Russians, Americans, French, Romanians, Poles, Indians — the word *Jew* never came up in conversation. *We* were Anglo-Saxons.

"Israelis are not Jews. They're Hebrew-speaking Gentiles," said an accountant from New Jersey who lived next door to us.

"Not my people. More like *goyim*," an American rabbi I ran into on the Mount of Olives told me, fixing me with scorching eyes.

"I agree with all your negative comments and barbs," a scholar who had settled in Israel a few years earlier confessed.

"So why do you continue to live here?"

"Because it's the only sensible place for a Jew."

At times I felt more at home among the Arab merchants in the cavernous passages of the old city, who treated us to Turkish coffee and tea with mint leaves. One invited us to sample the spinach pastry his wife was frying. Countless children played in the surrounding squalor. Almost in a whimper, he confided that he had once been the proprietor of a prosperous business confiscated by the Israelis after the Six Day War.

The same evening I sought justice for the Arab from a friend with government leverage. I had barely given him the gist of the heart-breaking saga when he cut in. "This isn't the one in the oil business by any chance?"

"Yes," I nodded.

"With a summer house in Jerusalem and a winter palace in Jericho?"

"Right!"

"Drove a Mercedes and owned a fleet of trucks?"

"You know him?"

"No," he replied. "They all tell the same story. I've lived here for over twenty years and I find nothing but good. Yet you have a new horror story to tell every evening."

By December, the capital drenched in rain, we longed for falling snow, Santa Claus, and the frenzy of exchanging gifts and cards. On Christmas Eve, curious, Terrye and I set out to attend midnight mass, something that would never have occurred to us back home. On the way to the Church of Nativity, we were stopped by a police roadblock. Only Christian tourists were allowed into Bethlehem.

In Jerusalem, in the old city, pilgrims packing the Church of the Holy Sepulchre spilled onto the cobbled streets, listening to the proceedings on loudspeakers. Rejected, on the way back, we knocked on the bolted door of the YMCA. It creaked open and the Arab watchman appeared from behind.

"May we see your tree?" Terrye asked demurely.

He inserted the plug. The tree came to life, giving us lumps in our throats.

And without chocolate bunnies and painted eggs in stores, there was no knowing when Easter would roll around. We asked a young Israeli friend who taught swimming at the same YMCA.

"Easter?" he scratched his head. "What's that?"

We mentioned the Last Supper.

"Oh, you mean the Christian Passover."

By this time our children were conversing in Hebrew, and Terrye, loving every moment of our new life, blossomed, gaining confidence and new insights. Every time I talked of returning to Toronto, she would steer me to the lobby of the King David Hotel to watch the garishly dressed tourists returning from the hot spots, meeting with government dignitaries, arranging the unveilings of institutions bearing their names.

With six months behind us, my roots still refusing to take hold in the Jerusalem stone, the journalist advised me: "You must give yourself at least a year."

In the diaspora, I was special, a child of the Holocaust. In the Jewish state, I was just another survivor.

Life was a daily struggle and people craved the material world I had run away from. "You're twenty years too late. We don't need idealists," they told me. Just to make ends meet, many of them held two and three jobs, frantically running from one to another.

When I told an elderly cousin of Papa's who lived in the religious enclave of Mea Shaarim that we had a two-story, four-bedroom house with a garden in Toronto, she dismissed me with a fishy stare. Often she'd visit, lugging bags of food.

"You're refugees and we must help you."

I noticed Hebrew translations of many popular American novels and couldn't understand why my book hadn't found its way here. My New York agent pointed me to his sub-agent in Tel Aviv, the largest literary agency in the country.

"It's been on our shelf for several years, but so far publishers have ignored it," was the response.

Promptly, I addressed myself to the three top publishers. One didn't reply, the second thanked me for bringing the book to their attention, but unfortunately, their year's slate was brimming. The editor at the third, however, was encouraging and invited me to drop in on my next trip to Tel Aviv.

The rising sun's rays, spreading like an oriental fan across the ancient land, filled me with hope the day I set out, accompanied by a friend from Montreal who was trying to find himself in Israel. The address on the letterhead led us to a bookstore. The clerk at the counter pointed up the stairs.

"It's the editor's day off, but his assistant will see you," said the typist.

The academic behind the desk spoke a Warsaw Yiddish. "We've had enough of the Holocaust. Every person in this country is a story. Write something to make us laugh."

I don't know what I said on the way back, but when the Jerusalem skyline appeared on the horizon, my Montreal friend remarked, "Mornings, you're Moses, leading the Jews to the Promised Land. By evening, you're Hitler."

"This time around we'll hold out for a hefty advance and a healthy advertising budget," wrote my agent. "This new manuscript is nothing short of a masterpiece, and I expect it will be a best seller."

I was still wallowing in my sudden good fortune when another letter from him followed. Doubleday wasn't so enthusiastic, he said, but seeing that I was one of their published authors, he thought he could squeeze an advance of five thousand out of them if I agreed to a major rewrite.

I instructed him to submit the manuscript elsewhere. The familiar rejections came flying.

I called the advertising agency, threw my commercial reel and portfolio in the car, and headed for Tel Aviv. In a tumbledown building in the industrial part of town, I followed a sign to the third floor and faced a receptionist with hairy armpits, in a sleeveless frock, fanning herself with a manila envelope. After I presented myself, she hollered something in Hebrew and received a response from a male voice of equal volume. Continuing to fan, she pointed to a door.

"Mr. Kuper," the voice boomed. The man was tall and of military bearing. "When I heard through the grapevine, as they say where you come from, that you were hiding out in Jerusalem, I saw an opportunity and gambled that you'd respond."

He strutted about. "We are a small, developing nation and lack the sparkle, the glitz, the zing, the pizazz of America. Come, let me show you." He led me to a room where several artists sweated at boiler-room speed. When I stopped to address one, my host yanked me away.

"Would you like to see my work?" I asked when I could get a word in edgewise.

"Your reputation has preceded you, Mr. Kuper. I wouldn't presume to be your judge." Glancing at the Coca-Cola clock, he said, "My goodness, it's almost noon." After introducing me to his wife, stuffing envelopes in the mail room, he escorted me past the human fan. "I'll be in touch."

Within the week we were invited to a party at his home in an exclusive suburb of Tel Aviv where Moishe Dayan resided. The look was not unlike California: sprawling split levels with TV antennas dotting the roofs and sprinklers keeping the manicured lawns green. Even the door chime had a North American ring to it, not at all like the guttural one of our residence in Katamon. Mrs. Advertising answered the door, bedecked in an ankle-length gown, her fingers, wrists and neck aglitter.

Abstract canvases and non-figurative sculptures were displayed in the airy living room. Waiters with bow ties mingled about, popping champagne corks and offering tidbits. Terrye and I looked out of place in our simple attire. Several of the guests had flown in from Switzerland, Los

Angeles, even Australia. There were a few local army types, a sprinkling of government officials, trendsetters, and a voluptuous woman claiming a family connection to Abba Eban. Lobsters, caviar, shrimp, and other nonkosher concoctions appeared on the table and were consumed over laughter and chatter that drowned out the daily skirmishes. In this din, it was hard to fathom the agony of the young airman pictured in the press that day who had been shot out of the sky over the Suez Canal.

The host paraded me around. "This is the brilliant young man I've been telling you about," he said. And when we were leaving, he clasped my hand. "We must talk soon."

He followed it up with an invitation to a business dinner. Before setting out, I called his office to confirm the time with his wife. "She's at home today, preparing for a very important guest," the receptionist said, and I thought I heard the swoosh of the envelope.

The same chime resonated, summoning the lady to the door. "I suppose you didn't bring everything with you," she commented, eyeing my attire — the very same that I had worn to the party. "My husband will be out in a moment." She escorted me into the living room. "He's showering after his yoga lesson. In the meantime, can I offer you a real scotch?" A skeptical look affixed itself to her face when I told her I wasn't much of a drinker.

At which point her husband appeared in white shoes, freshly pressed slacks, and matching polo shirt. Bing Crosby without the golf club. Grasping my hand in both of his, he castigated his wife. "Darling, didn't you offer Mr. Kuper a real scotch?"

"I hope you're not too hungry." The wife beckoned us to the dining table. "I simply threw something together when I got home from the office an hour ago."

Soufflé, broiled fish, baked eggplant, and croquettes appeared as if out of a magician's hat. Reaching for the wine bottle, the husband stopped midway. "Darling, what will our guest think? Surely you know that cabernet sauvignon is never served with soufflé." He backed up his chair. "Hopefully, we still have a sampling of the splendid '59 Rothschild Semillon in the wine cellar."

"Relax." I patted his arm. "Your guest is a simple Polish peasant who knows zip about wine."

"Ho, ho, ho," the two twittered. "A big advertising man like you? Very funny indeed."

We were having dessert when I decided to take the plunge. "What is it you have in mind?"

It caught him off guard. "A talent like you has many options. You could join a company such as ours. Naturally, we would pay you handsomely. God forbid the competition should snare you! For us, it would be disastrous. You could also establish your own shop. That would be even worse. You'll sweep all of us into oblivion. Your wisest choice would be to buy an established agency."

Editing the scene in my head, I cut to a close-up of him waiting for a reply, followed it with a quick shot of the wife raising an eyebrow, and zoomed in on me, biting into the flaky strudel as if I hadn't heard him. "It sounds as if you're looking to unload." I reached for the coffee.

"Ho, ho, ho," they chorused.

"What's it worth?"

"Five hundred thousand."

I angled on myself draining the coffee, then to a quick reaction shot of the wife, and back to him.

"Or you could acquire fifty percent, for shall we say, uh, half that amount," he said.

"And should I decide to take you up on your offer, what sort of salary did you have in mind?"

"The hour is late and you have a long trip back."

I never expected to hear from him again. But he called, inviting me to be a judge at an international poster exhibition he was organizing. By the time he hung up, I had agreed that I owed the country at least that.

I arrived early and the exhibition hall was locked. I waited, but no one showed. Arabs tending flower beds looked at me quizzically and shrugged when I made inquiries. I paraded outside the building and peered in a window. The walls of the large room were bare, not a poster in sight. At an outdoor café, I ordered a coffee and sat back enjoying the warming sun when I spied Bing Crosby coming towards me, followed by a racially mixed entourage.

Startled by my presence, he stopped in his tracks. "Didn't anyone get in touch with you to tell you it's been canceled? Someone broke into the building and stole all the posters."

The following day, I saw my name in the *Jerusalem Post*. As one of five international judges, I was quoted as saying, "It was difficult selecting the winners, as all entries were of inordinately high caliber."

"Nine months and you expect miracles?" Our friend the journalist was discernibly shaken. "You owe it to yourselves to give it a full year."

Ellen cried, not wanting to go back.

When the journalist saw us packing, he was resigned. "At times I've entertained the idea of spending a year abroad. What do you think are the prospects in *galut** for someone like me?"

*   diaspora

16

ONLY THE OLD guilt prevented me from kissing the Canadian soil upon our return in August 1971. Everything looked rosier through renewed eyes. It was a blessing to have a place to come home to. The Israelites wandering in the desert also yearned to return to the comforts they had left in exile. How many lessons did I need? Shamefully, I now realized that I had done everything not to succeed in the Jewish homeland. As righteous as the cause was, and I believed in it wholeheartedly, I simply could not bring myself to place my children on the sacrificial altar — to watch them one day, dressed in uniform, going off to the front.

When the euphoria of being back died down, reality set in. I had no job, no car, our bank account was almost empty, and the children needed clothing. I was thirty-nine years old and lost. The phone rang. It was BB, Canada's advertising whiz, wanting me to "Come back, *Bubale.*"

When I declined, he threw me a challenge: to create and produce a pool of eleven TV commercials in less than a week on a modest budget. It more than made up the year's salary, and it was six times more than Doubleday would have advanced for a year's work. I instructed the agency's comptroller to make the check payable to Kuper Productions Ltd.

The first assignment under my own banner was a commercial for a circular saw, featuring a do-it-your-selfer building a dog house. Studying the beauty shot in the camera, I concluded the dog was overshadowing the product, but I had fallen in love with the frisky little mutt. The handler, who had four more just like him, was delighted when I offered to buy him.

When I came home that night, Ellen snatched the pup my from hands, exclaiming, "*Motek!*", Hebrew for sweet. The name stuck.

IT STARTED INNOCENTLY enough with a letter from my half-sister, Tamara, who wrote from Chernovtsy that as she was growing up, she lived in hope of one day being together with her big brother, whom she only knew by name. "Jankele" was a magic word in her vocabulary, she said. His letters were eagerly awaited, and his parcels were cause for celebration. Like a god, Jankele could turn dark nights into sunny days.

In my album there were photographs of her as a pretty little girl holding a doll, in a school play, as a teenager posing in front of a monument, at her wedding with her dark, handsome young groom, and later with one child, then another. She was exceptionally beautiful, with a radiant smile and Papa's sparkling blue eyes. Stretching my imagination, I could easily see in her my fraternal *buby*. Yet when I searched within, I felt no connection.

In her letter, overflowing with endearments, Tamara implored me to get immigration papers for her, her husband, and their two children. Her appeal touched me, so I discussed it with Terrye, sought advice from others, and for weeks on end debated with myself. When I turned to Uncle Jacques, he was candid: "As usual, your father wants to export his problems," he wrote. "Don't do it. You'll regret it for the rest of your life."

I couldn't just flatly refuse her. "Migration to Canada from Russia would be a difficult and lengthy process," I wrote, advising her to go to Israel, "where there are numerous agencies to assist newcomers." To ease my conscience and her disappointment, I appended that there it would be a mere formality to bring them to Canada.

Six months later, a telegram arrived from Haifa: "Come and get us. Tamara." I thought I'd keel over.

I recommended that they settle in for a while and that I would visit them in due course. To sweeten the bitter pill, I wired a bank draft, sufficient to quench their thirst but not enough to develop an appetite.

One letter followed another, each one more desperate than the previous, all directed to appeal to the blood bond between us. When I refused to cave in, offering practical advice, she tightened the emotional screws. "We left everything behind — our furniture, clothing, whatever we possessed — for our parents to live off. Otherwise, they'd starve."

Shame, Jankele! Shame! a voice accused. Where would you be today if others hadn't helped you?

"You were a refugee once yourself," Tamara wrote. "So you must understand what it's like!"

My guilt thrived in fertile soil. I walked about talking to myself and dispatched another modest sum, with a plea that they sink roots.

A funereal silence greeted me, broken months later from the city of Ashdod. Although the tone was more optimistic, they were lonely. Could I pull strings to have them transferred to Ashkelon, where they had friends?

I was acquainted with an individual involved with Israeli causes, and by coincidence, he was taking his annual trip.

"I went to see your relatives in Ashdod," he reported upon his return. "They have a spacious, newly furnished two-bedroom apartment, a fridge full of food, and a brand new Volvo station wagon. They look happy, well dressed, and content. Your sister's a beauty with an angelic smile. Her husband is a good-natured fellow. We downed a few glasses together. Their children are delightful. After half a dozen phone calls to the right people, I got them a choice apartment in Ashkelon facing the sea and a good job for your brother-in-law with the municipality."

Tamara had also appealed to Uncle Shmil-Leib, who wrote me, "Your sister is a bit of an actress, Jankele. Don't be taken in by her tears."

No sooner had my head cleared than a registered letter arrived, postmarked Italy. They were in a refugee camp outside Rome, having fled the outbreak of the Yom Kippur War. "We were petrified for our children," lamented my sister. "My dear brother, I love you and I won't rest until we're with you. I beg you, send us papers."

I did nothing, in the foolish hope that an angel from heaven would appear to whisper nuggets of wisdom into my ear. Meanwhile, pressuring letters continued to fill our mailbox. When I couldn't be dislodged, a new singer joined the choir. "Do as your sister commands!" wrote Papa.

I hardened my stance.

More than a year had elapsed when I answered the ring of my telephone and a captivating voice said in Yiddish, "This is Tamara. Is that you, Jankele?"

"Where are you?"

"Brooklyn. I would like to see you, Jankele." Her warmth reached out, begging to connect.

A shiver sprinted through me. I envied those who had siblings and tried to imagine how my brother, Josele, would have turned out. Would he have resembled me? Possibly he would have become a famous scientist and discover the cure for cancer.

Still, it was with misgivings that I journeyed to New York accompanied by Terrye. After checking into a hotel, we caught a show and had dinner, and the next morning, a Sunday, when I suggested a visit to the Whitney Museum,

Terrye accused me of delaying tactics. The cab ride from Manhattan to Brighton Beach in Brooklyn took almost an hour.

The driver coursed his way up to a tenement building, where a young couple with two children sat anxiously on the front steps. As we climbed out of the taxi, they rushed forward, hugging and kissing us with passion.

"Jankele! Jankele! My big brother!" Tamara held onto me, shedding tears.

Though a little heavier and a few years older than I had pictured her, she was even more beautiful than in her photographs. Gazing at her, I saw Papa looking back at me.

Her husband, Izzy, a casting agent's dream for a young Stalin, had lost some of his boyishness, but the look of wonderment still dwelt in his eyes. I was taken aback when his lips pressed against mine, his bushy moustache irritating my mouth.

"Come and kiss your uncle and aunt," my sister addressed her children in Russian. Holding onto bicycles, the boy, eight, and the girl, younger, stared at us, boredom painted on their innocent faces.

As soon as we entered their well-equipped apartment, a bottle of Russian vodka materialized. *"Na Zdrowie,"** my brother-in-law toasted.

Imitating, I downed mine in one gulp and choked. He gave me a hearty slap on the back, an immediate refill, and chided Terrye for not joining us.

The conversation was halting, burdened with pauses and translation delays. Tamara was on the verge of grasping the new language. Other than a few Hebrew profanities, Izzy spoke only Russian.

"What is a beekooklee?" he asked with a scrunched up face, pointing to a word in a tabloid.

"Bicycle," I said, leaning over his shoulder.

---

*   to health

Wide-eyed, he pointed, "Poozlee?"

"Puzzle," I deciphered and convulsed with laughter.

Both children were already adept in the new tongue, Brooklyn accent and all.

After a lunch of chicken soup that Tamara had prepared and another round of vodka to seal the meal, we went for a stroll on the boardwalk.

Old people sat outside rows of neglected tenement buildings, exchanging gossip in Yiddish. Along the boardwalk, more of them, bundled as if for winter, rested on benches facing the sea, waiting for the day to pass.

The boardwalk was crowded with joggers and families out for a stroll. A mangy stray sniffed about for something to snatch. Below, invaded by bathers, the sandy beach was humming with activity. A game of volleyball was in progress. Radios blasted, vendors hawked their wares, children frolicked in and out of the ocean. A couple, their bodies bronzed, pecked at each other playfully, while from the distance, the sound of an approaching siren could be heard.

My niece and nephew paused at almost every kiosk, whining for chips, hamburgers, knishes, ice cream. Tamara, too, was attracted by the smells, glitter, and sizzle. I found myself playing the good uncle, reaching for my wallet and performing the magic gestures.

When I began to sniff for information on Papa, Tamara eyed me curiously.

"When I was a little girl, he was away in Siberia, so I hardly knew him. But since his return . . . ," she paused to wipe her eyes, "I love him very much. I love him so much, I could almost die."

I had been punctured by a finely honed knife.

"Your father is the finest man I know!" added her Izzy. "Never a bad word from him. And so smart. Everyone likes him."

I lay bleeding.

Continuing to play the big brother, I asked, "What do you need?"

"An air conditioner and a Polaroid camera," she replied decisively. In Toronto we lived without air conditioning and only weeks earlier I had acquired a Polaroid for my work. I handed her two crisp hundred-dollar American bills.

"Jankele, no!" she protested unconvincingly.

"Take it! Tamara, take it!" her husband sanctioned. She stuffed the money into her apron pocket.

Izzy, a plumber in Russia, but unable to find work in the New World, had accepted a job in a chocolate factory. One evening when I answered our phone, Tamara was in hysterics. A chemical compound had burned the soles of Izzy's feet and he had been rushed to the hospital. The following morning I dispatched several hundred dollars.

The company employing him refused to take responsibility for the mishap and the newcomers sued in the hope of collecting a bundle. The legal aid lawyer assured them they would be millionaires, but months later, when the hearing reached the court, they walked out empty-handed.

Healed, my brother-in-law once more pursued a plumbing job. But he was not in the union, had no command of the language, and was foreign to the city. He met with no better success.

"What will we do, Jankele?" Tamara lamented on the phone. "He's been to hundreds of interviews."

"It's easier to get hold of a doctor than a plumber in New York or Toronto. Why can't he find work?"

"He has no luck! That's all!"

I located someone in New York whose cousin was married to a plumber. When I told the tradesman of my brother-in-law's plight, his whisky voice almost shattered the phone. "I'll hire him sight unseen!"

Tamara thanked me and the heavens. When the phone rang the following evening, I had an inkling it would be her. After our conversation, again I placed a call to the New York plumber.

"If your brother-in-law is a plumber, then I'm the Pope!" he shouted, and hung up.

Like many Russian immigrants in Brighton Beach, Izzy became a cabbie. Not long afterwards, because of some infraction or other, his license was revoked. For a while, he and Tamara were assisted by Jewish benevolent agencies. When that dried up, Tamara became a supermarket cashier.

Nightly, I listened to their tragedies, often being reminded that had I brought them to Canada, their lives would have taken a brighter turn. Finally, they concluded, that to get ahead in America, one had to be self-employed. Izzy and a friend decided to go into an appliance-repair business. They already had the location and each was to invest five hundred dollars.

"Can you lend us the money?" Tamara's voice was muffled by tears. I promised to consider it and immediately dispatched a money order. While I wallowed in hopes for their imminent prosperity, Tamara was on the line, bubbling with excitement.

"How's the business progressing?" I asked.

"Oh, that! We didn't trust the partner." She then informed me that her mother was visiting.

Bombarding me with blessings and greetings in a high-pitched voice, and in a Yiddish strange to my ears, my stepmother referred to me as her "dear child" and begged that I visit her in Brooklyn, so that at long last she could cast her eyes upon me and hold me close to her heart. Listening to her outpourings made me uneasy, as if I were betraying Mama. To diminish my guilt, I answered abruptly in impersonal tones. It reminded me of the first time a plate with some pork in it was set in front of me. Though starving, I swallowed only a few mouthfuls in the hope that God would deal with me kindly.

After her mother left to go back to Russia, Tamara increased the pressure to bring the entire family out. The major obstacle was my half-brother, Mikhail, serving in the army. After his stint, he came home a patriot, refusing to abandon the motherland. Papa, exasperated, was prepared to leave him behind, but Lena wouldn't even consider it.

Through pleading, persuasion, and God only knows what other inducements, Mikhail finally relented, but by then he was married and had fathered a baby girl. New applications had to be made and the entire process reset into motion. Months later, and still no exit visas, Tamara spent hours crying into my ear.

The sending of parcels continued; Papa's monthly pension was scarcely enough to sustain them for a week, and Mikhail had been dismissed from work because of his intent to emigrate. "Don't be so accepting," I wrote Papa. "If you want out, fight for it."

His reply was so uncharacteristic, I suspected its origins. He could no longer endure living in a basement unfit for humans, he said, and their economic situation was so desperate that if I ever wanted to see him again, I should turn heaven and earth.

Once again I sought my lawyer friend Muni's help to re-enlist the ear of the sympathetic senator with connections leading all the way to the Russian minister of foreign affairs. A cable from External Affairs in Ottawa expressing concern for one Aaron Zelik Szlomowicz Kuperblum and his family was sent to the Russian Foreign Ministry in Moscow. The bureaucrats, who for years had played games with Papa, suddenly treated him with civility, handed him the documents, shook his hand, and wished him a safe journey.

But now another cog stopped the wheel from turning. Mikhail and his wife were having marital problems. He was willing to abandon her but not the child. If he wanted the child, however, the wife had to be part of the baggage. When he agreed, she presented him with a new demand: her aging mother wanted to come along. All that was required was money for air fare and exit tax. It was a terrible expense, and Tamara offered to pay half if I would cover the rest. Feeling magnanimous, I proposed to foot the entire bill. The money was to be paid in dollars to a contact in New York, enabling Papa at his end to collect rubles at the black market rate.

When I asked my secretary to get me a bank draft, she cracked, "For someone who's an orphan, this sure is turning into an expensive family reunion!"

IN THE SUMMER of 1979, the entourage landed in Italy and soon afterwards joined the Russians in Brighton Beach who had transformed the Brooklyn neighborhood into "Little Odessa." Several weeks after their arrival I flew to New York to greet them.

Twelve years had elapsed since I'd last seen Papa, and there was little evidence of any change. At seventy-two he looked as fit and spry as the day I had see him off at the Toronto airport.

The larger apartment Tamara moved to accommodated everyone. New furniture crowded the rooms. Frivolous acquisitions were in evidence. A lady's mink coat hung in the cupboard. Izzy sported a heavy gold chain around his neck. The bathtub, converted to a storage zone, was stuffed with discards, reaching the ceiling. A leaky faucet emitted a monotonous dripping. The cold water in the shower would shut off without warning, scalding the occupant.

My nephew Edyk, who by now was calling himself Eddy, spent copious amounts of time in front of the TV watching baseball. When the last inning was over, he would leave, returning with a can of pop to scan the channels for another sporting event. The second television set was claimed by his sister, who glued herself to the game shows and soaps.

Izzy regained his license and went back to his taxi, clocking in twelve- to fourteen-hour days. When he came home, he looked for company to down a vodka or two with him.

I never did get to meet Mikhail's mother-in-law, or his wife, who took up with another man upon their arrival. The child, a sweet little girl with Slavic features, long, blonde locks, and the lithe body of a potential ballerina, was left in Mikhail's care. No doubt she resembled her mother, for she bore no likeness to those in whose midst she now found herself.

Mikhail was in his thirties and was very intelligent. It gave me a queasy sensation when I noted his resemblance to me and saw traces of my offspring playing in his features.

Puffing endlessly on cigarettes, he had little to say, secluding himself in his room. When the family sat down to eat, like Papa, he excluded himself.

My stepmother Lena was a massive woman with stringy, graying hair, growths on her face, and legs that had difficulty supporting her body. Her plate was full, conducting the family ensemble: looking after Papa, acting as surrogate mother to her son's child, and catering to Tamara's children. Whatever strength was left, she spent on her daughter.

To my horror, my stepmother attempted to treat me as though I, too, were an infant, by tucking me into bed.

Beginning to gray and having accumulated more poundage, Tamara glided about the apartment, her eyes glistening with happiness. I envied her, wishing I could partake of the emotion.

Papa went about his life no differently than he had during his stay with us. He rose early, jogged, showered, and ate his *kasha* (now uncooked — he had arrived at a new nutritional theory). By the time the others got up and congregated at the breakfast table, he was in another room, his nose in a book.

"Grab your mandolin and come join the party, Zelik," called a dark-haired young Kisel. "No one makes more delicious *latkes* than your wife Edzia."

On the other side of the partition dividing the kitchen from his workroom, Papa sat glued to the newspaper. "Enjoy!" he replied, without permitting himself even a glimpse.

Into the second day of my visit, Papa suggested that the two of us go to the beach. The activity and jabbering was deafening; the place was buzzing with Sunday bathers. In the distance a steamer, tugging a barge, crossed the horizon. Nearby, a vendor was peddling hot dogs, and at the point where the coast and waves met, a group of children were building a sand castle.

No sooner had we settled ourselves than someone nearby turned on a ghetto blaster, the vexing noise blaring at full volume. When I suggested we move to another spot, Papa scrutinized me.

"I often hear complaints from others: the beach is dirty, the water is polluted, it's too crowded on weekends, the smog is unbearable, and there are too many cars. In the meantime, their lives pass them by. Even if you plunked them in paradise, they would find something to criticize. You're right, Jankele, the music is loud and it's not even the kind that I particularly favor, but instead of seeing it as a disadvantage, I think to myself: How fortunate to be living in freedom, on such a beautiful beach, enjoying the rays of the sun and listening to somebody else's radio! How lucky can a man be!"

I reached out to hug him. Happiness spread across his face. We lay on our backs staring at the painted sky, interrupted only by seagulls fluttering their wings. Papa told me how he was prevented from taking out the mandolin I had bought him years earlier. And rather than allowing it to be confiscated, he had thrust it into the hands of a startled bystander.

A joke I had heard in Israel came to mind: "If a Russian immigrant walks off the plane at Ben Gurion Airport not carrying a violin case, then he's a pianist and his piano is en route."

"Papa, you live a separate life." I feared my words may have set off a land mine, but Papa wasn't ruffled.

"For years I've been after them to jog with me, to eat what I eat," he said sadly. "But who listens? Tamara once told me that if she had to abide by my diet, she'd rather die. The Mama is a sick woman, has diabetes, and no matter how hard I tried, I couldn't make her see the light. After all, I was away for eight years and she brought up the children on her own. By the time I returned, it was too late, the pattern had been established. At first I used to argue, beg, threaten, but when I realized it was useless, I decided, for my own health and their peace, to keep quiet."

Papa and I dunked ourselves in the ocean, splashing each other, and were carried back to shore by the incoming tide. "Life is like the sea: one wave covers another," theorized Papa when we were working the towels on our wet backs. We threaded our way back along the beach, our bodies gilded by the sun. "Jankele, I brought you something from Russia." My ears perked up, the little boy still waiting for Papa's demonstration of love. "Unfortunately," he continued, "it was stolen."

The glimmer faded. "What was it?"

"When I left home in '39, I carried *Zaidy* Josef's hammer with me. Imagine, I guarded it all these years and thought it would have special meaning for you."

"I would have loved to have it, Papa!"

"I know, Jankele. You are fused to the past."

17

IT FELT STRANGE to suddenly have a father I could call and converse with at will. I telephoned him almost daily, sometimes just to listen to his voice and hear him laugh, but when the novelty wore off and the long-distance bills mounted, I confined the calls to the discount periods.

"My father lives in New York," I heard myself telling friends. "My father plays the mandolin . . . My father loves opera . . . Excuse me, I've got to call New York and speak to my father." I could point to a living and breathing connection.

The postman delivered a large envelope with a story in it. "Perhaps you can see to have it published, Jankele," Papa wrote.

One day when my car was being repaired and I rode the subway to my office, I took along the manuscript and read:

FEELINGS OF MUSIC
by A.Z. Kuperblum

During our stay in Italy, I had many friends among the hundreds of Soviet Jews who were waiting for permission to emigrate to the countries of their choice. One day I was sitting on a park bench facing the sea, hoping someone I knew would pass by. But no one came. I always carried the book my son wrote, *Child of the Holocaust,* reading and rereading it, hoping to improve my English. Ready to trek home, I noticed a middle-aged man in a stylish, light-colored suit, slowly approaching. I motioned with my hand, inviting him to sit beside me. He smiled, thanked me, and holding out his hand, introduced himself, "Alessandro!"

In turn, I told him my name. We shook hands and sat down. I had been in the park since eight o'clock that morning without a soul to talk to and suddenly . . . such luck! I asked my new acquaintance where in the Soviet Union he hailed from. He looked at me in a way that told me that he spoke only Italian. We sat in silence, put our hands on our knees, and stared straight ahead.

Suddenly, I had an idea. I said, "Signore Alessandro!" Immediately he turned his head to me and I began to call out the names of past heroes of Italy: "Giordano, Bruno, Galileo, Garibaldi, Leonardo da Vinci." Alessandro moved closer and began speaking with great enthusiasm. The only thing I understood was something about Leonardo da Vinci and the *Mona Lisa.* At any rate, I was glad my new acquaintance had a chance to talk and get things off his chest. A few minutes later, we assumed our former poses. What could I do to get my friend to talk some more? I knew that the Italians are a musical people, so I began to call out the names of some of my favorite composers: "Beethoven, Grieg, Schubert . . . !" When I came to Guiseppe Verdi, his eyes came alive, and at that moment I began to sing an aria from Puccini's opera *Tosca.* A smile appeared on Alessandro's face. He picked up my beat and we sang a duet. He had a fine voice, and we moved from one aria to another, from one opera to another. When we reached the point of having to search our memories for more, I recalled an old Yiddish song that held a special place in my heart. My *Zaidy* Josef and *Buby* Chana used to sing it: "Raizele, Der Shoichets Tocheter."* The lyrics, by the Yiddish poet Segalowicz, were set to the music of "Come Back to Sorento."

As I sang my beloved song in Yiddish, Alessandro recognized the melody and sang along. We put our arms around each other, and staring out at the sea, sang at the top of our voices. An audience applauded when the song was over. I was unaware that people had stopped to listen. After that, Alessandro bid me *arrivederci,* and explained in such a way that I understood, that he had come from Rome only for the day. We embraced, and he said, *"Grazie, grazie . . ."* several times over.

I went to the park every day and sat on the same bench, my hands on my knees, and watched the waves rolling in to shore and out, in to shore and out, and reminisced how Alessandro and I had sat with our arms around each other and sung that unforgettable Yiddish song, "Raizele, Der Shoichets Tochter."

Lunching with a friend that day, I bragged about Papa's story. My companion, a tall, beak-nosed copywriter who delighted in puns, invariably responding in jest to serious questions, suddenly became solemn. "My father, that son of a bitch, even on his death bed, never told me he loved me."

THE VOID AT my own wedding still fresh in my memory, it was gratifying to have a Papa when our Ellen decided to get married. Her wedding took place in a synagogue, complete with bouquets of spring flowers, a cantor's resonating

*   Raizele, the ritual slaughterer's daughter

voice, hundreds of guests, and an array of spiffy-looking ushers and doll-like bridesmaids.

There was also a bona fide *zaidy*, his wife beside him, walking down the aisle to the accompaniment of a solo flute. Tamara and her entourage flew in from New York. Under the terms of the custody agreement, Mikhail's daughter could not leave the United States and he would not attend without her. The orchestra played, the guests took to the floor, and with mercurial speed, the waiters dispensed the traditional dishes from heavily laden trays. Sitting at the head table without so much as lifting a utensil or a glass, Papa watched the assembled guests scraping their plates clean. Even from afar, I could read his mind: "I pity these poor souls, making a graveyard out of their stomachs!"

After Tamara and her family left, Papa and Lena stayed behind. We drove to the farm for the weekend, where Papa, like a child in a playroom, strutted about, inspecting weeping willows, smelling wildflowers, and skipping pebbles across the pond. Sunday, when we were preparing to return to the city, he insisted that he and my stepmother remain, and scoffed at our concerns.

"Surely, there's a store nearby where I can get apples, *kasha,* and black bread!"

"But you wife doesn't eat that," said Terrye.

"For sure they must have pork and potatoes."

"And how do you propose to get there?"

"I'll walk," he grinned.

"We're talking miles."

"It's good for the legs."

I scribbled down the important phone numbers, made him practice dialing, and ordered him to call me daily. Then I drove him to the general store and loaded up with provisions. Crossing our fingers that when we returned on Friday, they would be alive and the place would be intact, we piled the children, the dog, and ourselves into the car and took off.

When I didn't hear from Papa by noon the next day, I dialed.

"Allo!" he answered hesitantly, and broke into laughter when he heard my voice. "I'm glad you called, Jankele. We could use some sugar."

"Look in the pantry. There's a large bag there."

"That?" he chuckled. "We need at least ten kilos."

"What for?" I asked, camouflaging my concern.

"Jankele, it's a surprise. I know you'll be pleased." His voice was soft, oozing charm.

"We'll bring it with us on Friday."

"We need it right away." Now he sounded desperate.

I phoned a farm neighbor, a Yugoslav who spoke Russian. That evening she reported back. "I was sworn to secrecy," she teased, and would say no more.

After work on Friday, I called the farm. "More sugar, Jankele!" Papa begged. We packed and joined the heavy traffic leaving the city for the weekend.

Our farm lodgers met us in the courtyard. Motek, the first out of the car, jumped all over them. "Feh!" Papa scooted him away. He reached down to kiss the children, but when he spied the sugar, he grabbed it and dashed inside. A mound of partially rotten apples lay on the kitchen table, and the floor was littered with peels, while steam emanated from a large cauldron. All about were containers filled to the brim.

"Oh, no!" Terrye gasped.

"Say nothing," I whispered, with a smile on my lips but not in my eyes.

"Aren't you surprised?" Papa was radiant, pointing to the lifetime supply of applesauce.

"What a surprise, indeed!" I responded.

"Are you pleased? Really pleased, Jankele? As soon as you left, I started looking for something to occupy us. Then I saw all that fruit just going to waste. What a shame! So we got to work. Look at the tree. Not only did we pick up the ones that had fallen, but the tree itself is naked."

"Those apples are infested with worms," Terrye said, a little too loud.

Papa asked for a translation.

"She said the apples are sour, Papa!"

"Ah!" His eyes twinkled like stars in the sky. "But the applesauce is as sweet as sugar."

The following weekend, before we even had a chance to unpack, he boasted, "The surprise of all surprises, Jankele," and led us on a tour. On an enormous field boulder, embedded by the side of the house, Papa had chiseled "A. Z. Kuperblum," and on another, "Jack Kuper." A chilling reminder of how far apart we had drifted.

"What kind of name is Kuperbum?" voices taunted.

"How do you spell it?"

"Your father will kill you when he finds you've changed your name," warned Uncle Shmil-Leib on his visit after our marriage. Not long afterwards, he sent a photograph of himself posing in front of his store with a new sign: "Tailleur Kuper."

"I'd give anything to be able to sign my paintings 'Jankele Kuperblum'!" said an artist friend with an Anglo-Saxon name.

Scavenging through the toolshed, Papa had come across cans of leftover paint and a dried-up brush and had set himself the task of rejuvenating the flock of lifesize metal herons, Canada geese, and other feathered creatures we had acquired from a sculptor friend who lived nearby. In time, the metal had rusted, adding character. Now the torsos of the birds were covered with the glossiest black, the beaks were red, and the eyes were sky blue, just like Papa's. Terrye restrained herself from laughing, but I couldn't see the humor.

"Why can't you leave well enough alone?" I squawked at him. "Don't I have enough problems without you adding to them?" Shocked by my outburst, he withdrew into himself.

For the rest of the weekend, we avoided each other, but late Sunday, when we were leaving, he advised, "A person should think ten times before uttering a bad word. Once it leaves the lips, it can never be retracted. The damage is done forever." After I apologized and he accepted it readily with a hug, he said, "Now that we're friends again, what would you like me to do here? You're the boss, so you must provide work."

My heart pumped double time. "Papa, you're on holidays. Relax! Take it easy. Nothing needs doing, other than cutting the grass."

"Grass is my specialty."

"Have you ever driven a tractor?"

"How difficult could it possibly be?"

"Don't you dare even think about it. You hear?"

"All right, if you say no, it's no!" He held up his hands, in surrender.

"It's all a show. He's doing it for you," Terrye commented, on the way home.

Throughout the week I worried about the mischief he was getting into. Sure enough, on the weekend, we discovered that he had dismantled a stone wall around the rockery and was feverishly reconstructing it.

"I'm a specialist in this field," he proclaimed. "Wait till you see it when I'm done. You'll be pleasantly surprised."

To my amazement and pleasure, he fashioned it with skill and artistry. Even friends admired the results. Encouraged, Papa ripped up the walkway parallel to the driveway and phoned me at the office demanding screening sand and tons of flagstone. Primitively executed, it was a work of art, so in keeping with the quaintness of the place.

Papa kept up his health regimen and reading and sporadically plucked on the mandolin he had brought on his first visit. He injected his wife with serum to control her diabetes. Often they sat together under a tree, playing cards.

Relaxing on the porch, looking at the stars and listening to the crickets, he ruminated, "All my life I have dreamt of living in a place like this. Oh, the things I could do here! Where you have weeds around the pond, imagine a bed of stones. It would be so beautiful, I know it would please you. Life would be much easier for you if we were all together." He waited for a reply.

Perhaps he was right, I thought. What started out as a weekend escape had become an albatross around my neck and the cause of quarrels and recriminations with my wife and children.

Still a teenager after our return from Israel, Ellen had invited a group of friends to spend the day at the farm and I conscripted them to help clear the fields of stones. After lunch, they had fled, leaving me with a distraught daughter.

"Papa, if you want to live here," I said, "it's fine with me."

"Oh, I really would, Jankele." He was a picture of contentment. "My problem is Lena. Her life revolves around Mikhail. She phones him three times a day to check if he has eaten breakfast, lunch, and dinner. How does he feel? Does he miss her?"

The calls were reflected on my monthly telephone bill.

"When I first became acquainted with her," he continued, "she was a librarian. That's how we met. She was interested in books, music, the theater. In those days I had someone to talk to. Now, all she wants to do is play cards. What do I care about cards? But to placate her, I do what she asks." He sighed. "Unless Mikhail and his little one are part of the package, I would never be able to convince her to live here."

"But Mikhail's daughter isn't allowed to leave the States," I reminded him. He shook his head in agreement.

"Then it's an impossible situation!"

"Such is life, Jankele. One has to learn to bend with it!"

18

LITTLE ODESSA BOILED over, not only with what America had to offer, but with the finest Russian caviar, rugs from Armenia, brass samovars, and mouth-watering smoked fish that had once spawned in Soviet waters. The Russian hit parade resonating onto the street blended with the tumult and babble of hurried pedestrians and cacophony from the subway ramp above. Shoppers had hungry looks in their eyes, elbowing their way at counters. Surely the supplies couldn't last forever!

Rarely did one hear an English word in the shops with Cyrillic signs. The prosperity of the new proprietors was reflected in their flashy cars, trendy clothes, and twinkling fingers. The neighborhood boasted some dozen restaurants, representative of the Soviet republics: they were modest affairs with few tables, where the owner cooked, served, cleared the dishes, and took the cash. But it was in the posh establishments, seating several hundred people, featuring stages, live orchestras, and emcees, booked seven nights of the week for several months in advance, that many of the Brighton Beach residents came to celebrate their birthdays, weddings, bar mitzvahs, and whatever else the entrepreneurs could promote. Instead of gifts, and to defray expenses, guests coughed up a hundred dollars per couple. The music deafened, tables creaked under the parade of dishes, and the vodka gushed — a never-ending fountain. Couples took to the floor and the joints jumped. America!

My brother-in-law lost his license for refusing to take a passenger to a feared destination, then regained it and bought a taxi. If others could prosper by saddling themselves with mortgages and debts, why not he? He hustled long hours, trading his boyish looks for a midriff paunch and a chronic backache.

Tamara became a teller in a bank, the good times leaving their imprint on her body. "What can I do?" she threw her hands in the air. "They all came to our parties, so it's not nice if we don't reciprocate."

Papa and his wife acquired their own apartment, one floor above Tamara's, and my half-sister called me for a contribution towards their monthly rent.

"If Papa needs help, shouldn't it come from his lips?"

Leading me as if on a tether, she spoke for Papa: "He feels he has no right asking, because he never did anything for you."

I bristled with tension. "For the first time in my life I am able to really help him. The problem is, something is preventing me." I only heard her breathing.

In velvet tones, bracketed with apologies, Papa called, repeating the request. I resented it no less, but grudgingly agreed.

Mikhail also moved to a place of his own, not even a block away, and the child spent most of her time at her grandparents', Papa escorting her to and from school. In a short time Mikhail became proficient in English, and although it was accented, acquired an impressive vocabulary. In spite of his qualifications, he also hacked cab. On Sundays he frequented the museums.

"A computer programmer earns well," I offered during a rare conversation.

"Money is of no interest to me," he said. "Driving taxi gives me time to think."

I had aspired to greater heights, but responsibility had led me to making commercials, some so mindless I couldn't believe I had a hand in them. Yet he, with education, brilliant mind, and opportunities, chose to drive cab.

"Jakub!" the barber in Lublin snapped at me, indicating the clean-shaven hulk rising from the barber's chair, reeking of fragrance.

I sprang up, ridding the client of the hair clinging to his clothes, but couldn't reach above his waist.

"How old are you, boy?" He loomed over me.

"Eight, almost nine."

He flipped me a coin, relieved me of the whisk, and brushed himself off. I ran for his overcoat, and even jumping, couldn't grasp the hanger. I pulled and watched helplessly as the garment fell onto freshly cut locks.

"That does it," the proprietor snapped.

"Please, sir, what will I tell my mother?"

"Come back in a year or two . . . when you've grown a few centimeters."

While life pulsated, acclimatizing the immigrants to the Brighton Beach rhythms, our own patterns shifted like pebbles of sand in a desert breeze. At age twenty-three, our son Mark, whom I had driven to hockey practice at five in the morning and who had inspired me to scream, "That's my boy!" when I heard he'd scored, was about to exchange wedding vows.

This time, even Mikhail and his daughter came. To initiate the festivities, we invited the family out for a dinner at a Chinese restaurant. Naturally, Papa excused himself and his wife stayed with him.

I winked at the waiter. "This is a special occasion." He returned shortly with a tablecloth and the customary teapot. When the platters of steaming, exotic dishes were passed around, Mikhail sat back waiting for Tamara to serve him. I pierced him with an icy stare.

Tamara shielded him. "It's his first time in a restaurant."

The next day at dusk, while elegantly attired guests mingled in a large hall on the outskirts of the city sipping champagne and nibbling hors d'oeuvres, Mikhail kicked a soccer ball in a nearby field. During the photography session, the ceremony, and throughout the meal, he looked gloomy and bored.

Breakfasting by the pool the morning after, I strove mightily to keep my volcanic anger in check when I saw his mother slice and butter his bagel. Later he asked her for a glass of water.

"Get your own water!" I yelled.

It struck him like a blow. Papa turned ashen.

Soon, the real reason for his presence in Toronto surfaced. A girl who had once known him in Chernovtsy and was now living in Canada had sent out feelers. Lena had contacted her, and between them they had decided that Toronto was as good a place as any to rendezvous.

"She's coming tomorrow. Be so good, Jankele, pick her up at the airport and drive them to the farm. Let them spend time together. Maybe something good will come of it." Papa was speaking on his wife's behalf.

I looked him in the eye. "I am not a chauffeur, and the farm is not a flophouse!"

Papa turned on all the charm he could muster. "Jankele, your farm is the ideal place for a young couple to fall in love. It may be your brother's only chance." When he realized he wasn't about to dislodge me, he petitioned that at least I find a hotel.

"Let him do it himself," I shot back.

In the end, Terrye came to his rescue and reserved a room at a motor lodge. Against my vigorous objections, she chauffeured Mikhail the next morning to greet his amour, arriving on an Air Canada flight from Winnipeg. The following afternoon he reappeared. The atmosphere was taut. Papa and Lena threatened to cut their stay short.

"Go!" I flared.

Terrye played the mediator. "He's your brother, and a guest in your home. You'd better apologize."

It was unpalatable, but as I sat down with him, I found myself probing the secret combination to Papa's vault, convinced that Mikhail was privy to it. He led me around a circle, culminating in a mounted attack of his own.

"You visit us, we visit you, but it's plain it's only a charade," he said. "And while I'm at it, what's the reason for this big house with a swimming pool yet?"

His outburst numbed me, and months after their chilly departure I still pondered his brutally candid assessment of our relationship. I couldn't help but respect him for it.

"LISTEN, JANKELE, WE definitely want to settle in Canada." It was Tamara on the phone. "It's so clean, so beautiful, no holdups, no killings, no rapes." My heart went into overtime. "We don't need anything. We know you're busy, so just tell me how to go about it."

I explained that the laws had tightened, but that there were venues, and gave her the name of an immigration lawyer. She reminded me not to trouble myself as, after all, they were capable, and I had enough on my own plate. A few days later she had an appointment with the Toronto lawyer; could I recommend an inexpensive hotel?

I was tempted to howl. I knew what she was after. "There's plenty of room in our house. Come, bring your husband, look around, take as long as necessary."

"Are you sure, Jankele? We don't want to be in your way."

In the end she came alone, visited Izzy's distant relatives, who were recent arrivals, and after her appointment told me the attorney wanted to see me.

She was investigating condominiums in the part of town

where Russian immigrants lived when I asked, "What does Izzy plan to do here?"

"With your connections, Jankele," she pinched my cheek, "surely you can push him into some kind of job!"

She still believed I could pull rabbits out of a hat. I hesitated to tell her that just to stay afloat, I constantly had to prove myself. The only easy entry I had was to a showroom owned by close friends where I could buy a mattress or a couch for less than retail.

At first, the lawyer didn't quite know why I had been summoned. After consulting his files, he said, "Oh yes! Your sister and her family can immigrate, provided they show a minimum of one hundred thousand dollars with which to open a business here."

"Are you still there?" I shouted into the mouthpiece, after conveying the counselor's words.

"Where will we get so much money?" Tamara sniffled.

It was the same salad, only a different dressing. I felt her anguish, but I had children of my own.

When I next heard from her, they had sold the taxi and purchased a Russian deli.

Tamara gushed with excitement. "All our friends who went into business have become millionaires, and driving a taxi is too dangerous. This way we'll work together."

"You should consult a lawyer," I said.

"Please! He was against it."

In spite of toiling seven days a week, with their children's and Papa's help, they barely eked out a living. The store, the size of a postage stamp, was in dire need of refurbishing. An antiquated freezer hissed, wheezed, groaned, and constantly had to be repaired. Expenses escalated and nimble fingers helped reduce the inventory. Adding to their distress, the local Russian Mafia representative paid them a visit, offering protection for a monthly fee. Somehow they struggled on until the lease expired and the landlord doubled the rent. They put the business up for sale. When there were no takers, they closed the door and walked away, leaving empty shelves and curling linoleum.

Once again my brother-in-law saddled himself with a cab, and Tamara settled in behind a desk in a doctor's office. Bored with school, Eddy became a chauffeur. Lena's health deteriorated, and she spent her days hobbling between hospitals and doctors' offices.

"An automobile also falls apart if you don't look after it," said Papa dryly, reconciling himself to the inevitable.

From Belgium came word that Uncle Jacques had died and his younger brother was suffering from Parkinson's disease. Unable to sleep, his pain excruciating, Shmil-Leib had to be spoonfed and helped to the toilet.

"Threw away his life!" Papa narrated on the phone from New York. "Occupied himself with business, percentages, stocks, destroyed his nerves. Never enjoyed a day's peace."

I couldn't help feeling the sermon was for me.

"Your brother is a foot-soldier, out in the trenches, risking his life," I defended. "You, on the other hand, are a general in the safety of a bunker far from the front."

"It just seems that way to you, Jankele." In the next breath Papa announced he was flying to Brussels to rescue his brother from the army of doctors on whom he had become dependent. "Only *kasha,* apples, black bread, and daily exercise can save him."

Papa was gone for months, then reported, "Every day I carried him on my back down the stairs into the fresh air for walks in the park. Two, three times a day I massaged his body, stimulating the blood to flow through his veins. Pigment returned to his cheeks, and by the time I left, he managed to hold a spoon and was sleeping like a baby.

"My brother's troubles stem mainly from his son," he sighed. "Shmil-Leib promised to buy him a house when he got married, but when the time arrived, they found themselves knotted in a squabble. He offered to finance a modest home, but his son licked his lips for something more luxurious. 'You're not my father,' he cussed him. 'I never want to see you again!' Shmil-Leib was excluded from the wedding, and later when the children came along, they were robbed of a grandfather. He should have left his son in Tbilisi. That boy brought him nothing but sorrow."

Shortly afterwards, Papa received a note. "This is my last letter," uncle had scribbled with an unsteady hand. "I am saying goodbye!"

"I must go back, Jankele," choked Papa.

I offered to finance the trip and called Brussels to expect him. Uncle's wife was pleasant and appreciative.

"I hope you're not offended if I lay my cards on the table," she said. "Your father means well, but he's more of a hindrance than a help. I have no time to be looking all over Brussels for *kasha.*"

Uncle was dead within the month.

His passing was followed by Lena's. I tried to comfort Tamara with the old line that time is a healer. I also conveyed condolences to Papa. Not surprisingly, he philosophized briefly about life and death and quickly changed the subject.

As when I offered to drive him to the grave of his beloved cousin, Hershel, who had passed away between Papa's visits, his face turned to granite and he didn't answer. Similarly, when I proposed that we call upon Hershel's brother, Abe, in his nineties in a nursing home, Papa responded, "He probably won't even know who I am!" Later when Abe died, Papa received the news without comment.

I was the only one who could tell him how his mother had ended her days in 1942: crossing the street, she had been knocked over by a passing horse and buggy. Five days later, broken-hearted, his father had followed her to her grave.

Papa never inquired, and when I broached the subject, he repeated, "The dead are dead and life is for the living."

"Foolish!" Papa scorned Tamara and Mikhail for visiting their mother's graveside every Sunday. "You think she knows who comes and who doesn't? It makes a difference to her? Feh! The only one who really profits from it is the florist." He would have been quite content to forego the placing of a headstone, had the two not badgered him. "One day," he promised them, not knowing where the money would come from. Just then, a thousand-dollar inheritance from Shmil-Leib arrived. I suggested a note of thanks was in order to the bereaved widow, knowing that although he nodded, he would never carry it out.

Tamara begged Papa to move in with her, but he was proud of his independence. I continued to subsidize his rent, Mikhail clothed him, and when shopping for groceries, Tamara bought extra. His pension covered his other needs, and twice weekly, the municipality provided him with a domestic to cook and clean.

"What's to cook?" he chided. "And my place isn't dirty. But the poor Polish woman needs a job, so I let her in. She swishes a wet mop around, one, two, three, I sign a piece of paper and get rid of her."

His routine never changed: he jogged, peeled his apples, strummed the mandolin, and frequented the library. The way he had purged Mama from his memory, so too, Lena disappeared. Not just from his life, but from his vocabulary as well. Gone!

It was an April ritual to await Papa's arrival at the airport terminal, when he came to celebrate my birthday. Sandwiched between attaché cases and designer apparel was Papa, in white sneakers, T-shirt, and jogging pants. Although he was approaching eighty, he could race up the escalator like a youngster, scaling the steps two at a time.

Other than essentials, his overnight bag contained offerings ranging from an obsolete Brighton Beach Insurance Company calendar to a Passover *Hagada,* distributed free to Russian immigrants by the Lubowitchers in Brooklyn. An ashtray from an obscure hotel, a jewelry box adorned with sea shells — someone's souvenir from Florida — a half-used bottle of foul perfume, a bar of soap, a Santa Claus toy, and a box of mildewed chocolates. Once, after his Lena's death, he brought what remained of a carton of alcohol swabs. He would deposit these discards on the kitchen counter without a word, as if he were merely the courier.

"Who are these for?" I would ask.

"Do I know, Jankele? Whoever wants." Papa smiled with a new set of porcelain teeth Tamara had funded.

"Papa, you eat chocolates?"

"Me? Feh! It's poison."

"So, why bring them for us?"

His face was remarkable for what it didn't reveal.

During one of his visits, he and Shaul had tossed a basketball around. Papa had taken a fancy to it, and before returning home, asked if he could have it. Without giving it a thought, I agreed.

"*Zaidy's* packing my ball!" Shaul's bottom lip quivered.

"I'll buy you a new one!" I said, and watched his eyes fog with tears.

Terrye came out of the trenches. "You think it's right to give away your son's basketball?"

"Why do you begrudge him a stinking ball if it gives him pleasure?" I replied. "My father is seventy-five. How much longer do you suppose he has on this earth? Besides, Shaul hardly plays with it."

"Your father has never brought our children so much as a fig. He's concerned only with himself." I resented the venomous words coming from her sweet lips.

Later, as we lay in bed, she tried to shoulder her way into the round of my back, but I was charged with injury. "You've rubbed salt into my wounds."

"My quarrel is not with him. It's with you."

It was a complaint I often heard from my children as well. They resented my preoccupation with Papa, griping that whenever he was around I reverted to being a child.

Without warning, Shaul, the little boy with whom I had

constructed a tree-house at the farm when he was twelve and who later joined a short-lived rock band, "the Migraines," turned twenty-two and embarked into matrimony. It seemed as if only yesterday I had arranged for his circumcision, naming him Shaul Mandell, after Mama's second-youngest brother, Shepsel, and Papa's brother Mendel.

Ellen had been the recipient of an eiderdown brought all the way from Russia, and at Mark's wedding, Papa had handed him a cheque. With Lena gone, Papa came to attend the nuptials empty-handed. He was sunning himself by the pool, listening to *La Traviata* warbling from the patio speakers, when I displayed a Fitz and Floyd platter I knew Shaul and his fiancée admired.

"You'll present this to the bride and groom."

"You're so clever, Jankele! You think of everything." He fingered the porcelain with wonderment and smiled in childish oblivion.

The newlyweds had left for their honeymoon and Papa was still with us in July when we were about to celebrate Terrye's birthday.

Simca made a card and designed paper to wrap her gift in. Ellen prepared her mother's favorite foods, secretly storing it in our basement refrigerator. Mark and Shaul deliberated as to what to buy their mother. Flowers and cards arrived. Papa could not help but notice the frenzied activity. Handing me several bills, he said, "Give Tobala something from me."

"What would you like me to buy?"

He grinned innocently. "Do I know from such things?"

"I'll tell you what, Papa, I'll help you select a gift."

On a tour of Hazelton Lanes in the fashionable Yorkville area, we came upon a record shop. I suggested a compact disc Terrye had mentioned. Unfortunately, the shop was out of that recording and the clerk tried to persuade me to select a different work by the same composer.

"What now?" A crease appeared on Papa's brow.

"There's another store not far away."

"Tsk, tsk! So much here and we have to go searching!"

Neither the music nor the composer was familiar, so we trekked from one store to another until some two hours later we landed our catch. An exhausted Papa reached for his wallet, and when the clerk handed him the bagged purchase, he tried to transfer it to me.

"Praise God, that's finished!" he sighed with relief. As I led him past our parked car, he looked baffled. "Where now?"

"Wrapping paper, some ribbon, and a card."

"Oy, oy, oy!" he muttered. "So much trouble, just for a birthday!"

Back home, he dropped the purchases on the kitchen table and made for the stairs. "Not so fast," I said. I showed him how to wrap the gift and forced him to sign the card. The present tied with a yellow ribbon, the card affixed, he passed it to me.

"Papa, it's for Tobala."

He presented the gift to her with adolescent awkwardness. "I you give for birthday," he said, pecking Terrye on the cheek, smiling from ear to ear. A once-in-a-lifetime experience for him, as it was for me witnessing it.

"FEH!" PAPA MADE a face at intermission when we left the Yiddish concert I had dragged him to. Even when he professed enjoyment, I suspected he would have been happier to have stayed home. However, at the circus, he mirrored my own youthful excitement, squealing and clapping his hands, mesmerized by the trapeze acts, howling at the clowns, and enchanted by the performing animals.

Those who met him were astounded by his vitality and cheerful disposition. Everyone received a generous smile and a chair, and we were prompted to serve refreshments. He loved an audience, especially a Yiddish-speaking one.

"This took place a few years back." He hypnotized his listeners with sparkling eyes and engaging smile. "While jogging along the boardwalk in Brighton Beach, a man stopped me. 'I see you here every morning,' he said. 'Mind if I join you?' 'Why not?' I replied. 'It will be more enjoyable!' By his appearance and manner, I knew instantly he had left the old country years earlier.

"We ran together, exchanging a few pleasantries, but after a while, gasping for breath, he stopped. 'Carry on without me!' he wheezed. On the return, he fell in beside me keeping pace. 'How far do you run?' he asked. 'Five kilometers, every morning,' I answered. He was astonished. 'You're in such good shape! How old are you?' I was seventy-five then, but why should he know that? So I told him, 'sixty.' 'No wonder!' he said. 'I'm sixty-five . . . and I run two kilometers. But when I was sixty, I could also run five.'"

Like a seasoned thespian, he paused allowing for laughter and picked up when it subsided.

"After our daily jog we would rest on a bench and trade thoughts. He once owned a butcher shop and was now retired. His children were grown and married, his wife was already in the next world, and he lived by himself. One day when I told him I felt useless and would like to find something to occupy myself with, he jumped as if scorched by scalding coals. 'I know the owner of a large hardware store and he's looking for someone to lug heavy boxes.' 'Lugging is my specialty,' I told him. 'The problem is,' he revealed, 'the man is orthodox and only hires observant Jews.'"

His listeners hooked, Papa paused to blow his nose. "What was there to do? I put on a hat, not only to appear pious, but to conceal my white hair, and in a fringed garment borrowed from a neighbor, presented myself. The owner looked me over, asking my age. I thought to myself, if I have to lie, I might as well go all the way. I told him 'fifty-five.' 'Fifty-five!' he bellowed. 'You're way too old to be lifting heavy loads. Do you have any idea how much these boxes weigh? I am only forty-eight and can barely lift one.' I walked over to where the cases were stacked, picked one up and danced with it. That seemed to satisfy him.

"'What synagogue do you belong to?' he asked. What do I know of synagogues? So I answered, 'The one around the corner.' He mentioned a name. 'That's the very one. Exactly!' I concurred.

"Just when I thought the worst was over, he piped up with, 'Who's the rabbi there?' 'Oh, I have such difficulty with names,' I told him. 'It's the one with the beard.' Pulling on his own beard, he pondered for a moment. 'I can see you're a God-fearing Jew and in good shape, but at fifty-five, God forbid, if something should happen to you, the insurance wouldn't cover it and your wife could sue me for whatever I'm worth.'"

Applause followed laughter. Papa hushed the crowd.

"'Not to worry,' said my boardwalk friend, and led me to an even better opportunity. Only this time, I had to be a cook.

"Following directions, I went to an apartment building where after pressing the buzzer, a voice invited me to come up to the twenty-first floor. There I was met by a middle-aged woman who led me into an elegantly furnished residence. A man in a wheelchair mumbled in English, repeating over and over: 'I told him it should be two dollars and fifty cents, but he charged me three dollars. I told him two-fifty, but he charged three.'

"The woman sitting opposite poured tea and offered cookies. Then she said, in Yiddish, 'Before I tell you why I summoned you, I'd better give you some background. When my brother was studying architecture, he swore that by the time he was thirty he would be a millionaire, renowned, married with two children, one boy and one girl, and the creator of the most magnificent building, in which he would reside. The edifice of his vision is the very one we're in, Mr. Kuperblum. He also found the woman of his dreams, but she would not marry him unless he transferred the property to her.' She stopped to add milk to her tea. 'And like a fool, he obliged. Shortly after the wedding, she visited her parents in Florida, not returning for months. During that time, my brother received an envelope containing photographs of her cavorting with another. He lost his mind and here he is.

"'He has to be watched twenty-four hours a day. I can't leave, even to get my hair done. The hairdresser comes to me. If I don't take a vacation, I'll go out of my mind. I need someone who has the talent and stamina to keep him amused. I'm told you play the mandolin and tell not a bad story.' I nodded and told her that my English was still poor. 'No problem,' she said. 'My brother understands Yiddish.'

"'Is it also a fact that you're an excellent cook?' 'It's my specialty,' I smiled. 'I once owned a large restaurant in Warsaw.' She led me to a pantry stocked with more foodstuff than I had seen in all my years. Bottles of every beverage one could imagine, all kinds of chickens, ducks, steaks, chops, fish, vegetables, you name it, were stacked neatly in an enormous freezer. 'You'll have no reason to leave the premises,' she assured me. 'I'll give you fifteen hundred dollars for three weeks.' In my entire life I never had so much money, and in my mind I already had spent it. 'When can you start?' she asked. 'Immediately,' I answered. 'Very good. Be here tomorrow morning.'

"I was halfway out when she detained me. 'One more thing, Mr. Kuperblum. What would you serve him for breakfast?' I didn't want her to think I would serve him what I ate, so I said, 'For breakfast, I would fry him up a couple of hamburgers with salad on the side.' She stared, open-mouthed. 'Hamburgers and salad, for breakfast?' Obviously I had guessed wrong, so I quickly added, 'maybe potatoes as well.' 'Let me think about it, Mr. Kuperblum,' she said, and escorted me to the door."

No matter how often I heard him tell the story, it remained fresh. With each telling he altered it slightly, garnishing, flavoring, trimming unnecessary fat. But as much as I joined with the others in appreciation, I felt his tales were deceptions.

"Papa, why not reveal what really happened in your life?"

"Isn't it up to the writer to beautify and make it appealing? Reality is boring! Who would be interested?"

"I would."

It sent a current of gloom through him that persisted the rest of the day. However, after his return home, he sent me an account entitled, "A Remembrance of the Four-Year-Old Jankele Kuperblum." On the verge of my own discovery, my spirts seesawed between anxiety and elation.

"'If you're a good boy,' said Jankele's mother, 'and go to sleep, tomorrow Papa will take you for a hike in the forest.' Jankele kissed his parents goodnight, climbed into bed and closed his eyes.

"They left early the next morning, and outside they met Papa's younger brother, Mendel. 'Come Jankele, I'll put you on my shoulders,' said Mendel. But little Jankele would not hear of it. A short time later he tired and begged to be carried."

Papa's carefully formed Yiddish characters melted before me, carrying me back in time.

"In the forest clearing, they spread a blanket. 'Jankele,' asked Mendel, 'would you like me to tell you a story?' 'I love stories,' replied Jankele. Whereupon his uncle sat down, crossed his legs and began: 'Once upon a time, there was a boy who strayed into the woods and got lost.'"

I had read only two pages with many more to go before realizing that it was just another one of his fantasies. Mendel's voice was Papa's, and the four-year-old Jankele was simply bait.

"*Kompinator! Kompinator!*" a voice accused. It was mine.

19

OTHER THAN CARING for the grounds, weeding the vegetable patch, and taking garbage to the local dump, little else needed tending on our farm. It was now sought after by house and garden magazines vying to feature it in their illustrious pages. Ironically, I talked of selling.

"You'll see, Jankele, you'll soon have a flock of grandchildren and everyone will congregate and spend the best of times," said Papa.

Once I accepted his counsel to keep the farm, I itched to finally, once and for all, correct all the compromises, mistakes, and poor decisions I had made. The first order was the demolition of a cottage, abutting the century-old farm house. I had spent a lot of effort to give it a reason for existence. But after everything was said and done, it was still freezing in winter and stifling in summer. It sat on decaying logs, and the crawl space provided a haven for rodents. Even its shape, long and narrow, disturbed me.

Early one morning, we set out with sledgehammer, crowbar, and working gloves. Papa couldn't have been happier. But halfway, his mood changed. "I'm thinking, Jankele, when everything is functioning as it should, and you can finally relax and enjoy what you've created, you search for new problems. What have you got against that lean-to? All the bother to tear it down, then the expense and headache of building something in its place. What for? Like attaching a superfluous nerve to your system."

"Papa, if everyone thought like you, we'd all be living in cellars."

"You're not getting younger and it's time you stopped pushing a full wheelbarrow uphill and started walking down with it empty." It made sense, and by the time we arrived, he had me convinced.

We sat in the gazebo, intoxicated by the aroma of lilac bushes. A cow mooed in a distant field. Otherwise the deathly quiet was interrupted only by tweeting birds and an occasional car speeding along the concession road, pursued by a cloud of dust.

Papa inhaled deeply, expanding his lungs. "The air is so fresh here, Jankele. So healthy! You're lucky to have a place like this!" Stone still, staring blankly into space, we swatted the occasional fly. Out of the blue, Papa deliberated about the world becoming so overcrowded, predicting that people would be forced to live on barges afloat on the ocean.

The conversation drifted and I asked, "How did you and Mama meet?"

He looked up at the sun, squinting his eyes. "One Saturday afternoon I was strolling through the park in Pulawy and came upon an attractive young woman weeping. I sat down beside her and offered her my handkerchief. At first she would have nothing to do with me, then she poured her heart out. She was hungry. I invited her to a restaurant, then walked her home."

"That's it?"

"No, Jankele." The memory was paining him. "That was your mother's younger sister, Esther. She died of typhus when you were very young."

"I remember her, Papa. The doctor who treated her had a missing arm."

"Not a doctor, only a *feldsher*,* and so in love with her."
He glided his tongue across sun-dried lips. "Your Aunt
Esther was stunning. When I took her home, I saw such
poverty. Unimaginable! A small house, smelling of mildew
and so many mouths to feed. I took a shine to the eldest,
Etta Liba, your mother."

"Etta Liba? Mama's name was Edzia."

"That was her Polish nickname. Her father, a towering
man, could take a tattered pair of boots and with a bit of
spit and polish give them new life. He'd be gone for weeks
on end, visiting markets in search of a customer. That
night he was hand-stitching a shoe, griping that his sewing
machine was out of commission. I walked over to the
machine, which was taking up precious space under the
kitchen window, sat down and pressed on the treadle.
Nothing moved.

"'I'm a specialist in this field,' I told him. I had never laid
eyes on such a contraption, but figured, how difficult could
it be? At any rate, I tinkered with that careworn piece, all
the time admiring your mother from the corner of my eye.
Eventually, we exchanged a few words, I lent her a book,
and later, we started to see each other on weekends and
finally every evening. Not long after, her family moved to
Zyrardów, and we promised to write, but never did. A few
months later I left to work in Warsaw.

"I slaved over a cobbler's bench in a stifling garret with
four others. One day the boss's wife hollered for me to come
down. We had distant relatives in the capital, but I hadn't
informed them of my presence and wondered who it could
possibly be. I rushed down the creaky stairs, and there was
Etta Liba. I was so surprised. She wept that the poverty at
home had become so unbearable, she had no choice but to
leave. Here she was in the big city and didn't know what to
do. I suggested we get married, and two weeks later we

---

* medic

exchanged vows in Zyrardów, where you were later born. There were twelve or thirteen people at the ceremony, mostly her family and a few friends."

"No one from your side?"

"It was too far and who could afford it? You had to take the *statek** to Warsaw, and from there, a train to Zyrardów. The fare alone was forty or fifty *zloty,* and the average daily wage in those days was about three. I think my parents sent a card."

"Was Mama pregnant? Was that why she came looking for you?"

"Jankele!" Papa recoiled, as if from a boxer's jab.

"I wrote to Zyrardów and they have no record of my birth." I cross-examined him. "How do you explain that, Papa?"

"Because I registered you in Pulawy, where we lived — I'll explain." His frown metamorphosed into a smile. "In her last month, your mother went to Zyrardów to be with her parents. While she was boarding the train in Warsaw, she lost her ticket. Seeing her in distress, a compassionate porter came to her rescue and she arrived at her parents' doorstep just in the nick of time. That very night, you were born. I went to bring you both home to Pulawy, and on the way back I found the baggage handler and reimbursed him. What a fine human being! I'll never forget him! There are people who say that all Poles are terrible anti-Semites. You see Jankele, you can't generalize!"

"What kind of person was Mama?"

Speaking slowly, as if censoring his thoughts, he offered: "Your mother kept a clean house. Before the Sabbath she would wash the floor, mop, dust, polish. She was also a fine cook. In her spare time she would knit and embroider. You may remember the hanging in our kitchen, the strawberries looked so real."

I couldn't, but another, of chefs leaning into a cauldron,

* ferry

stood out in my mind. It had Polish words embroidered on it: "Where many cooks meet, there's nothing to eat!"

"Your mother was a linguist, spoke a good Polish, and was fluent in French. She dressed you in a white sailor suit and taught you: '*Bonjour, Maman. Bonjour, Papa.*'" He savored the memory. "Her German was even better."

I remembered Mama on the street, shivering from the unmerciful cold, a frayed rope around her shoulders affixed to a baking tray laden with strudel squares. Passersby paid no attention, and those who stopped to inspect walked on. On the verge of tears, she prayed, "Dear God! What will I do?" A group of German soldiers suddenly congregated, and I was astonished at the ease with which Mama conversed with them. Laughing and devouring the strudel that I had seen her bake that morning in a friend's oven, they pressed money into her hands. She hugged me, and jubilantly we rushed back with the empty tray to make more.

I turned to face Papa. "What I wouldn't give to have a photograph of her!" Hard as I tried, I was unable to pull her into focus. I could see the shape of her face, could picture the sadness in her large, moist eyes, but the pieces refused to merge. "Do any of my children resemble her? Sometimes, when I look at them, especially my Simca, I see fleeting glimpses of Mama."

"Yes, yes!" he responded, but it was clear that either time had robbed him of memory, or he surmised it was the answer I was seeking.

"How come you don't have a Mommy?" Simca asked at age three.

"She was killed by the Germans." I tucked her in.

"Why?" she asked, after I had turned off her light.

I turned to Papa again. "Mama was beautiful, wasn't she? She had long, black, silky hair, large, dark eyes, tall and slim. Am I right?"

"Your mother was cursed with a goiter, Jankele," Papa

said, and scratched a mosquito bite on his leg. "Remember she wore a scarf around her neck?"

Mama rose to thank the summer camp director and his staff for the rich experience they had given the deprived children of Pulawy the summer of '39.

"Mama!" I pulled her dress. On our walk home, I picked up my grievance. "No one else spoke. Why did you have to?"

"Your quarrel should be with those who didn't speak."

"You embarrassed me," I whined. "You always embarrass me."

So many years later, I remembered that when she stood, her scarf had slipped, revealing the aberration.

Papa looked askance, scanning the vista. "Your mother was an unhappy soul. You couldn't draw a smile out of her. Nothing was right. Nothing was ever good enough. A malcontent, chronically complaining." He sighed.

On hands and knees, I scrubbed the floor, straining to reach under the bed with the sopping rag. Mama pointed to grime wedged between the splintering boards. "Just like your father," she said, commanding me to rewash the floor.

Papa went on. "For example, she would needle that a friend of hers lived in a better apartment, was married to a greater provider, attended theater, and frequented restaurants. At the time, I wondered if her unhappiness was because of our economic situation, but in the end, I concluded it was genetic. Her mother was also an injustice collector!"

"Mama said you were irresponsible."

He swerved. "In her eyes maybe, but remember, Jankele, a smile can accomplish more than a sledgehammer. She had no reason to complain. Every day I would put in at least seven, eight hours sewing twenty shoe uppers. After that I would deliver them to the factory and pick up skins for the next day. I was never afraid of work, but a cobbler in Poland, if he worked a day, he could squeeze through, and if on the next day he didn't work, there was nothing to eat. I always made sure there was enough on the table."

The scar-faced boy at the *Tarbut* Hebrew School flaunted a shiny *zloty* pilfered from his mother's wallet. After class he led me to a grocery store, and in a nearby stable, hiding like mice, we feasted on kaiser buns with freshly churned butter.

"There were problems between you and Mama."

"It's not pleasant for me to talk about this," Papa said. He closed his eyes, started to say something, changed his mind. "When you were two or three years old, your mother went to visit her parents, who by then were living in Warsaw. She was supposed to be gone for a few days, but didn't return until some three weeks later. You kept asking, 'Where is Mama?'"

"Someone to see you, Jankele." Papa's calloused hand guided me to another room. A lady with long, dark tresses, large, dark eyes, and painted lips, floated towards me, her arms outstretched. I ran to her, crying, "Mama!"

Papa was in mid-sentence, ". . . and that she wanted a divorce. Her parents kept a boarder, a truck driver who had proposed to marry your mother. Naturally, I was distraught and left for Warsaw to confront him. 'I have to marry a woman with a child? What a silly idea!' he scoffed at me. My self-respect at a low ebb, your mother and I didn't talk to each other for maybe two or three months, after which I began to steer our lives back on track."

"I remember there was also bad blood between Mama and *Buby?*"

"Your mother was critical of mine, and vice versa. For example, when we would visit, *Buby* would ladle out two bowls of soup. Your mother refused to so much as pick up the spoon and expected me to do likewise. How could I insult my own mother? So naturally I ate not only mine, but the second bowl, too, and this offended your mother. Often I would pay my mother a compliment and attribute it to her daughter-in-law. 'Oh, she's getting smarter, beginning to understand a thing or two!' your *Buby* would beam. Similarly, I would tell your mother that *Buby* had said nice things about her."

Though painful, I continued to dredge. "Why did Mama want to leave you?"

He shrugged.

"Papa, you remember the neighbor I introduced you to? The farmer whose wife left because he came to bed smelling of manure?"

Papa was baffled. "I never smelled. I was always clean and properly dressed, with polished shoes."

"Then what was it?"

"If a person tells me it's night and I see it's day, I don't shout, 'You're crazy!' Instead, I try gently, tactfully, to show that the person has made a mistake. On the other hand, your mother constantly derided others and herself. She regretted marrying me. I wasn't educated, spoke a poor Polish, was too short, and so forth. She bemoaned that had she not met me, she would have emigrated to America."

"Why did she call you a *kompinator?*"

"*Kompinator?*" He mulled it over. "I never heard her call me that. I've always traveled the straight road. Never cheated anyone, never took advantage, never harmed nor hurt a soul."

Papa started to walk and I followed him to the back of the property. Admiring the view from the hill, we eventually ended up at the pond.

I asked what had attracted him to communism.

"My greatest pleasure, always, was to see children of different nationalities sing and dance together."

The Soviet film *Circus* unreeled to the accompaniment of chase music. A Caucasian woman with a black baby bundled in her arms is running for her life through a metropolis, pursued by a hoard of obese men in top hats, black tails, and silver-handled sticks. As they near her, she leaps onto a passing train and the music segues to intrepid strains as she is whisked off to the U.S.S.R. Performing high atop a trapeze, the audience, a potpourri of nationalities, cradle the baby, serenading it in various tongues, ending with a Yiddish lullaby.

"Papa, for this, you became a communist?"

"I was never a communist, Jankele. In fact, up to the age of fifteen, I attended synagogue and laid phylacteries. But when I became acquainted with Gorky, Sholem Aleichem, and Sholem Ash, as well as the great American, English, and French writers of the time, whose works became available in Yiddish translation, religion lost its grip on me."

"Was that when you moved in with a Gentile friend?" I asked. He looked perplexed. I continued. "I remember hearing a story about you leaving home. Your father went to get water at the town pump and when he saw your roommate in your winter coat, *Zaidy* was terribly upset. It had taken him years to save up for it."

"Where did you dig up such a grandmother's tale?"

Indeed, how had it lodged itself in my memory with such clarity of detail? "Something else," I went on, enjoying the journey. "One day on my way home from *cheder,* I saw you. I was terrified you were coming to punish me, so I ran. 'Jankele, wait! Jankele, wait!' You pursued me, but I managed to lose you and hid in the market square. At dusk, I crept home and stood at the door for the longest time, fearing to enter. When I did, you told me you had chased after me to buy me a sweet."

He displayed an injured smile. "Did I ever lift a hand to you?"

I couldn't recall an instance.

"In my entire life, I never struck you, nor anyone else! It's not in my nature."

I tried to stop, but demons propelled me and I dug up the episode with the spinsters. He gazed at me as if forever.

"I would take money that wasn't mine? Never!" he

scowled. "After the German bombings, the house we lived in was decimated. You and I used to go there to dig in the rubble, to retrieve my sewing machine. One morning, I don't recall whether or not you were with me that day, two German soldiers and a city official, a Pole, spied me from across the street. The shingle with my name on it had survived and was dangling on its bracket. 'Kuperblum,' read one of the soldiers aloud. 'That's a German name.' 'He's a Jew,' the official said. They took me to a nearby garrison where I spent the day hauling ammunition boxes and sacks of provisions.

"I was young and healthy and had little difficulty performing the task, but many other Jews, elderly and weak, couldn't lift the loads. One man fell, spilling a sack of salt. The German picked him up by his collar, dragged him to the river's edge and held his head under the water. When he released his grip, the poor soul had expired. That evening I told your mother about it. 'Others are fleeing to Russia, what are you waiting for?' she said. Whatever money I had, I gave her, and left with only a slice of dry bread in my pocket."

"So, it was Mama's idea!"

"I didn't even have it in mind, but she insisted."

"I remember that morning," I ruminated. "It must have been hard for you to leave."

He blinked. "What choice did I have? At the depot when I lined up to buy a ticket for Lublin, a German was plucking Jews from the queue, driving them off. We were forbidden to travel. But luck was with me and I managed to persuade a decent Pole to purchase one for me."

I was tempted to ask how he paid for it.

"At every station, the train doors would open and a voice would thunder, 'Any Jews?' I could hear the laments coming from other coaches. An elderly woman was booted off and fell face down like a sack of potatoes. Fortunately, no one betrayed me."

"They thought you were a soldier."

"You have an amazing memory, Jankele! That uniform was a blessing. Polish POWs returning from captivity were treated with more civility, even by the Germans. Nevertheless, it seems I was suspect because when I found a seat, some passengers moved away. That's how it was. Even a small child could point a Jew out. At any rate, I got to Lublin, spent the night, and the following day set out for Wlodawa, walking some two hundred kilometers through dense forest. There were others, but one person attracted less attention, so I kept to myself. I not only feared Germans, but also Poles. Life was cheap, and a Jew was easy prey."

Running beside him, I snaked my way through the pine trees. In the next instant, I was behind the camera directing a young Yves Montand in Papa's shoes.

"In Wlodawa, I met up with an uncle, my mother's brother. He knew a local family, and they invited us to stay the night. These people led an almost normal life behind shuttered windows, blessed Sabbath candles, and ate gefilte fish with *challah.** During dinner, uncle broke down and decided to return to his family. 'They'll kill you there,' I warned him, but he took no heed."

Branded in my memory was a version Mama had related: Outside Wlodawa, Papa knocked at a farmhouse door. The peasant woman allowed him in to warm up, and when he pleaded for food, she asked for money or valuables. He had nothing. Noticing a sewing machine, he sat down to tinker, and removing the bobbin, demonstrated that the machine was jammed. Not to worry, he was a Singer sewing machine specialist. Fiddling with it, he replaced the part, and presto, it performed like a charm. The grateful peasant served dinner and allowed him to spend the night in the attic.

My resourceful Papa made me proud. So many decades

---

* braided egg bread eaten traditionally on the Sabbath

later, my sentiments hadn't altered. The blemishes, imperfections, and frailties made him human and real, but Papa wished to be perceived as a saint.

"I've never cheated anyone in my life!" He gazed at me, my image reflecting in his eyes. "Jankele, I am puzzled as to why you carry such dark thoughts about me!"

Was my memory playing tricks? How did these accounts find a nest in my head?

Masking his momentary depression with a zesty smile, he said, "After my uncle left I made my way to the Bug River. The moment I set foot in a small rowboat standing idly by the shore, a couple of German soldiers appeared, and I faced the barrel of a gun. 'A Jew, let's kill him!' heckled the younger.

"The older one ordered me into the boat and rowed me across to the Russian side. It shows you cannot judge an entire nation. I expected to be welcomed by comrades. Imagine my shock when I was apprehended, and like a criminal, thrown into a dungeon and the next day, ferried back again by the Russians. I followed the river's shore and passed a German driving several hundred Jews to God only knows where!"

As he was talking, I was editing the footage, debating which version was more riveting. His or mine?

"By sundown, I came upon a fisherman who offered to take me across. Don't think I didn't fear he might push me overboard. It was common. As it turned out, he was decent, never even asked for money. Moving at night like a stalked animal, I made my way to Brest-Litowsk, and the moment I found work, I sent parcels. I earned five hundred rubles a month and a parcel cost at least three hundred, plus postage."

Mama allowed me to untie the string and unwrap the box encased in burlap. I unveiled individually bagged treasures of beans, tea, noodles, bread, marmalade, and a chocolate.

"Papa, why didn't you take us?"

He stared at his toes wriggling in the water. "An impossibility," he said emphatically. "It was too dangerous with children. But the moment I legalized my status, I applied for your visas. By the time I had them in my hand, the war between Hitler and Stalin had broken out."

I held onto Mama's coat sleeve as she rapped gently on a door. An unshaven man in winter underwear, furrowing a hand through his hair, studying us with sleepy eyes, held the door ajar. "Excuse the mess," he apologized, clearing a space for Mama to sit. Clothes lay scattered on a dresser, chairs, the floor. Empty bottles and drinking glasses crowded a night table and a terrible stench permeated the dim room. He slipped into a pair of soiled pants held up by suspenders and sat on the bed that occupied most of the space.

'How do I know I can trust you?" Mama looked troubled. A black cat appeared from under the bed, jumping onto his lap. "One hears of frightening stories."

He stroked the cat gently, and the animal arched its back. "Unfortunately, our profession has been invaded by amateurs."

"I wasn't thinking of amateurs," Mama looked him straight in the eye. "I had in mind . . . bandits, murders."

"I'm from Lwow, but I can give you names of your kind here in Warsaw who will vouch for me." He rolled a cigarette. "It's simple. You leave my fee and a password with a friend or relative and only after I've delivered you safely to the other side do you divulge the secret word. On my return, I present myself, mouth the password and only then collect. It's that safe."

"Jankele, you'll soon see your father," a hopeful Mama said.

Whatever we still possessed, she sold at the old market. At night I watched her smoothing out the crumpled bills, counting and recounting, placing one on top of another, neatly tying them into a handkerchief.

"You can't trust those Ukrainian bastards!" warned the thick-necked husband of a friend Mama took Josele and me to say goodbye to. "Don't you know their tricks? Are you so naïve, Edzia?" He stormed about the room in a dressing gown and slippers, picking his nose and shaking his puffy fingers. Fear invaded Mama's dark eyes and I sensed she regretted the visit. "He escorts you to a forest, makes you crawl until you reach a barbed-wire fence, then leads you to an opening and points to an observation post flying a red flag. You entrust the rogue with the word and creep through the hole in the barrier and are welcomed by Russian soldiers. The fixer returns to Warsaw, spits out the magic word and collects. Everybody's happy, right? Wrong! The fence is not the border . . . the soldiers are not Russian . . . and the forest is layered with victims."

Dangling our feet in the stagnant pond, Papa and I gazed at our reflections. "Make no mistake, Jankele, your mother held me in very high esteem, and I her. I'm certain, had there been no war, we would have patched things up and lived happily."

I had made a dent and in an attempt to break through, I resorted to a diversionary tactic. "Do I remind you of her?"

"Many times. The other day when I asked, 'Jankele, perhaps you can give me five hundred dollars for the club I belong to,' you made such a face."

"You told me it was free."

"The swimming and the other sports activities are, but sometimes they organize a trip to a museum or a picnic, and for that they charge. I thought it would be good for me to get out and meet people. After all, I'm alone now. You said it was difficult for you." He persisted with the assault. "That your business wasn't going well. You were helping your children. I didn't sleep that whole night, you reminded me so much of your mother. Another thing," he carried on, "you never telephone to ask, 'Papa, what are you doing? How are you feeling? Are you hungry? Are you in need of something?' After all, I'm already elderly, in my eighties."

"So, I'm exactly like Mama?" I tasted the bittersweet sensation.

BEFORE RETURNING TO Brighton Beach, he reminded me that I owed him a treat.

"Papa, ice cream is made of sugar and fat," I chided him.

"Once a year," he laughed, "how much damage can it do?" And when I asked what flavor appealed to him, he answered, "What's the difference? You decide, Jankele." By the time we reached home, the cone had disappeared, Papa threw the napkin to the curb, wiped his hands on the back of his pants, and said, "And next summer, we'll do it again."

20

A VOICE LACED with a Russian accent was at the other end of the phone. "I am Boris," he spoke calmly, leaving spaces between words. "My sister is visiting from the Soviet Union, and she has regards from your brother."

"My brother? It must be a mistake."

"Oh, yes?" responded Boris, with a horrifying matter-of-factness. "Solomon Kuperblum."

I suggested that we meet right away.

He came with his sister, wife, daughter, and mother. In his thirties and only a short time in Toronto, Boris owned the house he lived in and a humming baking business. They sat in our living room, taking it in. His vivacious little girl hoped to be a model, his wife rattled off the various trips they had been on since settling in Canada, while his sister, a perpetual smile on her lips, added nothing.

The mother, elderly and with silver hair, unravelled the story in a droning Yiddish. "In '42 my father was the manager of a shoe factory in Omsk. Many people were employed there — your father, Aaron Zelik, among them. My younger sister occasionally visited, and he took a fancy to her. Not long after, they got married and had a son, Solomon."

I felt the blood drain from my body. "You don't really mean married?"

She smiled demurely. "Of course! By a rabbi under a *chupa*!"

"In 1942?" I could barely utter the year.

There was a dusting of snow in the ghetto. We kissed Mama's family goodbye and mounted the waiting *droszka*.*
The coachman who had entered the ghetto carrying Jews evicted from the Aryan side, searched for Christians evacuating the sealed zone. Before agreeing to take us to the *statek*, he demanded payment.

We sat behind him, our bundles on the jump seats. The horse galloped, the sound of hoofs harmonizing with the disconcerting clatter of the worn wheels. A German soldier, matched by a Polish "blue" and a Jewish Ghetto policeman, were on both sides of the gate. As we neared the checkpoint, the driver pulled at the reins.

"Dear God," prayed Mama, "perform a miracle!"

The ones guarding our lane joined their counterparts, busily inspecting a wagon hauling milk into the ghetto, frisking the terrified driver, checking documents, burying their heads in milk cans, and surveying the vehicle's underside.

"Keep going," ordered Mama. The moustached Pole lashed the animal across its bony back.

I expected bullets, but heard only the pounding of Mama's heart. I looked up in search of God's face.

Before boarding the *statek*, Mama warned us not to attract attention, and in no circumstances to speak Yiddish. Fortunately, the passengers, stuffing themselves with steaming sausages, ignored us. Even so, several stops before Lublin, Mama panicked and whisked us off the ferry.

By the time we reached the Jewish district of Lublin,

* horse-drawn buggy

after a two-day journey on foot, our knuckles were so frozen we could barely open our hands.

Only weeks later, Mama bundled us up again. Our vision obstructed by snow and chased by tormenting wind, we arrived in a forlorn *shtetl*, where we didn't know a soul.

A year later, *Zaidy*, together with his two younger sons, somehow managed to leave the Warsaw Ghetto behind. With shovels flung over their shoulders, pretending to be road workers, they trekked hundreds of treacherous kilometers to reach us.

Sickly, with a flair for drawing, Uncle Shepsel found work digging ditches for the Germans, while Moishe roamed the market to see what he could pilfer.

Zaidy left every morning, his tools in a burlap sack dangling on his back, and he would reappear after dark to give us crusts of stale bread, frozen potatoes, an occasional onion, half-rotten beets, and even an egg. Once, when he came home with a chicken, Mama wouldn't look at it. It hadn't been slaughtered by a *shoichet*.*

In the winter of '42, when *Zaidy* didn't return, none of us slept. At daybreak, Moishe went looking. Just before curfew, catching sight of him returning with *Zaidy*'s tools, Mama threw her head into her lap. "Oh no!"

Moishe had come upon a farmer hurling frozen earth into a pit. "Three Huns on horseback shot the beggar in cold blood," the farmer told him.

Noticing the cobbler's tools strewn about, Moishe fell onto the mound. "He was no beggar!"

The peasant snorted. "I always filled his bag, knowing all along he was our Lord Jesus Christ, just testing my generosity."

When the snow melted, Shepsel and Moishe left to work on farms, and Mama, traipsing through villages, traded packets of tobacco for eggs. Josele on her shoulders, I at her

---

* ritual slaughterer

side, we trudged across bogs and the rutted roads of villages. She often complained. Her legs ached, her feet were swollen. Other times, infused with hope, she'd give voice to a Polish children's song:

Riding in an open wagon
Children, country bound,
Wide eyes taking in the wonders
Of the sights around.

Look! There lies a white-washed cottage
Made of straw and clay.
In a field a lonely scarecrow
Scares the birds away.

In a meadow by the river
A stork takes off and flies,
Stork! Stork! cry the children,
Klak! Klak! he replies.

In one isolated village, a young peasant couple took a shine to me and begged Mama to leave me for the summer to tend their goats. She refused. A bag of flour, potatoes, half a loaf of bread and a pitcher of milk later, she reluctantly submitted.

After a few sundowns, Mama reappeared with red eyes and face lined with worry.

"I want to stay," I told her. "They're good to me." I pulled from her grip.

"I'm afraid they'll convert you."

Not long afterwards, a weighty peasant woman, helping a limping Uncle Shepsel down from her wagon, showed up outside our window. Fixing her eyes on me, Mrs. Paizak proposed I take Shepsel's place until his injury healed. Mama shielded me, but I ran to the gregarious stranger who dispensed hope from her mouth and sugar cookies from a cotton pouch.

Boris's mother brought me back to the present. "But the

marriage didn't last long. He constantly beat her. She walked around with a black eye and so bruised, until one day she threw him out, telling him never to return. Eventually my sister remarried a fine man who reared the boy as his own. Solomon kept the name Kuperblum, and once or twice Aaron Zelik went to see him. Then your father went to America without leaving so much as an address."

I'm in a deep sleep and this is a nightmare, I concluded. When I wake, these faces will have been swallowed by the light of dawn.

IN TIME A LETTER arrived, postmarked Omsk. Solomon, a professor, was married and had a daughter. His mother was gravely ill. He wanted to know what my interests were. Who were my favorite authors? He sought my views on a variety of subjects.

Oddly, I identified with him, and enclosed the address in Brighton Beach, encouraging him to write Papa.

"Well, isn't it wonderful you have another brother?" An enchanted Papa was on the phone. "It's important to repopulate the earth with Kuperblums, Jankele."

I vowed not to grill him, but he had a need to unburden himself.

"At the time I was working in a factory in Omsk, when a young woman came home from the front to have an abortion and to return to the battlefield to rejoin her lover. Desiring to keep her from the war zone, her parents persuaded her to have the baby, and to protect her honor, they asked if I would give the child a name. Why not? I was alone and needed someone close to me, and at the same time, was saving a poor Jewish girl from everlasting shame."

"Are you saying he's not your son?"

"Absolutely!" He couldn't have been more emphatic.

"Does he know?"

"As far as he's concerned, I'm his flesh and blood." He didn't sound convincing.

"What are your feelings towards him?"

"None." He may have wanted to placate me but only succeeded in disturbing me more.

"It sounds as if you don't like him, Papa!"

"Last time I saw him, he was drinking vodka, *feh!*, and asked me for money yet." I pictured Papa's grimace.

"And?"

"I gave him what I had."

"Apparently he's a professor, highly respected! You should be proud."

"I must confess, I'm surprised," he conceded. "Jankele," he faltered, allowing the words to slip out as if inadvertently. "I think he's hoping you'll sponsor him to Canada."

"You think I should?"

There was no response.

Many a time I regretted not heeding Papa's advice to leave well enough alone at the farm, but in the spring, when I picked him up at the airport and drove there, the renovation was at an end. On the approach, his eyes widened. "It's wonderful, Jankele!" He marveled at how I had succeeded in integrating the new with the old. After inspecting the walkway stones which had been broken by hauling trucks, he repaired the damage, then turned to planting trees. "When they mature, they'll bear the most delicious fruit."

Searching further, he found a pile of fieldstone behind the barn and threw himself into erecting a wall at the farmyard entrance. He worked with difficulty, reminding me of Paul Muni in prison garb and shackles, in *I'm a Fugitive from a Chain Gang*. I aimed my video camera and was distressed by what was in the viewfinder.

"Papa, leave some for next weekend," I pleaded.

In the city, instead of his usual jogs, he took brisk walks, sometimes pausing at Ellen's to take her Davida for a promenade in a carriage. Where before he took Motek for long runs, now it was just a stroll in the ravine.

"Dogs are for guarding," he lectured. "Tamara has a dog as big as a fly. Taxi, they call him. Feh! He won't eat anything but cooked chicken breasts. Half the world goes to bed hungry and they cater and fuss over him as if he were an infant."

One evening, perusing Roman Vishniac's photographic essay *A Vanished World,* Papa stopped at a page picturing a little bearded man with the traditional cap, vest over white shirt, and bottoms of trousers stuffed into out-of-shape boots.

"Looks just like the Jew I sold your *zaidy*'s sewing machine to, back in '36," said Papa, as if commenting on the weather.

I studied the subject gripping a shoe firmly in one hand, holding pliers in the other, and pulling at a nail. The caption read: "A shoemaker. Warsaw, 1937."

"Papa, look!" I pointed to the peculiar sewing machine in the background.

Squinting, he brought the book to his eyes and erupted with glee. "That's the very one I fixed when I was courting your mother."

No sooner had he come than it was time to leave.

"You never ask me to prolong my stays. Why don't you show me a little love?" he said.

"You're welcome to remain as long as you like, Papa. No one tells you to go."

"No one tells me," he mocked. "It's not the same as being asked to stay!"

"Please stay."

He fused his eyes to mine. "I'll think about it." Then he announced he intended to spend the rest of the summer in the Pocono Mountains, where he had a friend and a patch of a garden behind Tamara's trailer.

The night before his departure, he noticed me fiddling

with the tape recorder and sat back smiling like a guest on a TV talk show. "Well, what would you like me to say?"

"Whatever's on your mind." I adjusted the mike.

"You are the interviewer," he grinned.

"When you left in '39, you kissed us goodbye as if you were going to the corner store to pick up kaiser buns for breakfast. You never looked back. How were you able to tear yourself away so easily?"

"Is it on?" he whispered, pointing to the recorder. I nodded. He cleared his throat searching for a voice and a tone. "How else does one leave? Kiss and look back and kiss again? Back and forth, what's the point?"

"Why didn't you come back after the war?" I was reminded of the hare I once trapped.

"Do we have to discuss this now?"

"When then, Papa?"

"I searched for you."

"How did you know I had survived?"

"I saw your name in a Yiddish gazette. To this day I remember your address in Lodz . . . 49 Kielinskego. My letters came back unopened."

"By then you were already involved. Tamara was born in '44."

"I had an understanding that if any of you were alive, I'd go back."

"Then Tamara would have grown up without a father?"

"That's how it was in those days. A woman was lucky to have a child. There were many women and few men. Millions died on the battlefield. I was still young and didn't want to miss the opportunity of having more children. Besides, what was there to come back to?"

"Your Jankele! By '46, you knew I was alive."

The veins bulged beneath his skin; his middle finger drummed nervously on the library table. "I stayed up nights writing letters all over the world."

"In your fantasies, Papa. Had you wanted to find me, you

could have." I sounded like a prosecutor. "Strange, you searched for years, but merely days after your arrest, your wife located me . . . just like that." I snapped my fingers.

The tempo of his tapping escalated, irritating my ears, as he searched for an object to rest his eyes on. When I continued the interrogation, he snapped at me derisively, "Why do you insist on opening these festering wounds? Perhaps you would have been happier had I come to you a broken man, old and crippled, unable to care for myself! You were dreaming of a tall, valiant father, who single-handedly would take revenge on the Hitlerites. Just like in the movies. But after the war I was physically and mentally a wreck, a walking corpse who could neither think clearly nor look after himself. I would have been a burden to you."

"Why can't you admit you blundered?"

After a pause, he resumed, his voice rising in emphasis, as if reading a speech. "Jankele, my dream was that we should all be together. With whatever strength I still possessed, I wanted to atone for the sins you accuse me of. I also hoped to exercise the *dybbuk** that dwells within you, and help you acquire a new outlook on life built on love and trust. That, I'm certain, would be the best medicine for your festering wounds, which until this day, I see, haven't healed. But you built a wall around you that gets wider and wider by the day. You chase for Kuperblums all over the world but ignore the ones so close to you in Brighton Beach."

"You wanted to dump your family on me, Papa," I hurled at him.

"Together, life would have been sweeter for all of us."

My temper escalated. "For me, it would have been hell!"

His stare intensified and was followed by a nervous twitch. "Then I guess it's better that things worked out the

---

*   the soul of a sinner which, after his death, transmigrates into the body of a living person way they did. They'll find their way in Brooklyn." He underscored the remark with his trademark hand gesture, leaning back and crossing his arms. "As for me, it's a tragedy that we're not together. Wouldn't you be happier if I were to live with you? Then we could call it 'our farm.'" He succeeded in dragging a laugh out of me.

"It's great having you near, Papa. Unfortunately, the opportunity has presented itself rather late."

"Then let it be." He fell into momentary silence. "But maybe it's still possible that I could live with you." His eyes bore into me.

"Why not?" I mouthed without appetite.

"As I age and won't be able to look after myself, I may have to come to you." His voice quivered.

"Papa, you're only eighty-two and you run five kilometers a day."

"It gets harder by the day."

When he was packing, he reminded me of the notebook he gave me in '67. "I've been thinking about what I wrote then and would like to correct a few thoughts." It was still in the same drawer where I had pitched it. I handed it to him.

At the airport, I pressed bills into his palm. "For your club, Papa."

He gripped my shoulders. "Jankele, let's forget the past. Let's, as of this moment, start anew." My heart melted. I threw my arms around him, and after a kiss, we went our separate ways.

21

"WHAT FOR, CHILD?" asked Papa, when I talked of journeying to Poland. "There's nothing there for you."

Terrye also tried to dissuade me from retracing the nightmarish steps. Others advised me never to set foot there again. A friend who took the trip, planning to stay weeks, returned within days. When he had knocked on the door of the only brethren in his *shtetl*, asking, "How does a Jew fare?", the occupant, pointing to a crucifix, responded in perfect Yiddish, "Can't you see I'm now a *Goy!*" and slammed the door.

Yet the land of my birth haunted me as if cloaking a secret, and I was drawn, though not without fear. I saw myself deplaning in Warsaw, confronted by a shadowy figure pointing a loaded revolver at my temple: "Finally caught up with you, Jankele Kuperblum!"

Clearing customs in Warsaw, Terrye and I found ourselves outside the terminal, our luggage at our feet. When booking our driver from Toronto, his wife had assured me he would meet us, yet now there was no one holding up a sign with our name. Just as I was beginning to fret, a man with a pleasant expression materialized. *"Pan** Kuper?" he said, sucking on a pipe.

*   Mister

I was flabbergasted. "How did you know?"

"Instinct." Jan exhaled a puff of smoke.

After we checked into the hotel, I asked him to take us to Pawia Street, where I had once lived. When we taxied up to the intersection of Pawia and Smocza, I thought we were in suburbia. Where were the hustle and bustle, swarms of people shouting, pushing, jumping on and off rickety streetcars, street vendors peddling herring, fresh bagels, sour candy, and ladies' stockings.

"Cigarette holders! Glass cigarette holders!" My own voice rang in my ears, promoting the goods I had unearthed from the rubble of a bombed factory.

Where 32A Pawia Street had once stood there was now a parkette with children romping on a teeter-totter. I was hoping to at least find the number, but even that had been obliterated, leaving only the laughter, quarrels, and songs echoing in my head. Around the corner we came upon a gutted structure, a remnant of the Warsaw Ghetto. A few blocks away loomed the impressive monument to the ghetto uprising. I was snapping pictures when a derelict approached. "For good luck," he said in broken German, offering a postage stamp of the same memorial.

I dug into my pocket. "Are you a Jew?"

"No," he protested, shifting his eyes, then snatched the bill from my hand.

At the entrance to the gas station, on the former site of the Umschlagplatz, where the Jews were assembled for deportation to Treblinka, a flower box with a few wilted carnations and two protruding wrought-iron candle holders, bereft of candles, were connected to a crumbling section of a brick wall. The inscription, in both Polish and Yiddish, had long since faded.

The performers at the Yiddish Theater were on vacation. We were told they were mostly non-Jews who performed in the Yiddish language rather convincingly.

Adjacent to the theater was an exquisitely reconstructed

synagogue. It soon became apparent that the *shamus,*[*] wearing a cardboard *yarmulke,* wasn't Jewish. There was no rabbi and no worshippers. A synagogue for tourists.

As we emerged into the sunlight, an elderly couple rushed towards us, their arms outstretched. "Leave us a few dollars!" they beseeched in Yiddish. They weren't married, only *shnored*[**] in partnership.

Although he was a seasoned cabbie, Jan had difficulty locating the Jewish Historical Museum. In the foyer, illuminated by a naked lightbulb, sat an undernourished woman behind a desk. The director, a lean, nervous man, greeted us warmly and took us on a personal tour. The barely lit exhibits — photographic blowups of Holocaust scenes — were covered in dust. Construction barricades blocked our paths. The director explained that they were in the process of renovating the interior. He smiled pathetically. "It's been going on like this for the last ten years. Poland's roots are withered, sapped of their nourishment. Unconsciously the people recognize this loss, and hence the sudden curiosity for everything that connects them to a Jewish presence." In almost a whisper, he related how, following the Six Day War, he was dismissed from the Polish army for poisoning his children's minds with Zionism. In his defence, he pointed out that he was childless. They acknowledged their mistake, yet he was not reinstated and his pension was terminated.

Back in his office he pulled out a thick ledger. I looked over his shoulder. *Jakub Kuperblum, born Pulawy, 1932.* "Is that you?" I didn't trust my eyes. It had my address in Lodz. "Your file is upstairs." Unfortunately, the clerk in charge was away and no one else had a key to the room. "Come back tomorrow," the director advised.

I did, and the archivist, a shell of a man with watery eyes,

[*]   caretaker
[**] panhandling

came wobbling down the stairs and had me follow him to the fourth floor, where he fumbled with a large key, trying to unlock the heavy door. The room was cramped with cabinets and shelves overflowing with documents. Here, too, the smell of cement permeated the air and everything was covered with layers of dirt. Sitting on the only available chair and scanning through an index, he announced dryly, "Sorry!"

"What happened to the deposition I gave in '45 at the orphanage in Lublin?"

He threw his arms into the air. "There is the slightest possibility that it may be on the third floor," and he was gone. I looked about, touching a document here, a photograph there, precious treasures turning yellow and brittle. The archivist returned. "He's at the doctor's today."

"Doesn't anyone else have access?"

He gave me a sober look. "This is not America."

The next day, the archivist descended the stairs to retrieve the file of my lost years. When he reappeared, he spread his arms in a gesture of helplessness.

The Jewish cemetery on Okopowa Street, a stone's throw from Pawia, was decaying with neglect. The monuments of prominent writers, philosophers, and religious leaders dated back hundreds of years. Some of the graves and crypts had been vandalized, others had eroded with the passage of time. Jan told us Catholic students devote one day a year to pulling weeds and clearing fallen branches.

In the bitter winter of 1940, scavenging for firewood, my twelve-year-old uncle Moishe and I zigzagged between these graves, petrified of waking the dead.

On our third day in the Polish capital, we passed the skeleton of a multistory building. Jan told us that the structure, which had been designated to house government offices, stood on the site of the largest synagogue in Warsaw. "But when the Jews of America got wind of it," he explained patiently, "they applied proper pressure, and construction came to a halt."

The story was disturbing enough, but what was even more distressing was that it was not being told by an anti-Semite, but by a man, who when witnessing me weeping, had joined me in my sorrow. Yet he too had swallowed the line about Jewish clout.

A well-informed source gave us a different version: "It was contracted to a Swedish company, but when our government detected the foundation had been improperly poured, they refused to pay. Likewise, the Swedes wouldn't remedy the problem unless they were compensated. The government didn't pay, the builder didn't finish, and the eyesore remains, a monument to bureaucratic mismanagement. As to the holy ground of the former synagogue, it lies next to the abandoned project."

HEADING EAST OUT of Warsaw along the two-lane highway, we came upon a road sign for Pulawy. In the town a grocer, noticing me focusing my camera, engaged me in conversation. "That was where you lived," he pointed to an empty lot. "I remember the shingle above your door, 'A.Z. Kuperblum, kamasznik.'* Your father made uppers for shoes."

I used to gaze out our front window at the massive Catholic church across the street and watch the worshippers climb the countless stairs, occasionally on their knees, and imagined they were ascending heaven. When I misbehaved, Mama, pointing to a nun, would threaten me with the *Baba Yaga,* ** and I lived in constant terror of those black-clad figures. Scrutinizing the modest church with grown eyes, I counted less than a dozen steps leading to its portals.

---

*   cobbler
**   a Slavic witch

"I'm not a Jew!" the town's *meshigine** bellowed, running up those same stairs. He lived in a dingy basement and roamed the *shtetl* collecting stones for the house he planned to construct for himself and his blind daughter. The amused Germans riddled his body with bullets and watched him cascade like a barrel to the sidewalk.

When we barged into the municipal offices, a pretty blonde threw us a furtive glance. I apologized for the intrusion, explaining that we were passing through and I had come for my birth certificate.

My birth date was shrouded in mystery. Although I knew the year I was born, sometime around Passover, I didn't know the exact date. At the end of the war when documents had to be procured, I selected April 16th, as that particular year the first Passover *seder* fell on that day. Papa was emphatic that my birthday was April 11th. However, I had the clear impression he wasn't all that certain.

"When were you born?" she asked.

"Nineteen thirty-two," I replied. "Either March or April."

She reached for a tattered log. "If you were christened in Pulawy, then for sure you're in the church records."

"I was never christened," I caught myself saying apologetically. "I'm a Jew."

She gaped as if she had come face to face with an extinct species. "I'll have to check the archives. Come back tomorrow."

"By then we'll be in Lublin."

"That's the best I can do."

I snapped a picture of the house where my friend Franek Zielinski once lived. When I was wandering through the countryside pretending to be a Christian, I had borrowed his name. I would have loved to know what became of him.

My face pressed against the car window, we coursed our

*   crazy

way around Pulawy for more than an hour. Among the hosts milling in the streets, the park, the market, I couldn't find a familiar face. The place I had lived in during my formative years was changed beyond recognition, and I was a stranger in its midst.

ALL THREE LUBLIN HOTELS were fully booked. After a complicated process of referrals, a couple on the outskirts of the city agreed to put us up for one night. They were gracious hosts, giving up their own bedroom and billeting Jan in the attic. Dinner was delicious, and after the dishes had been washed, they offered to show off their city by night. We piled into their Russian-made car and headed to town. A ten-minute drive later, the baroque railway station loomed before me.

In the summer of 1945, not a *grosz* to my name, I had arrived and spent the night here on the waiting room floor. The next morning when I stepped outside, the first Jew I met rebuffed me. The role I had played for three years living among peasants had become *me*. I not only spoke like a peasant boy, but with my feet caked in dirt and my head shaven, I was one. Worse, I couldn't remember one Yiddish word.

Our hostess, oblivious of my history, but sensing it when I wept, wrapped her arms around me, shedding tears of her own.

The next morning Jan drove us around in circles in an attempt to retrace the route that eventually led me to the orphanage. Around noon we parked the taxi and went looking for an eatery. The uphill street felt strangely familiar. To my astonishment, I stumbled upon the courtyard where I had lived for one week that summer of '45 with a couple who claimed to be my cousins. A haberdashery now occupied the premises. I entered to inquire and the proprietress shrugged. "But," she added, "there's a *paskudny Zyd** upstairs, and he knows everything."

At the far end of the landing, in a room no larger than a cupboard, a bearded man wearing a skullcap was bent in half, repairing umbrellas. "You speak Yiddish?" I said, hoping to make up for my stormy entrance.

"First say *shalom aleichem*,"** he responded. I obliged. "Now sit and tell me what brings you here," he said.

Without sitting, as there was nowhere to sit, I asked about the couple. He remembered them well. He told me that Lublin, once boasting countless synagogues, a famous *Yeshiva*,† and numerous holy men, now had difficulty convening a *minion*‡ in an improvised prayer house. At one point I reached for my wallet. "What are you doing?" he stared, his eyes bulging. "Give your money to Israel! To Israel!" he sobbed and pushed away my hand.

At Majdanek, just outside Lublin, a monument resembling a flying saucer hovers over the victims' ashes. Several of Papa's brothers and his only sister perished there. The inscription reads: "Let our fate be a lesson to you."

From there we headed for Piatki, the town that was as famous for its thieves as Chelm was for its fools — according to popular lore. The bearded pests of that town who spoke a peculiar language and worshipped a different God had been liquidated.

In the winter of '43, a man with a disfigured arm and his young wife had given me a lift to Piatski in their horsedrawn sleigh. German soldiers were patrolling the streets. She was expecting, and I was to be her helper, but the baby was born half-human and died within hours.

I knocked on the door of the shack still standing near the

---

*   a mean Jew
** Peace be unto you
†   Talmudic academy
‡   quorum

fire station. "Do you know who I am?" The woman spread her arms as if to embrace me, then quickly withdrew.

"I don't remember a thing," she trembled.

I had pictured her as tall and skinny. She was still slender, with the same face and the same silly grin, but the years had dwarfed her. "During the war, you brought a boy here from Malinowka," I said.

"I was a young girl then. I remember nothing," she said defensively. I tried to assure her I meant her no harm. "No!" she hissed and closed the door.

"Where's her husband?" I asked a next-door neighbor.

She crossed herself. "Died long ago. She hasn't been the same since the day she gave birth to that pig baby."

After my services were no longer required, I had found employment in an adjoining village with the Kozak family. Adam Kozak was a quiet, methodical man, who instilled in me the love of work and an appetite for peasant philosophy. After liberation, thinking I was the last living Jew, I peeled off my mask. Mr. Kozak received the news calmly. However, when I made plans to leave, he flew into a rage. "Had the Germans discovered you here, we would all have been killed! You'll stay and work till your dying day! You owe us your life!" Sunday, when the family left for church, I fled.

The taxi snaked its way along the grooved course and parked at the river's edge where I used to swim and water the cows and horses. Gielczew looked very much the way I had left it in the summer of '44. In my mind's eye, I could see the humble cottage two or three properties from where I was standing, but when I got there, I found a hut unlike the one I had left. The entrance was on the side instead of the front, and the straw roof had been replaced with tin.

A hunchback, who reminded me of a leprechaun, sat on a stool staring from across the road.

"Where does Adam Kozak live?" I asked.

He looked into my eyes. "The moment I saw you step out

of the taxi, I knew right away you were the boy who used to follow Kozak around like a puppy dog. Always working, helping, never resting. He encouraged you to play with the other children, but you only wanted to work. You wore a cross around your neck, and every Sunday went to church. The entire village envied Kozak. I used to scold my own children, 'Why can't you be more like Franiu?'" The distant memory made his eyes water. "You often came here to play with my son. Don't you remember? And to think in the end you turned out to be a Jew! It's hard to believe!" He told me that Kozak, his wife, and the eldest son, Stefan, were no longer alive.

"Then who lives there?"

"Stefan's widow."

I recalled being at their wedding and drumming on a wooden chest, accompanying the accordionist. "And the others?"

"That was Antek who just drove by on the hay wagon. His farm is along the road."

I had always pictured Antek as a young, quiet twenty-year-old, in Polish army uniform, leaving for the front in '44. Now he was in his sixties and reeking of cow dung. When I inquired about his sister, he indicated a blue-washed farmhouse. "Cesia is already a grandmother. She's in the fields." He sent someone to fetch her.

Her place was not unlike that of her parents: the walls were decorated with religious pictures, and throughout there was the stench of sweat, pork, and spoiled vegetables. Instead of the peasant food I remembered and longed for, we were treated to chicken soup with egg noodles served in individual bowls, a far cry from when we ate from a communal pot. Antek was silent. He couldn't eat. The atmosphere was tense. They all avoided my eyes, as if they were expecting me, at any moment, to explode, point fingers, and spit in their faces. But I had not come as an accuser, nor a judge. I was there to see them. Or was it for them to see me?

I rose and before I knew it I was anointing them heroes, draping them in courage, telling them they were decent people for sheltering me during those dangerous times when we shared a tragic moment in history. Choking with emotion, I professed delight to be in their midst, but somewhere in mid-sentence my hand started to shake, spilling the vodka from the glass, and I broke down.

They responded positively to the role I had cast them in, and in turn toasted me. "Imagine," Cesia said, "our children have everything, and they're such ingrates. You were all alone, no one to love you, yet such a good boy. So appreciative for the smallest favor." She reminded me that after my departure, I had sent two letters, to which they had not responded. After Kozak's death, they intended to contact me, but by then they had lost my address. "My father," she recalled, "predicted you would become famous."

I was curious about how he had reacted to my defection. In their version, Kozak tried to prevent me from leaving because he feared for my safety. Was their memory failing, did they think mine had, or had they altered history in the hope that time would wash away the truth?

When we were ready to depart, I squeezed bills into their weathered hands. They kissed and hugged me with passion. The fact that I was a Jew didn't seem to figure. I was a member of the family. Then why, deep within, did I still fear them?

"You should tell Jerusalem about how you were saved," said Stefan's wife. "As righteous Gentiles we are entitled to a monthly pension."

Neighbors gathered outside wanting to touch me, as if by contact they too would be blessed. Terrye had already entered the taxi when a man in a heavy coat pushed his way to me. "Franiu, I was your best friend. We chased

rabbits in the fields and picked mushrooms in the forest."
My blank expression more than disappointed him.

The villagers waved as we passed in the taxi. Voices
echoed, "Franiu is here! Franiu is back!" making me feel
like an actor returning to take a bow for a performance
given some forty years earlier.

A FOREST THRIVES on the site of the former extermination
camp Sobibor. Terrye and I walked down the long gravel
path leading to a granite sculpture of a terrified mother
cradling a child. The inscription says that thousands
upon thousands of Jews, Poles, Gypsies, and Russians
perished there. On the way out I plucked a few flowers,
and my wife reached for two pine cones from under an
evergreen tree.

The highway led to Malinowka. Jan made a sharp turn
onto a dirt road. "This isn't it," I complained. "The smithy
should be right here."

We climbed out to ask some locals if they knew the
blacksmith, Tekalewicz. To jostle their memories, I showed
them a snapshot of myself with the Tekalewiczs, taken by
a traveling photographer in '43. The peasants fingered the
print with great interest. It struck me that we were at the
opposite end of the village but couldn't go farther, as the
road narrowed. As if out of nowhere, a bare-chested, mus-
cular young man appeared, asking questions, eyeing us
and Terrye's purse.

"You can only get through by horse and buggy. Come, I'll
take you." He reached to open the taxi door.

A familiar terror surfaced. I snatched the photo, yanked
the door shut, and ordered Jan, "Let's get out of here!"

Kilometers later, I wondered what had compelled me to
ever want to see the blacksmith again. Immediately after
the war, when I returned as Jankel Kuperblum, he pulled

a gun on me, threatening to blow my head off. What would I have said to him now?

As Franek Zielinski, a Catholic orphan, I roamed the frozen fields and snow-covered villages during the winter of '42 — a night here, a day there, entertaining children, chopping wood, hauling water and generally making myself useful. I was doing well until word spread that the boy with the golden voice was infected with rabies. I was driven off like a rabid animal.

Late one afternoon I had knocked on the door of the Golombeks, a couple and their hearing-impaired teenaged daughter. They apparently received my entry into their lives as a blessing from Jesus, swallowing my fabricated story as gospel. However, when word circulated that the Germans were to conduct a house-to-house search, they revealed what they had suspected from the start, and with teary eyes, escorted me to the gate.

Nothing looked familiar. "Golombek," I explained, "dealt in black market meat during the war." The puzzled peasants shook their heads.

But one stepped forward pointing to a dwelling. "It's Golombowski you want! Right there! The meat business was only a cover. He was the leader of the local underground and the woman was not even his wife. After the war he went into hiding, was caught and sent to jail for opposing the new regime."

"The place doesn't look familiar," I said.

"That's it all right."

"And his daughter?"

"There was no daughter."

We left, and on the way, stopped two old timers returning from church. The first walked on as if he hadn't noticed us, but the second was more accommodating. "I'll show you," he said, and squeezed in next to the driver. In the next village, he trumpeted, "This is it." It was not at all like the place of my memory. Nevertheless, I tapped on a window, and a young man in his late twenties appeared. The spitting image of Golombek. The same face, Golombek's smile.

"That's my uncle, all right," he confirmed. "But his name was Bolek Golomb."

"Possible," I agreed, but nothing, not even the staircase leading to the attic, seemed to be in the right place. "Where's your uncle now?" I asked.

"He died four years ago."

"And his wife?"

"She's also gone, but his daughter is married and living in Wroclaw. My father will know how to get in touch with her." He went to wake him.

"That's my brother, all right," said the father, picking the wax from his ears.

"How do I get in touch with his daughter?"

"That shouldn't be too difficult, but his son lives closer."

"Son?" I swallowed hard. "He had no son."

"Is that so?" He smiled, a smile not that dissimilar to Golombek's. "Bolek had three sons and one daughter, all a year apart."

"There should be a pharmacy just ahead," I said to Jan as we entered the *shtetl*. It soon came into view. The very one where Golombek had purchased the medicine to cure my dreaded scabies itch.

The Warsaw taxi stopped in the market square and we stepped out to inspect: small one-story houses with tin roofs, leaning as if in a Chagall painting, and not a Jew in sight. Faces peeked out from behind lace-curtained windows and doors, eyeing us curiously. Spotting my camera, they became alarmed. Were they still expecting the rightful owners to return? After the war, a few survivors had come back, and had ended up floating in the river with knives in their backs.

When I spotted a bearded man sitting under a tree, I wondered, Could he be my brother? Perhaps on that fateful night when the *shtetl* was emptied of Jews Mama had entrusted Josele to peasants, and here he was. I was tempted to question the stranger, but feared making a fool of myself.

To get to the Paizak farm by horse and wagon took a lifetime. By taxi, the trip was over in a blink, but when we neared the homestead, we could see that the buildings were gone. An urchin leading a herd of sheep directed us to a block house in another part of the village. Children were in the yard. One of them sprinted into the house and returned a moment later with a heavy-set, white-haired woman.

Mrs. Paizak's beautiful daughter, Genia, had had long dark hair and emerald eyes. She was about twelve or thirteen. We used to romp in the wheatfields, roll on the ground, and tickle each other until we cried from laughter.

The last time I had seen her, she was young and radiant, about to be married. We now embraced, and the song she taught me when they had renamed me Kubush, emanated from her lips. Tears rolled down her cheeks and not once did she take her eyes off me. I, too, cried, and when I turned, there wasn't a dry eye in sight.

A majestic eighty-seven-year-old Mrs. Paizak soon appeared with Genia's husband, a quiet, unassuming soul. I remembered him when *he* was a dashing young man, courting the effervescent Genia. The entire family — sons, daughters, wives, husbands, and numerous grandchildren — posed for my camera.

On that black day when I found Mama and Josele gone and our place looted, Mrs. Paizak had helped herself to the few cooking utensils that were still there. A rusty old pot would have been a treasure for me. I sauntered into their kitchen, but like everything else, some forty years later, even the cookware had altered.

When we were alone, Genia confided that at the end of the war she had been gang-raped by a band of so-called partisans. "I'm lucky to be alive," she cried. Ever since, she had been afflicted with one thing or another.

Browsing through old photographs, we came upon a snapshot of Mrs. Paizak's eighteen-year-old son, Stashek. She told me he had been murdered by bandits years earlier. "You are the only son I have now. I always loved you as if I had carried you in my own belly," Mrs. Paizak cried.

For a while she had kept both my young uncle Moishe and me, until Stashek threatened to drag us to the Gestapo, tied to the tail of a horse. Tyrannized, she evicted us.

At the mention of Moishe, Mrs. Paizak unleashed a barrage of invective, painting him in unflattering shades. Me they had found more palatable. I didn't protest, didn't accuse, didn't attack. Whereas Moishe had condemned them for treating us like dogs, to save their own skins.

After the meal, Genia's eldest son hitched the horses and everyone got into the wagon. As the animals began to trot, Mrs. Paizak and Genia broke into song. When their children didn't join in, the old lady shook her head sadly. "We didn't teach them because when the other children hear Ukrainian songs, they call us foreigners."

On the site of their old farm, beams lay decaying in overgrown grass. Before I knew it, we were approaching the back fields, where for days Moishe and I roamed until hunger and cold drove him to despair. It led to a quarrel and in turn to our parting. He headed towards the river and disappeared into the blinding snow and I never saw Uncle Moishe again.

I asked Genia whether we were at the right place. "Don't you remember, Kubush? This is the meadow where you looked after our cows and sang so beautifully." I looked about. A row of weeping willows lined a narrow creek. They were much taller now. Other than that, there was nothing tangible to hold onto. I missed the cows grazing, the haystack, the resident stork, the crows circling above. My friend who played the flute in the next field was also gone.

When I pointed the camera to snap a picture, I expected my finger to refuse to activate the shutter. I desperately tried to conjure up the scene of some forty years earlier. To recall a feeling, a glance, a thought that would reawaken a terrible secret long buried in my subconscious. Was I responsible for Moishe's death? Had I really said, "Go! I'll have a better chance without you. You look so Jewish"?

Ready to leave, we offered Mrs. Paizak a lift into town, where she lived with a granddaughter. On the way, the old lady pointed to a field of corn. "That's where your grandfather is buried."

There was barely enough space in Mrs. Paizak's room for the narrow cot on which she rested her tired body. She volunteered the name of the Jewish family who had once owned that very cottage, then rattled off the rest of the town's former residents, who were now no more than a memory, and in most cases not even that.

At one point I asked under what circumstances she had met us. Mrs. Paizak took a deep breath, spat into a corner, and crossed herself. According to what unravelled from her fertile imagination, she had first encountered us in the Warsaw Ghetto when she smuggled in food to the starving Jews. On one such mission she piled all of us, Mama, Josele, *Zaidy*, the cobbler, uncles Moishe and Shopsel, and me into her wagon, covered us with straw, sneaked us out under the noses of the watchful guards, and drove us all the way to the *shtetl* where we settled.

In *Child of the Holocaust*, describing my return to the *shtetl* after liberation, I wrote:

Someone may recognize me, I thought, and I walked slowly, unassumingly. I wanted to stop and talk to someone, but thought that my questions could betray me.

A street, another street, one turn, then another, and now to my left was the place where we had lived. I wanted to stop and go in, examine, look around, inquire, but I feared even to look in that direction.

I must look, I must, I kept saying to myself. Perhaps my mother is there; perhaps everyone is there; perhaps they've all returned and are waiting for me.

I didn't stop to look, I did not really look, but shifted my eyes to catch a glimpse. Instead of the house, I saw flat ground and a few well-tended trees.

"Dear God!" I whispered. "Dear God!"

I wanted to stop and take a good look, but I didn't, for my fear would not allow me to; I just walked on, as if that flat ground and the young growing trees were of no concern to me.

Yet now I heard Mrs. Paizak say, "The house where you and your mother lived is now a hair salon." She gestured towards a row of store fronts adjacent to a cluster of trees.

It didn't look at all the way I remembered it. I closed my eyes and my mind and begged Jan to drive on.

The Hollywood Radio and TV Awards honored the best of the year. Hopefuls arrived from far and wide. I heard my name and was transformed into a defendant at a trial. The prosecutor looked strangely like the emcee.

"You directed these commercials, Mr. Kuper?"

"I also wrote and produced them," I offered, "although others are claiming credit."

"Did the product sell?"

"Beyond expectations," I answered smugly.

The face turned sullen. "Are you aware how many people died as a result?"

"Died?" I blanched, and looking past him, caught the impassive stare of the aging judge, a lookalike for Spencer Tracy. "I only made the commercials, your honor."

That night, in a Lublin hotel, my sleep was invaded by a new episode of the recurring nightmare. A plumber called to repair a leaky faucet senses a foul odor coming from below. Soon detectives with cameras descend on the scene. They dig the cellar and discover the skeletal remains of a woman. It's only a matter of time before they'll sniff me out.

The next day, we were heading towards Warsaw when I ordered Jan to turn around. Something disquieting was tugging me back to the *shtetl*. By the time we reached the hair salon, the sun was melting on the horizon. With a hollowness in the pit of my stomach, I cautiously approached the window where Mama used to look out.

A solitary candle barely illuminated the tiny room, and a voice that was once mine asked the question of generations past, "Why is this night different from all other nights?" How fortunate we were to be together, celebrating Passover 1942 with potato peels floating in salted water!

In the midst of the festivities, Mama broke down. "He ran away to save his own skin and left us for the slaughter!"

What had I done? What was I hiding? Demons tormented me. Gazing through the window of long-ago events, I realized that like Papa I had abandoned her. In Papa's absence, I had become the target of her chronic complaints. Papa had left me to look after her and I had failed. Like Papa, I ran away from her and had been running ever since, pursued by a sense of guilt.

22

THE SMELL OF AUTUMN lingered in the air. Brilliant hues appeared on leaves, and flying in formation, flocks of Canada geese headed south. It was too cold to swim, but we sat around the pool hoping to prolong the summer. In the late afternoon chill I was tinkering with the malfunctioning garden lights when the phone rang. I hurried to the garden table, shaded by the umbrella that would soon be stored, and picked up the receiver.

"Jankele!" The tone of Tamara's voice told me something was amiss. "Papa is sick," she choked. "He's been complaining of a lump in his groin. It's so painful he can't sleep. I had to drag him to a doctor. They just called," she sobbed. "It's cancer. He must never know!"

Terrye found me hunched over in a chair. Sadly I recalled the years of waiting to reshoot my life, or at the very least, put it on fast reverse and re-edit. By removing a few frames here, transposing a scene there, adding a pleasant voice-over, appropriate sound and music, a few dazzling effects, I could turn it into a winner. A good editor could accomplish miracles even with mediocre footage.

Daily I was on the telephone to him, trying to make up for the times when I could have, should have, and didn't. He answered my queries with his familiar cheerful disposition.

We chatted about many things, but mostly he asked about the farm and little Davida. I sent photographs of her and a video of our weekend retreat, with emphasis on his handiwork.

He bubbled with delight. "Jankele, when I come to you next April, I'll make improvements. A few of the stones don't sit right."

"Papa, I can't wait for you to get started on lining the pond."

"That's my specialty." He managed a robust chuckle. "Our farm!"

To prolong the conversation, I made small talk. "Have you heard from Solomon?"

"I write him and he writes back."

"What does he say?"

"I sent him a present." He sounded as if he had overcome a hurdle.

"That's good, Papa. What was it?"

He caught himself. "I can't tell you, Jankele."

"Is it a secret, Papa?"

"Five hundred dollars." He breathed so softly I wondered if I had heard right.

"That's nice, Papa." I was happy for him and the brother I had never met, yet I felt the familiar ache, and heard "*Kompinator!*"

I dreaded the telephone's ring.

My secretary interrupted a production meeting. "Your sister's on the line."

"He had a heart attack during the night," cried Tamara.

The plane for New York was late taking off and when it finally soared, the ride was turbulent. The passenger next to me wouldn't stop prattling. I closed my eyes in the hope of luring pleasant memories, but all I saw was the ambulance with Papa in it, racing through the littered streets of Brooklyn, its siren blasting.

Papa was in a ward. I approached his bed with trepidation, but to my relief, he had color in his cheeks and looked well.

"So, Papa, what are you doing here?" I goaded him. "You should be on the boardwalk jogging."

"I knew the moment I let doctors near me, they'd make me sick," he replied ardently.

"You've had a lot of practice being healthy, but never learned how to be sick!" I said. He flashed a smile.

After the usual questions, he reminisced about the time he spent with Davida, pushing her on the swing in the park. "You, *Elter Zaidy*,"* he imitated her, with a shadow of a laugh, then detailed a design he had worked out for the pond. "I'll need lots of stones, Jankele."

"You can have all the stones you want, Papa."

When I leaned over to kiss him, he handed me a cassette. "A special surprise!"

Landing in Toronto and picking up my car, I inserted Papa's tape in the player. Mama had a favorite song. The melody still lingered, but I had forgotten the lyrics. Time had erased them from his memory as well. Gunning the engine along the multilane highway into the city, I heard him singing Mama's song, accompanying himself on the mandolin.

> *I set out on a journey with four horses abreast*
> *A rattling wagon disturbing the night*
> *The road lays covered, the blizzard plays havoc*
> *The snow blows, blinding my sight.*
>
> *Giddy up, my horses, giddy up, my eagles*
> *Hold your heads up and be proud*
> *Pull at the wagon, carry the load*
> *Giddy up, raise up a cloud.*

Short of breath, he strained to heights he could no longer reach, his tenor voice sounding more like a prayer, a lament, an attempt to deflect agonizing pain.

---

*   great-grandfather

I sang along, and soon Mama joined in. For a blink I could see her clearly, her head raised high, her sad eyes glued to mine.

> At a roadside tavern, I stop to rest
> And decide to have just one sip
> I drank away the wagon, my horses too
> And came home with only the whip
>
> Yes, yes, my wife, yes, yes, you're right
> There's nothing left for the Sabbath, my dove
> Sh, don't worry, sh, don't complain
> Yes, there's still a God above.

Upon Papa's release from the hospital, again he refused Tamara's offer to move in with her. Where he once jogged five kilometers with ease, now he traversed the path in a wheelchair, the onlookers on benches staring with pity. For Papa, who spent so much of his energy guarding his health, the humiliation must have been unbearable. Many of them had never exercised in their entire lives, ate what they pleased, day or night. Yet here they were, in good enough health to make it to and from the boardwalk on their own, while he had to be pushed like a child in a stroller.

Further examination revealed that the cancer had spread and was advancing like a barbarous army, determined to ravage his body. He was unaware, because no one told him. Or perhaps for our sake he feigned ignorance.

The telephones buzzed between New York and Toronto. Papa's voice was deteriorating.

"Do you want me to come?" I asked.

"If you're not busy, Jankele." He could barely breathe.

"Jankele, Jankele!" He tried to form a smile when I reached his bedside, and I caught a glimmer of his old self. A few words later, he clutched his torso, the suffering cast on his face. I massaged the area, and gradually his eyes closed. I tiptoed into the living room and slouched into a chair.

"My God!" I cheered when I discovered a shop on a narrow cobbled street in Grenade close to the Alhambra. A craftsman was languidly polishing a mandolin-like instrument. "What is it?" The Spaniard picked one off the shelf and displayed it by its neck. *"Dombra?"* I asked. He nodded. The surprise of all surprises for Papa's eightieth birthday.

Friends going to New York agreed to hand-carry it, and I arranged with my sister to pick it up from their hotel and keep it under wrap until November 17. At the agreed hour, my brother-in-law, stuck in a traffic jam, didn't show, and our friends left, anxious not to miss the curtain.

New arrangements were made, and this time when Izzy arrived, he was informed they had just checked out. And so it went — mishaps, misunderstandings until finally the *dombra* was safely concealed in Tamara's closet.

On his birthday Papa called to thank me. Unfortunately, the eight-string instrument I had lugged across Spain was not a *dombra*.

A cruel wind howled outside Papa's apartment in New York, and I was cold. On his instructions, a window had been left slightly ajar. He always insisted on fresh air. Except for sipping some black coffee during the flight, I had not eaten, and my stomach growled.

I checked on Papa. He was sleeping soundly. I stuck my head into the kitchen and in my mind's eye saw Terrye and me at the rickety table with the mismatched chairs when we were in New York to attend Eddy's wedding. I had exchanged looks with my wife when Papa had served us cantaloupe wedges in large soup bowls. How trivial this and all my other complaints seemed now.

I dialed home. "Papa seems to be stable, and I'll see you tomorrow," I told Terrye. An oppressive silence reigned. I lay down on the sagging couch, covering myself with a blanket. I stared at photographs on the crowded dresser and the lids of my eyes started to droop. I slept. The garrulous ring of the telephone sent me running. Tamara was checking in.

I hurried to the bedroom. Papa opened his eyes, inhaled deeply, and reached for my hand. "My beautiful little boy!" he murmured. The words glided into my ears and percolated down through my body. I was his little Jankele and he, the Papa I had been searching for. I had an aching desire to imprison the moment.

He turned his head from side to side, squirming in pain. I stroked his unshaven face. He continued to writhe, his excruciating laments deafening me.

Tamara surfaced within minutes, followed by Mikhail. Soon two police officers entered, scrutinizing the premises, asking questions, filling out reports, to the accompaniment of Papa's piercing cries for mercy.

"For Christ's sake, we asked for an ambulance!" I gritted my teeth. Satisfied it was not a drug scam, they radioed for help.

Three unkempt and disheveled medics, not unlike the ones on television, stormed in, lugging all manner of paraphernalia. One, chewing gum, sat on Papa's bed requesting the exact information the police had just acquired. Another inattentively flicked his cigarette ashes. The overweight female with twine-like hair obstructing her vision, sniffled, cursing the flu.

At long last they lifted Papa into a wheelchair, and covering him with a blanket, marched towards the door. Papa, sapped of strength, his screams inaudible, shivered.

"Wait!" I obstructed their path. "His feet!"

"Don't matter," said the one with the cigarette dangling from his mouth.

I was ready to massacre. "This is my father! What do you

mean, it doesn't matter?" Someone handed me slippers, but I couldn't force his limp feet into them.

"Let's go!" commanded a voice, and a firm arm shoved me aside.

Neighbors gaped at the waiting ambulance with the flashing light. We followed the rankling siren in Mikhail's old car. The hospital buzzed at full speed. Weary doctors rushed to and fro, pursued by the public address system. Patients sat in corridors or lay on stretchers waiting, while a constant parade of ambulances dispensed casualties of robberies, muggings, shootouts, and an array of other mishaps. Visitors munched on doughnuts and sipped drinks from the procession of automats.

Tamara, Mikhail, and I paced the corridor. A frazzled intern in a white coat appeared. "Aaron Zelik Kuperblum," he said, consulting his clipboard. "Tell me quickly the patient's history," he demanded on the run. As soon as Mikhail started, he was interrupted. "Shall I let him die, or keep him alive for a day or two in pain?" We looked at one another. "I'll be back," he said, disappearing behind the portal. After many hours of anguish, the physician finally reappeared. He had nothing to report, and suggested we go home and check on Papa in the morning.

By the time Tamara turned the key of her apartment, a few neighbors were already leaving for work. I lay awake, my mind racing like an editing machine on fast forward. The penetrating ring of the phone brought me to my feet.

"Hello!" I heard Tamara's groggy voice followed by a suppressed cry, crescendoeing into an anguished wail.

I was grateful to Mikhail when he offered to go first to identify the body. He went into the room and we heard his racking scream. Tamara was next. I admired her courage. I was unprepared for what awaited me: on a high table was a stretched-out cadaver, head pulled back, mouth gaping, closed eyes facing the fluorescent lit ceiling. Is this my

Papa? It was so final! So cruel! I shrieked from the depths of my being.

The funeral was to be on Sunday. Our children, our son-in-law Stephen, Terrye, and three-year-old Davida flew in. The service was simple, performed by an elderly rabbi in traditional garb and beard, who attempted to weave a story of a man he had never known or met. The small gathering was supplemented by a few of Tamara's friends and a sprinkling of Papa's boardwalk cronies, huddling in a single clump at the graveside.

Papa's was the last available spot in the gigantic community of the dead, squeezed between two others of the same meager proportions, next to the fence, bordering a busy highway.

The rabbi chanted the ancient prayers, the pine casket was lowered, and the two black grave diggers began to cover the opening.

"*Zaidy*, why are you crying?" Davida looked up at me.

"Because I'll never see your *elter zaidy* again."

"Why not remember him the way I will?" She reached for my hand to comfort me.

In the afternoon, I took a stroll along the boardwalk and watched the angry waves accost the frozen shore — one dissipating, the other behind, roaring to life. Later I climbed the stairs to Papa's apartment. It was eerie unlocking the mottled door. Like a gremlin, I peeked in drawers, opened cupboards, hoping to find the notebook he had reclaimed from me. I was more anxious than ever to know what it contained.

I came across some wrinkled photographs scattered in a drawer. Most were ones I had sent through the years, but a few black-and-white snapshots, frayed at the edges, were unfamiliar. Papa posing with an array of friends. He looked young and fit, his hair coal black — a captivating smile and sparkling eyes staring at the camera lens. They had been taken during the time he had professed to be a physical and mental wreck. I claimed these, together with the proxy *dombra*.

PAPA'S FOOTPRINTS ARE everywhere and his memory haunts me. The fruit trees did not survive the harsh Canadian winters and the names on the boulders have slightly deteriorated. Terrye has nurtured an enchanting herbal garden around them. Fascinating plants with exotic scents and captivating names sprout in the spring and grow into clumps and bushes: cultivars of lavender, thyme, balm, parsley, mint, coriander, and more, surrounded by a symphony of edible flowers.

Death, with its power to dwarf differences, has made me forget what my complaints were. I miss his face on my birthdays. Terrye tells me I have acquired his laugh. When I speak, I sometimes hear his voice, and mornings, when the blade scrapes the foamy lather off my face, he stares at me from the other side of the mirror.

Acknowledgements

I AM GRATEFUL to many people who assisted me in this endeavor, particularly my literary agent, Beverly Slopen, for not letting me rest until I set pen to paper.

Susan Pacaud struck the match that got me going.

My appreciation to Robert Fulford and Malcolm Lester for their letters in support of a grant. And to Eileen Thalenberg for a flavorful translation from the original Yiddish of Papa's story, "Feelings of Music."

I am especially thankful to Mary Betel for her linguistic skills in acting as interpreter on my return trek through Poland, to Muni and Carol Basman for lending an ear and heartening me with their laughter, to Edna Sandler, who was an enthusiastic reader of my first jottings and offered valuable comments, and to Gary Ross, who pointed me in the right direction.

My friend, Marek Nowakowski, scoured libraries in Warsaw for the lyrics of the children's song that Mama sang.

My children, Ellen, Shaul, and Simca, read the first draft with great sensitivity, and Mark took the photograph of me that appears on the jacket.

One couldn't ask for a more supportive and enthusiastic publisher than Jack Stoddart. And I offer warm gratitude to Donald G. Bastian at Stoddart Publishing, for his dedication and perceptive understanding of the work, as well as to Kathryn Dean, who labored over the final editing.

I owe a special mention to teachers Doris McCarthy, for rescuing me from oblivion, Irene Prior, who introduced me to the principles of dramatic structure, and Dawson Kennedy, who taught me that the essence of design is simplicity. As well, Selma Kushner and another lovely lady, whose name escapes me, who resided in an apartment on Bathurst Street, for helping me with my lessons in the days when I struggled with the English language.

And then there is my indebtedness to my loving wife, Terrye, who not only lived much of the story with me, but also shared in the formidable task of committing it to paper throughout its many incarnations.

Finally, to all those who recognize themselves in this book, thank you for having been part of my life.